ALSO BY KARL PILKINGTON

THE WORLD OF KARL PILKINGTON
HAPPYSLAPPED BY A JELLYFISH
KARLOLOGY
AN IDIOT ABROAD
THE FURTHER ADVENTURES OF AN IDIOT ABROAD
THE MOANING OF LIFE

KARL PILKINGTON

CANONGATE

Edinburgh · London

FIRST PUBLISHED IN GREAT BRITAIN IN 2016
BY CANONGATE BOOKS LTD, 14 HIGH STREET, EDINBURGH EH1 1TE

WWW.CANONGATE.TV

1
PHOTOGRAPHY COPYRIGHT © AJ BUTTERWORTH, JODIE KRSTIC, MUS
MUSTAFA, SIMON SMITH AND ME & YOU PRODUCTIONS LTD

ILLUSTRATIONS COPYRIGHT © ANDY SMITH
PHOTOGRAPH P.106 © MUSEUM VICTORIA CC BY. PTERONURA
BRASILIENSIS, GIANT OTTER, MOUNT. REGISTRATION NO. C 30005.
PHOTOGRAPHER: JON AUGIER

BRITISH LIBRARY CATALOGUING-IN DATA
A CATALOGUE RECORD FOR THIS BOOK IS AVAILABLE
ON REQUEST FROM THE BRITISH LIBRARY

ISBN: 978 1 78211 731 5
EXPORT ISBN: 978 1 78211 734 6

TYPESET IN ITC SOUVENIR BY ALLIANCE CREATIVE

PRINTED AND BOUND IN THE UK BY BELL AND BAIN LTD

CONTENTS

IF YOU GO to a fancy restaurant these days you normally get given something that is called an 'amuse-bouche' – that's French for 'amuse mouth' – which is basically an appetiser that they serve before the food you have actually ordered turns up. The whole point of it is to whet your appetite. More often than not it looks like stuff they've just brushed up from behind the cooker and stuck on a broken Jacob's cream cracker. I tend to eat it just cos it's there but I very rarely enjoy it and it isn't a part of the meal I remember when looking back. To me, an amuse-bouche is like an introduction to a book, in that you could easily do without it.

I thought I'd finished writing this book. I had handed in the six chapters to the publishers and was all pleased with myself that after almost nine months of sitting in front of my computer, it was finally complete. Except it wasn't. Jenny at the publishers said she wanted some more. Jenny is never happy. If God had handed her his Ten Commandments for approval she would have suggested he write another three. 'Why do I need to do an introduction?' I asked. She explained that an introduction should inform the reader of why I travelled around the world looking at the topics I've written about. I said that I had written over 120,000 words and all this information was already in each chapter, but she insisted that an introduction was still required. So I am sat here feeling like a marathon runner who's been asked to do a lap of honour. I know the saying is that you should never judge a book by its cover but I'm asking you not to judge this one by the introduction. I don't know what to say that I haven't already covered, and would prefer it if you just went straight to the start of chapter one now. But for the benefit of keeping Jenny happy I'll keep going with this introduction even though I don't believe in them.

I think if a book has been well written you shouldn't need any explanation at the start. I only got round to watching *Star Wars* for the first time last year and thought it was odd that it had all that scrolling text about 'in a galaxy far far away' at the start of the film explaining the background to the story. I thought I'd downloaded the bloody Kindle version of it due to the amount of text there was to read. I wonder if Jenny was involved in *Star Wars* and demanded it had that intro added on afterwards.

I've just remembered an introduction to a programme I watched years ago that was so daft it made me laugh even though it wasn't supposed to. It was a travel documentary presented by Neil Morrissey (the fella off the TV show *Men Behaving Badly*) called *Neil Morrissey's Excellent Adventure in Jordan*. Now, just like Jenny at the publishers, TV execs also like the start of a programme to cover what the show is all about and why Neil Morrissey has been picked to present it. This is always a tricky sell for any programme as it's most likely that he just did the show cos it was a paying job and didn't have much else on at the time. But being honest doesn't always work for TV. If I was in charge I'd have just called the show *Amman Behaving Badly* (Amman is Jordan's capital city). This would immediately make Neil the perfect presenter for the show, no more questions asked. But they didn't think of this, so to justify his involvement the opening line to the series was 'I'm Neil Morrissey and I've always been fascinated by the desert'. It makes me laugh just writing it. He said it with such seriousness, which made it even funnier. Now, I've never met Neil, I'm sure he's a lovely fella, but I don't believe for one second that he has 'always been fascinated by the desert'. I would bet £100 that he was forced to say that line by some TV exec so any viewers wondering why Neil had been chosen to host the show now knew it was because he's fascinated by deserts.

And now, like Neil I'm being forced to explain and justify why I filmed *The Moaning of Life 2* series. Well, first of all I needed to earn some money to pay off the mortgage. The second reason was that if I was going to be away from home yet again I wanted to look at topics in life that interest me. The first *Moaning of Life* series looked at issues that most people face through their lives like marriage and having kids, but looking back on it, the problem with those subjects was that I went into them with my mind already made up, as I already knew that marriage and having kids wasn't for me. So in some ways it was all a bit pointless. With this last series I wanted to look at themes that did play a big part in my life even though I didn't realise how big. The original list of topics I was going to look into were:

My Identity	Time
Intelligence	Food
The Body	Waste

Fascinating!

About two weeks before going away to film the Intelligence episode I lost interest when an ape that I was planning to visit and challenge to a game of Pac-Man in Japan pulled out due to its carer not being happy with the fee. So that episode changed to Art. I also didn't bother with the Food episode in the end either as I thought there were already too many cooking programmes on the TV. Which is a shame really as I could have opened the episode with 'I'm Karl Pilkington, and I've always been fascinated by desserts'.

I think that's all you need to know for now. I hope you enjoy the book.

AS I WRITE this I'm twirling a stainless steel teaspoon up my nostril. I have my reasons for this, which I'll explain in a minute. Hopefully that will keep you hooked enough to get you through the introduction to this next topic, which is art. If you're like me, you might struggle to read about art. I know it's really important and is a big part of everyday life – I mean you can't even buy a cappuccino these days without it coming with some sort of doodle in your froth – but it's boring to hear someone go on about it at great length. It's as dull as someone telling you about their dreams. They say that in reality, dreams only last two to five seconds, so why is it when someone tells you about one they've had, it lasts longer than the Harry Potter series? I've switched nostril now. It would be a lot easier if I had one of them two-pronged forks so I could do both nostrils at once.

The art I grew up with wasn't proper art. Money was too tight to throw away on things that hung on walls or sat on shelves collecting dust. The only art we had was the gear my dad had got off someone down the pub, or ornaments that people had bought us as gifts. I'm not sure any of us really liked what we had; it was just there to fill a space. I'd go to my mates' houses and they had a lot of the same stuff, as their dads drank in the same pubs as mine. A game of *Through the Keyhole* would have been impossible on our estate as all the front rooms looked the same. Apart from the fridge magnets. My mam went through a phase of collecting them, but my dad soon got rid, as when you closed the fridge door they'd all fall off. It was like playing a game of Buckaroo every time you had to put the milk back!

Even though I didn't grow up around expensive art, and I don't own any now, I do like art. I just don't like the pretentiousness that surrounds it. I don't want a critic telling me WHY I should like the art, and how every glance at some painting 'will evoke painful visceral experiences with forms that are tactilely appealing', when to me, it just looked like what the bloke did in my cappuccino froth. But then I've never been keen on people telling me what I should enjoy. I'm a big fan of fish and chips, but I won't bother if I can't have a cup of tea with them. To me, that's like Ant without Dec. Recently I was away filming and I'd decided to have fish and chips, but when the waiter came to take the order he said they don't do tea. The cameraman piped up and said a sommelier he knew had told him that the best drink to have with fish and chips is champagne. I said, 'What else does he suggest, a martini shaken and not stirred with a bloody Scotch egg!' Seeing as I didn't know what else to eat and everyone else had ordered, I took his advice. I wish I hadn't. It was like sticking Anne

Frank in an episode of *Cash in the Attic* – the two things should never go together. I should have known his mate was talking out of his arse. Since when have you gone in a chippy and they've stocked bottles of Cristal next to the cans of Dandelion & Burdock?

The thing is, there are seven billion people on the planet, we're not all going to enjoy the same things. I like stuff more when I've come across it by accident and without any preconceptions. I found out I liked calamari this way. I actually thought I'd shoved an onion ring in my mouth at the time. And I tried wasabi for the first time thinking it was mushy peas. That gave me a right shock and nearly blew my head off.

The weird thing is, even though I didn't enjoy my wasabi experience, the memory has stuck with me more than my enjoyment of the calamari. It's the same with art. I get something out of the stuff that I don't like as at least the emotions get going. We like getting wound up. Why else would people watch Jeremy Kyle? It gives us something to moan about. You have to have the bad to enjoy the good. Last night for me dinner I had a garlic Chicken Kiev. I loved it at the time, but now I'm paying for it as I can't get rid of the smell of garlic out of my nose. I read online that the solution is to stick a stainless steel teaspoon up your nose. So that's why I'm sat here with cutlery dangling from my nostrils like some sort of human wind chime. It seems to be working. I read that the nose can remember 50,000 scents so I don't know why it can't have a go at remembering one of the other 49,999 smells it knows right now! It just goes to show that even my nose goes for remembering the bad things over the good. Thinking about it, I should have some wasabi now. That would clear it.

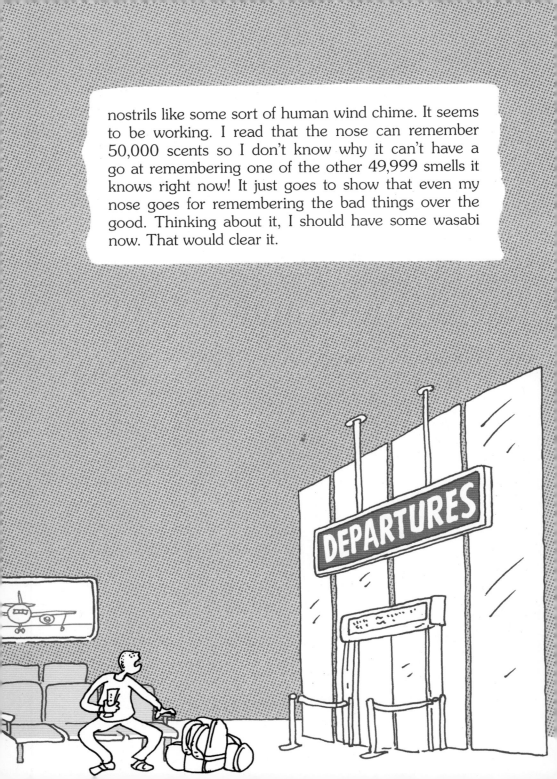

ART IN THE MUSEUM

My trip about art started in New York at the Museum of Modern Art. As much as I like art I don't like visiting galleries. One of the reasons being the whiteness. I can't handle it as I have really sensitive eyes. Instead of handing out audio guides, they should hand out sunglasses. I'm not alone with this problem, either. Look around in a gallery and everyone is squinting like Clint Eastwood. I wish they would wallpaper a few walls or use magnolia in places to calm it down a bit. One of the things that put me off the idea of going to heaven, if it exists, is the way it's always depicted as being really bright white, with everyone wearing bright white robes. It always looks like it would stink of bleach to me. Anyway, it's not just the white walls that give you a headache in a gallery, there's also the shiny, squeaking floors! No matter what shoes you wear you can't avoid causing squeaks. On a busy day it can sound like some sort of dolphin get-together.

The first thing that grabbed my eye in MoMA was the piece by Andy Warhol. It was the famous one of thirty-two cans of Campbell's soup which all look the same, apart from the contents of the tin. Vegetable soup, oxtail, tomato, clam chowder, chicken gumbo and loads more. I stood there looking at these for a good ten minutes, not trying to work out what Warhol was trying to say through his work, but just going through which soups in my forty-three years of life I hadn't tried. I may as well have been stood in Asda doing a food shop. In a way, I think that's where the art should be really – in everyday spots where normal people go. Post offices would be a brilliant place to show art as the queues take ages to go down. Whenever I have to go and buy stamps, I take a packed lunch, so what better space to show off art? Research says we spend about six months of our life queuing, so why not make it more enjoyable? It seems mad to have all these costly art galleries when there are loads of walls and spaces to fill elsewhere. Damien Hirst's shark could be displayed at a fishmonger's. Tracey Emin's bed could be in Bensons for Beds. If shopping on the high street is dying due to internet shopping, give us another reason to go out and shop.

I moved on from the tins in the museum and got to a pile of bricks. Normal-sized bricks. No cement. Just bricks laid out five by twelve, two bricks high, 120 in total. Now if this was in a builders' yard I wouldn't have stopped and looked, but I was in MoMA and knew this must be serious art. I gawped at it for a good fifteen minutes to try and work out what this was all about. The first thing I noticed was that they were fire bricks, the sort you have in fireplaces and kilns. I knew this as me dad used them when he built a brick BBQ outside our caravan in Wales. After that, everyone went and got one, and the smell of BBQs filled the air every day. I don't know if there was any truth in it, but there was a story going around that a woman had sat outside her caravan in the sun, wrapped herself up in silver foil to get a tan and ended up cooking herself alive. No one noticed as they thought the smell was just meat from another BBQ. I always think of that story when I see people wrapped up in foil like baked potatoes at the end of the London Marathon.

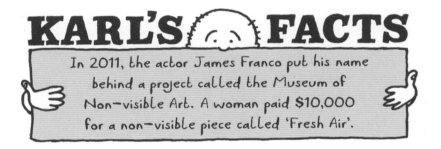

KARL'S FACTS

In 2011, the actor James Franco put his name behind a project called the Museum of Non-visible Art. A woman paid $10,000 for a non-visible piece called 'Fresh Air'.

There were no details next to the pile of bricks, so I wasn't even sure if this was a piece of art. They might have just been having an extension built. The thing with this is, I know that I could recreate it quite easily myself. Fire bricks are £2 to £3 a brick, so for no more than £360 I could have knocked one of these up in no time. After a while I came to the conclusion that the creator of this piece could just have been having a laugh. Perhaps you're supposed to think of the bricks as blocks. One hundred and twenty blocks. That's a load of blocks, and if you repeat that line over and over – 'a load of blocks, a load of blocks, a load of blocks' – it starts to sound like 'a load of bollocks'. That was my interpretation, anyway.

AN ORIGINAL WALL–HOL.

After having some time to take in some of the art on my own, Jamie the director had arranged for me to meet a critic. His name was Blake Gopnik.

KARL: I've been a bit confused so far.

BLAKE: Oh yeah? That's really good news. I wish I was more confused with art. I mean, for me the mark of a good work of art is when I keep looking at it, I keep being baffled by it. So anything that I immediately say 'oh, that's beautiful', 'that's a great work of human invention' or any of those kind of clichés, I think it's lousy.

KARL: I've just been looking at a pile of bricks and it sort of annoyed me a bit at first. I'm looking at it thinking this is a big joke. Then I'm stood there trying to work it out. Is there one answer to that pile of bricks?

BLAKE: There better not be. If there is, it's a crap work of art. I actually think that they look pretty damn good, and that a pile of bricks in a construction yard looks good too, so part of the point is just to make us rethink what it is to look at the world.

Fair enough, but a construction yard doesn't charge you $25 to get in. Blake took me over to a piece of art called 'In Advance of the Broken Arm', which was a snow shovel hanging from a ceiling. It wasn't a snow shovel that had been sculpted from stone or made out of glass or anything, it was just a bog-standard snow shovel. What with the bricks and now a shovel, I was wondering if I was in a museum of art or a branch of B&Q! To me this is art for people who have too much time on their hands. I can't imagine someone in a Third World country getting much from it.

Blake's eyes lit up when he saw the shovel. I reckon if he saw me today with the teaspoon hanging from my nose, he'd have me put in a Perspex box next to the pile of bricks. It was more interesting watching Blake's reaction to the shovel than looking at the shovel itself. But I like people-watching. When I was a kid I got into looking at paintings of normal people doing normal things by a bloke called Lowry. Kids playing in the park or factory workers making their way into work. They were simple images, but you can look at them again and again and see someone doing something you hadn't noticed before. I used to sit and do my version of these after I'd played out, drawing people I had seen watching a football game on the fields or people knocking around the shops.

BLAKE: I've probably written ten thousand words on this thing. And it still makes me wonder. It's actually weirder than it looks – most people don't realise this is not Marcel Duchamp's snow shovel from 1915; this was remade in the '60s. These pieces are called ready-mades. The whole point is you went and bought a shovel, and you put it up and that was it, that was the work of art.

KARL: How much is that worth?

BLAKE: That's probably the least interesting question you could possibly ask.

KARL: I know, but I'm looking at it and thinking it's a shovel, what's a shovel doing in here?! So go on, how much?

BLAKE: I don't know, they don't come up for sale very often. I guess not very much, ten million at most. Maybe more, maybe twenty. But not a lot in other words. Because pictures are selling, stupid bits of paint on canvas are selling for two hundred and fifty million dollars. I mean Marcel Duchamp's one of the biggest bargains you can get.

KARL: Ten million dollars? That's ridiculous.

BLAKE: Yeah, but it's all ridiculous. I mean, the fact that anyone has ten million dollars to spend on something that you can't use is sickening and criminal. My favourite thing in the world is to have my notebook, or to have a friend with me, and to spend at least an hour with one work of art.

KARL: What? An hour looking at a snow shovel?

BLAKE: Yeah! It's easy. You and I could do it easily, in fact. I mean, you spend two or three hours looking at a football match, right? Or a movie?

KARL: An hour's worth of thought, on a shovel? All right, so what should I do then? If I'm going to look at this and try and get more from it, what should I be thinking?

BLAKE: First of all, I don't think you should be thinking, I think you should be talking or writing, because the notion of contemplation I just don't buy. It has to be active. There has to be a real engagement with the work, just as if you're watching a football game. You're constantly talking, thinking, screaming at them. Scream at Marcel Duchamp, tell him that you think he's useless.

KARL: I feel a bit . . . a bit sorry for it.

BLAKE: For the work?

KARL: Yeah, because it was made to be a shovel and it's not. It's like looking at an animal in a zoo. Where you know it's not really doing what it's meant to do.

BLAKE: That's interesting. You've just said one of the most interesting things I've heard about a Marcel Duchamp. Can I pretend I said that?

KARL: You're just taking the . . .

BLAKE: No, I'm serious. To look at this from the point of view of the shovel is a genuinely original thought that has not been had. See, that's what happens if we spend enough time on it: new stuff happens. That's what art does, it makes new stuff happen.

The thing is, it would have been easy to just say it was all shit and walk away, but because I didn't, I had a good time chatting with Blake about art. Still think ten million quid for a shovel is ridiculous, though.

MAKING ART

The next part of my trip was not just about looking but actually getting involved in the art. First up, I was meeting an artist called Trina Merry. Her thing is to create art using human bodies and a load of body paint. She was making human sculptures of the twelve astrological signs by getting her volunteers to squeeze and huddle together to create the shapes. Once in position, she applied body paint to bring the image to life before she took a photo. I was looking forward to getting involved in this as it was something I could have a copy of once it was all finished. I've never been one for taking photographs. I only use my phone camera for taking a shot of the gas or electric meter reading so I don't have to write down the long number. I think this is because my mam and dad didn't bother with photos much when I was growing up. My mam hates having her photograph taken as she never likes how she looks and she always turns away or covers her face like some criminal coming out of the Old Bailey. God knows what we would do if she ever went missing as we'd have nothing to give the police to help identify her.

We were all pretty hopeless at taking photographs too. There would always be a finger over the lens or heads would be missing altogether. If anyone in our family had a photographic memory it would be useless, as everyone's heads would be missing. When we did take photos we never got round to getting them developed. We'd go on holiday to Wales for four weeks and only take one roll of film, so before taking any snaps there was always a big discussion as to whether or not it was worth taking a photo, which led to not many being taken. One roll of film could last for ages and by the time we actually got it developed, the photos showed me going from six to eleven years old!

The photo I remember the most from all my holidays growing up is one of Uncle Alf (he wasn't a real uncle, just me dad's mate) lying on the sofa in a caravan with a KitKat wrapper stuck to his head. I don't know how it was agreed that using one of the twenty-four photos for this was justified.

We didn't always remember to take the camera with us, either, so there are big parts of my life where there is no photographic evidence that I was around at all. The only evidence of my existence in my teenage years are the X-rays of the wisdom teeth I had done. These days, it's gone the other way – everyone is photo obsessed. Kids are growing up with every movement being photographed, and even before they have left the womb parents have enough scans of their kid to fill an album. It's no longer 'Here's Billy taking his first steps', now it's 'Here's Billy using the placenta as a trampoline'. They may as well have a photo of the dad's bollocks in there to show where they were before the womb!

I met Trina in a busy studio where dancers, artists and musicians practise their craft. She showed me a few images of her work that she had on her iPad. They were really good. There was one of around nine people intertwined to make up an image of a motorbike being ridden by a woman. There was one of a skull and another of a temple. On first glance you can't see the people involved, but on closer inspection you can see a lot more than you might expect.

KARL: Are they totally nude?!

TRINA: Yeah, they are totally nude. But in my work I try to obscure the body, because I don't want anyone to stick out solely as an individual. Except for maybe one focal person. It just depends how shy they are – if they need to cover up for whatever reason, I just throw them in back. People who are more confident, or if their body is needed for a particular piece, come forward.

KARL: Bit nervous now.

TRINA: Yeah, that is totally normal, to be honest with you – like we haven't even gone out to a café or had a dinner yet and you are going to take your clothes off for me!

Art seems to be the only place people accept nudity these days. The Greeks started it all off when they made naked sculptures of known athletes of the day. Apparently most athletes did their events in the nude back then, so this was the way people were used to seeing them. I saw one statue when I was in Greece of a fella sprawled across a rock, head tilted back, and his legs akimbo. He looked like a pissed-up bloke on a stag do, so I don't know what sport he did. I suppose he could have been the Freddie Flintoff or Gazza of the day.

To be honest, today's runners may as well go back to being nude as them Lycra pants they wear don't really hide much, do they? It's plain to see that if Usain Bolt went back to the old ways of running in the nude he would have an advantage getting over the finish line before anyone else. It can't have been easy running in the nude, though, having a couple of testicles slapping against your legs.

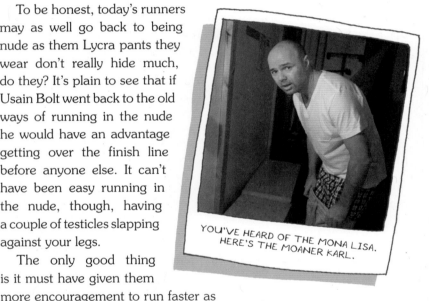

YOU'VE HEARD OF THE MONA LISA. HERE'S THE MOANER KARL.

The only good thing is it must have given them more encouragement to run faster as it would have sounded like they were being clapped along.

I popped on some jogging pants and a T-shirt and went into the studio where Trina tried to relax me by introducing me to all the other volunteers. It didn't help much as there were six girls and one bloke . . . who looked like Leonardo DiCaprio. I stood there in front of a big mirrored wall. I shouldn't have been there at all. It looked like S Club 7 with one of their dads.

KARL: Would everyone agree that it is harder for a man to be naked?

JAMES THE MODEL: I would agree, yeah.

TRINA: But you have one thing hanging out there – we have two.

KARL: No, no, no, but . . . I kind of think that they are all . . . the same. Breasts.

TRINA: You think that women are all the same?!

KARL: Breasts are, yeah. Everyone sees breasts every day, but you don't see knobs every day. There are loads of magazines with topless woman, it just goes over my head. If you suddenly took your top off – I would be like 'fine'.

JAMES: I think that male genitalia are much more offensive to the public eye.

KARL: I think it looks horrible as well. It's just not very nice. I don't think anyone wants to see it in a picture.

TRINA: I do. I think over fifty per cent of the population, females and homosexual males do want to see that. (giggles)

KARL: Not mine they don't.

TRINA: I don't look at the male that way. I don't want to make you feel uncomfortable. To be honest, I feel more uncomfortable when people are in their clothes, than when they are nude, because I am so used to these people.

KARL: Really?!

TRINA: Yeah.

Another problem I was worried about was getting a bit active down below. Being nude is one thing, but if it got excited, that could open another can of worms. Quite an appropriate phrase. I didn't know how mine would react as it has a mind of its own. I can be sat on a bus or train and the slightest tremor can set it off. It goes up and down all the time for no reason, so much so that I reckon it could conduct an orchestra by itself at times. I tried to subtly bring the matter up.

KARL: And if there's any sign of excitement?

TRINA: Sorry . . . what's that?

KARL: Just saying . . . if I get a little bit of excitement . . .

TRINA: (*blank expression*)

KARL: A little bit of movement, little bit of stiffness? Is that . . . ?

TRINA: Errmmm . . . you mean . . . ?

KARL: HARD KNOB!

TRINA: Oh. To be honest with you, I have painted, I don't know, at this point about a thousand people and it has only happened twice.

I've never been a fan of odds. And odds on knobs don't work. I can't control it. If it wants to get active, it just will. It could end up hailing me a cab back to the hotel if it gets out of hand. That's just reminded me of a joke.

HOW DO YOU SPOT A BLIND MAN ON A NUDIST BEACH?

IT'S NOT HARD.

Before we got into any positions Trina got us to warm our bodies up by doing some basic stretches followed by some slow walking.

KARL: What's this about, Trina? Why am I doing this slow walking?

TRINA: So, this is a practice that helps you to master your body and your focal awareness, so that you can stay concentrated inside the pose and use your body like an instrument, like a performer.

I was pretty good at it. They should do a race in the Olympics like this. Usain Bolt is the fastest man ever, so surely no one is ever going to beat him. And I don't get much enjoyment out of things that are over so quickly. It takes these runners longer to tie up the laces on their trainers than it does to do the race. Usain Bolt does the hundred metres in forty-one strides! The Red Arrows are another thing I don't enjoy as they are too fast. By the time you hear them above you, they've gone! So let's see who can do the slowest hundred metres.

Before anyone got nude, Trina got to work on designing how the lion of Leo would be put together. One by one we were called over and added to her vision. I couldn't make out what she was doing. I couldn't see the shape of a lion at all. I was called over and was asked to kneel down and get into a tight ball, and was crammed in between the others. This wasn't going to be as easy as I first thought. As we all crunched together, Trina and her assistant came over and moved arms and legs into place, criss-crossing limbs up and over each other. If I'd have had an itchy leg it would have been difficult to locate which leg was mine to scratch. An arm was pushing against my head while my face was being pushed into someone's knee. It was like playing Twister on the London Underground in rush hour. This went on for around thirty minutes, then Trina told us all to relax. I was pretty stiff and had problems standing up as my legs had seized up. I wandered around the studio looking like a newborn deer. As I was starting to get the feeling back in my legs Trina asked everyone to quickly trim any hairy areas of the body before she applied any paint. Now, trimming my body isn't a job that can be done quickly, as I'm quite hairy. I eventually gave in to Suzanne having a cat recently as she argued that I get more hairs on the sofa than any cat ever will, and she's probably not wrong. I was half thinking of suggesting to Trina that instead of being part of the lion, I should play the role of a hairball that the lion has coughed up.

I lifted my T-shirt and showed Trina and the other models my hairy chest, and I swear there was a gasp. Some men are described as being rugged, I'm just a rug. It's now my job at home to clean out the plug in the shower on a weekly basis as I shed that much hair. Some days it looks like I'm dragging Chewbacca out of the plughole.

KARL'S FACTS

The longest recorded chest hair measured 23.5cm and belonged to Zhao Jingtao from China.

I ended up borrowing an electric shaver and got to work on my body, removing a layer off my chest before handing the shaver to Jamie the director to sort stuff out on me back, which isn't thick hair, more like the little clumps of dust you get under your bed. Removing the hair made me feel even more nude and so I decided not to go and do the full monty. At the end of the day, I feel I have to keep something for Suzanne. The rest of me is out there on telly, the knob and balls are hers to see, if and when she wants.

Jamie said he knew I was never going to go through with it so had brought me some pants. He got them out and they were the finest pants I had ever seen in my life, and when I say finest I don't mean the best quality, I mean thin. Imagine wafer thin ham, and then slice it again! Jamie explained that they would make life easier for Trina to apply paint to as the material is the closest thing to skin. He wasn't kidding. I don't think I've ever had to handle something so delicate. A pair of pants made out of a spider's web would have been tougher. The strongest bit about them was the label. I eventually got them on and went back into the studio where I was greeted by the same bunch of people, but now they were nude. They applauded me as I walked in, as I think the pants were that thin they thought I was naked. I'm not a fan of being nude at the best of times, but with other people it's even weirder. I bought a hot tub recently to help with me bad back, and the salesman showed me a big seven-seater one and said I could invite mates round if I bought this one. There was a couple of problems with that: one being I don't have seven mates, and two, if I did, I wouldn't want them in a hot tub with me.

It's like phoning a mate and saying, 'I'm having a bath, do you fancy popping round and joining me?'

Trina started getting the main colour on our bodies to make us look like a lion. A light brown colour. It definitely took longer to do me due to my body hair getting in the way. I think I had more hair on me than Trina had on her brush. She was struggling to get through to skin so switched to a sponge and dabbed it on. Not many places were left untouched. She even dabbed between my cheeks. She kept telling me to relax as my arse cheeks clenched every time, but I couldn't help it; soon as the sponge touched my hairy arse, the cheeks closed like a Venus flytrap.

We crouched back into our rough positions, and Trina and her assistant got to work with more touching up while giving out instructions as to where we needed to move our feet or shoulders. This was so much harder than I thought it would be. Not only on the knees and legs, but I'm also not a fan of being in tight places. Last time I felt like this was when I was trying to get some trainers at a Sports Direct closing-down sale.

Suddenly my cheeks clenched again as someone was dabbing a soggy sponge on my arse. It was Trina. She stepped back and said she wasn't happy with what she was seeing. At first I thought she meant my arse, but she was talking about the whole thing and said we should all relax as she wanted to start again with a different design.

Everyone took this opportunity to grab some food, but because of all the paint, they couldn't put their clothes back on so it was a buffet in the buff. This wasn't that unusual for me as I tend to eat topless at home most days. I can be a messy eater. I've ruined loads of T-shirts from gravy splashes. Sunday lunch is the one that I make the most mess with, so I sit there looking like Peter Andre. I also prep my surrounding area like I'm about to do some painting and decorating before I have gravy.

Having food to look at was a bit of a blessing as it meant my eyes could relax a bit. They had been bouncing round the room like a squash ball trying not to stare at anyone's bits all morning, which is pretty difficult when you're in a room full of naked people.

Time was passing. We had already done around five hours in total. If it went on any longer, there was a chance I'd have to shave my body again. Trina announced she had a new design and planned on changing the lion's head.

This is where I would struggle as an artist. I wouldn't be able to start again on the same project. The saying 'if at first you don't succeed, try, try, try again' made sense years ago as you had no option, but now with Google it's easier to find someone else who can. Don't get me wrong, I'll have a go at doing something and put research into it beforehand. I'm always using YouTube these days before I take on anything. I'm pretty sure I would have done a lot better at school if YouTube had been around. It's like the best encyclopaedia ever, with the added bonus of dogs on skateboards.

Trina's new idea didn't change my position, so I was back down on my knees for another hour or so. Even though I wasn't doing much I felt shattered. It's funny how doing nothing can be so tiring. I always

have a go at Suzanne for saying she is tired after sitting on her arse all day, but full respect to her: it is hard work. I could sense that Trina felt under pressure with the time. The studio was only booked until 6 p.m., so she now had just thirty minutes to get it finished. I don't quite understand what happened but when I looked up from my pose I saw Trina was now undressed and getting involved in the modelling side of things while her assistant painted her. The room felt pretty tense now. It was like watching *DIY SOS* when they're trying to do up a house and the roof's off and it's clouding over.

TRINA: Do we look even? (*speaking to assistant*)

ASSISTANT: Stay in there, hold on!

KARL: Who?

ASSISTANT: Okay, now there is a space between the two guys . . . You have to tuck more down, Karl, you have to tuck more down.

KARL: Tuck more down?! Where? Here?

ASSISTANT: Between your chest and your . . . Tuck your head down, sweetheart, one mil . . . Okay, the head space is much better but there is still a space with Karl . . .

KARL: Mmmm . . . I can't move my neck down any more. I'm not a flamingo.

Trina's assistant asked everyone to hold still while she took a photo. 'Click' and it was done. I wanted to see the photo, but Trina said we had to clear the studio as our time was up. It was like a brothel being raided by the police as naked bodies ran about the place. I popped my clothes back on and she showed me the rough image.

TRINA: I am really happy with how the painting turned out. It looks great, and you were an awesome model even when your legs were going numb. You didn't even complain about moving.

KARL: Because everyone else was sticking with it and I didn't want to mess it up. Plus I wanted it to end. I was just thinking 'press the button, take the photo!'

TRINA: I was feeling the same thing myself . . .

KARL: I am glad that you are happy because I wouldn't be going back and doing it all again.

TRINA: You were very courageous, and you went for it, and I am like super proud of you and I really appreciate you doing that.

KARL: Well, thanks again for having us. Good luck with it all. All right, let's get out of here!

When I got home I looked at Trina's website to see if I could download the finished image, to find that she had done the image again. So I still don't have a photo of myself. What a bloody waste of time that was.

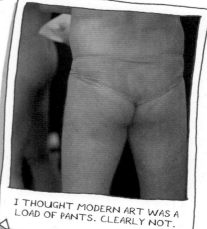

I THOUGHT MODERN ART WAS A LOAD OF PANTS. CLEARLY NOT.

PERFORMANCE ART

After being locked up in a studio all day it was nice to get some fresh air in Central Park. I love parks, and I'd say they do for me what galleries do for art lovers. It's natural art that I like – trees and lakes, insects and birds. I'm considering getting a dog, though, as I get strange looks from people when I'm walking through a park on my own. Dog or no dog, later that day I was definitely going to be getting funny looks as the plan was to get involved in some performance art in Central Park. In performance art, the artist is the body, and the live action they perform is the work of art. I suppose it's not too dissimilar to what I had been doing with Trina, except this time there was no chance to start again if it didn't work out, as it would be in front of a live audience.

In London, I used to see a lot of performance artists in Covent Garden. Getting to the shops was like walking through *Britain's Got Talent* auditions. Everywhere you looked there were jugglers, clowns on unicycles, sword swallowers, tightrope walkers, endless numbers of human statues and mime artists. I've done a bit of mime myself. It was when I was in the Peruvian jungle. I was in my tent and was really fed up, so I imagined unwrapping a Twix and eating it just like I normally do, biting the caramel off the top first and then the biscuit. It sounds mental but it kind of worked. After that I mimed eating an orange. That didn't work quite as well, as an orange does more to your taste buds, but the upside was I didn't have sticky hands. I did it again recently when I was thinking about buying a table tennis table. I stood there reaching for and hitting a nonexistent ball onto a make-believe table, but I got bored fairly quickly so binned the idea of getting one.

KARL'S FACTS

A Chinese performance artist has had one of his ribs removed so that he can wear it as a necklace.

The performance artist I was meeting was called Matthew Silver. He'd been doing his art on and off for nine years. I met him at the apartment he shares with a friend and a cat. On first impressions you could think Matthew was a proper mental, or homeless, or a stand-in for Tom Hanks in the film *Cast Away*. A gangly, thin man with a mass of hair covering his head and a smiley face. He looked like a dandelion. He invited me in and made me a cup of tea. I quickly realised he wasn't mental when he offered me a posh cinnamon herbal teabag. Not an official way to work out if someone is mad, I know, but then I've heard that one of the ways they work out if someone is a psychopath is by asking them if they like cats, so judging someone on their choice of teabags doesn't seem that daft. I've never got into these types of teas as you can't dunk biscuits into them. But I wanted to be polite so I accepted the offer. I didn't want to drink much of this tea, either, as cinnamon sends my heart rate through the roof for some reason, and it was already pounding thinking about having to perform in front of strangers in Central Park.

KARL: How did you get into this, then?

MATTHEW: Well, I was the class clown, I was always one of those characters. I go very simple, I go very raw and just like (*makes fart sound*) or (*makes chicken sound*) and then just dance in my underwear. I use awkward pauses to create tension, and usually because they are complete strangers they start laughing. It's freebase, it's all improv, it just happens, I just do it. I have a little technique, but the good thing about performance art is even a disaster can look amazing.

I think everyone would like to have the confidence to do what Matthew does. Most people don't take it any further than singing in the shower, but I don't even bother with that since I've moved to a house with a water meter. I try to get in and out as soon as possible. What I do like to do is dance for the cat. I mainly do it when I'm hanging around for the kettle to boil. I count while I'm dancing to see how long I can keep his attention before he looks away or closes his eyes. He's a tough crowd. I tell you, if Cowell ever leaves *The X Factor* they should get

my cat in. Or do a version of *The Voice* – three cats, once they all look away, you're out. Would be good that. I've gone off point, but all I'm saying is, we all like to show off and perform to ourselves (and cats), but it's a different ball game when there's a crowd.

Matthew handed me a pair of 'lucky pants'. They were Y-fronts, dyed bright green with 'LOVE' written across the arse. He said we should go onto the roof so he could show me the sorts of things he does. I popped on the green pants and he stripped down too, and then I gave him some help getting his props up to the roof. These were mainly toys that he had found, along with a wobbly stick and part of a highway barrier. He put on a motorbike helmet and carried a sign with 'LOVE' painted on it. He then went through his method.

MATTHEW: I like to just come out with a silly movement, you know, something like (*waves arms and dances on the spot*), really stupid, you know, and when you do it, you look at people's faces, make eye contact. You'll notice that people are actually smiling. You'll see people who are not into it, but then you'll see people who are into it, and if that person is into it and they're smiling, you can take it to another level. You could do my two favourites – fart sounds or the chicken noise. Eventually someone with an iPhone will start recording you, right? And then boom! That's your opportunity to come closer to that person.

KARL: What? Because they've got involved then?

MATTHEW: Right, they got involved. They gave you permission to . . . You know, if they're smiling or if they're videoing, they're involved. So you come up to them and you engage. You go up to them slowly, though, cos if you go in too quick you might scare the shit out of them. But if you just, you know, smile, they might be into it, you know.

Matthew's message was all around giving love to people, but that isn't really me. I find most people are a pain in the arse so I tend to avoid them if I can. I didn't even have an imaginary friend when I was a kid.

I thought about what message I would like to push in my performance and remembered the warm-up exercises I did with Trina where I had to walk as slowly as possible. I showed Matthew my skills as I thought I was quite good at that, and he liked it, so I suggested we both do it. Instead of spreading the message of love, I came up with spreading the message to slow down. New York is a place where everything is at a fast pace – it's the city that never sleeps – so it's a good message to get out there. I showed him my moves and he copied. He was impressed. Jamie the director just stared at me not saying much, which didn't really help. Who should I take notice of, Matthew who does this daily, or a bloke who makes TV? I decided I believed in the idea enough.

We went back inside and painted some cardboard signs with the word 'SLOW' to use during our performance.

KARL: What about money and stuff?

MATTHEW: You know . . . I perform when I can and lately I haven't been holding out the bucket. I don't ask for it. I let them give it to me, out of love, you know? Cos if I'm focused on making a certain amount of money, I'm not happy. I do all these great performances, I make a lot of people laugh, but then I'm like, oh, but I only made ten dollars. You know, today's typical person, if they don't make a certain amount of money they feel bad about whatever art they do. That's why art and money don't really work together.

I was confident. That was until he told me we might not be able to do this in Central Park as it was starting to get dark, and suggested Times Square instead. The idea of that made me nervous and I started to shake. Though that could just have been cos I was stood on Matthew's roof on a cold day in December in just a pair of green underpants, and I had less hair on my body than normal due to being shaved at Trina's body-painting session.

We headed off to Times Square to do our thing. In a way there was no better place to spread the message of 'slow down' as it's the most hectic place in New York. Thousands of people filled the streets. My heart was pounding like I'd eaten a full tub of cinnamon. Matthew had nothing to fear, he does this day after day. He doesn't even have to do anything, he just looks funny. He said I looked funny too in my costume of green pants, socks and trainers, and my back brace. The back brace wasn't part of the costume, though. I need it due to my bad back. I felt weak as I didn't have his hair and beard. I can't imagine he would look as funny or be as funny without the hair and beard. I've grown a beard now and again, but once it gets quite long Suzanne says I need to shave it as it doesn't work with a bald head. She says I look like a shuttlecock. To finish my look off, I borrowed his motorcycle helmet and a pair of shades. I'll be honest, I was shitting it. It was easy earlier on his roof when no one else was watching. We found our spot in Times Square and it happened. We did our slow-motion walking and added slow talking to it too. It's hard to explain now, but I think it worked. We improvised for around thirty to forty minutes. Crowds of people surrounded us, laughed and took photos as we told them to slow down in their busy lives. The fact that people stopped and watched means the message worked.

I got a proper buzz from it, probably more than I've ever got from anything else I've done. Don't get me wrong, I won't be getting invited to perform on the *Royal Variety Show* any time soon, but I thought the result was pretty good for something I'd not done before. The only problem I have with it as an art is that it's now gone. If people missed it, they missed it. Matthew has nothing to show for that night's work, and he will just have to start all over again tomorrow. He's like a council worker with a leaf blower – his work is never done.

I couldn't get to sleep for a few hours that night due to the adrenaline rush that I got. I sat in bed and googled 'performance art' on the internet to see if what I had done really counted as that. One definition I found said that 'performance art usually consists of four elements: time, space, the performer's body, and a relationship between audience and performer'. We'd ticked all those boxes. Now every year when I see Times Square on the TV for the New Year celebrations I can say 'I've played there'.

That's not bad, is it?

PAINTING A MASTERPIECE

My performance with Matthew was all about slowing things down. The next day I was due to meet an artist who does the opposite and creates artworks in record time. It's easy to think that stuff that doesn't take time to do is no good, but for art to be of any quality does it have to take years in the making? The ceiling Michelangelo worked on in the Sistine Chapel took him almost five years to complete. I've seen it and it is pretty good, but I think it's a bit daft to have a fancy piece of artwork in a building where people spend most of the time with their eyes shut praying.

Recently, critics seemed to go mad over the film *Boyhood*, the main reason being it took twelve years to make and the director stuck with the same cast over that time so you watched them age in the film. This fact seemed to take over from the storyline, and everyone just talked about how it was interesting to see the cast age. I watched it with Suzanne with her going on like 'Oh, look, hasn't he grown' and 'That hair suits him more than his last style'. It was more like going through a sodding photo album than watching a film. I didn't understand all the fuss. William Roache has been playing the part of Ken Barlow in *Coronation Street* for fifty years and the critics don't go on about him.

The artist I was going to meet up with was called Ushio Shinohara, a well-known Japanese painter (to those in the know). As soon as I entered his home/studio in Dumbo (Down Under Manhattan Bridge Overpass), the art district of New York, I could smell that familiar, chalky, damp smell of artists' paint. I recognise it even though I'm not around it much. Elephant shit is another smell like that. Ushio introduced himself. He was a small man, eighty-three years old with white fluffy hair, similar to my auntie Nora's, but unlike her, he had it in a flat Mohican. His hands were covered in so many specks of colour that when he put out his hand to shake mine I thought he was offering me some Skittles. I tried having a chat about his art but didn't get anywhere, as although he had been living in New York for almost fifty years, his accent was still strong and with my northern accent we couldn't make much sense of each other. I like being around people and having company, but

I don't always want to chat so I quite like meeting people who can't speak English as it gets rid of all the small talk. Han Solo had it right knocking about with Chewbacca – someone to watch his back and help him out without having to discuss what he got up to over the weekend.

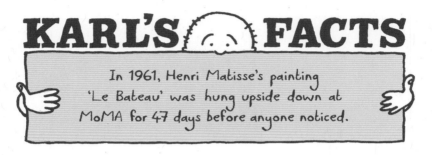

KARL'S FACTS

In 1961, Henri Matisse's painting 'Le Bateau' was hung upside down at MoMA for 47 days before anyone noticed.

The fact that Ushio couldn't understand me didn't matter anyway, as it was the art that was going to join us together. He got me to help mix up some paint so I could have a go trying out his painting technique. Only two colours were mixed: black and the brightest pink I have ever seen. The sort of pink that you only see in alcopops.

His wife Noriko appeared, a grey-haired trendy-looking woman, who handed me some boxer shorts to pop on. Not boxer shorts as in underpants, but actual shorts that a boxer wears to fight in. I always wanted a pair of these when I was younger, but my mam said the shorts were a waste of money as boxing was just another fad that I wouldn't keep up. After getting battered by a lad called Leeroy and hitting the canvas, my mam was right, I jacked it in. Today I'd be hitting the canvas again, but with my fists dipped in paint rather than my head. This was Ushio's technique of getting paint on the canvas. He started doing it in 1958 and has done thousands of huge paintings this way. It looked like he still had most of them rolled up and stacked in virtually every available space in his studio like some sort of carpet warehouse. He handed me a pair of boxing gloves and got me to tie sponges to them using string. Once the gloves were on, he told me to dunk one in the bright pink and the other in the black, then acted out what he wanted me to do to the canvas.

He wanted me to work my way across the big fifteen-foot-long canvas from right to left, thumping as I went, high up or low down, wherever I felt like. The main thing was not to stop. He slipped some goggles over my eyes and off I went. Thumping high, thumping low, left, right, right, right, left. The white of the canvas disappearing with every punch. The harder I hit, the bigger the splat. I was getting covered in paint with every punch as it splashed back at me. Forty seconds and thirty-five punches later I stepped back, wiped the paint from my goggles and looked at what I had created. As I took in the mess I had made, Ushio and Noriko applauded my efforts. They seemed happy, but I wasn't convinced. To me it was very similar to the mess Suzanne makes over the kitchen worktop whenever she makes soup in the blender.

KARL: How's that?

USHIO: Great!

NORIKO: Good, yes!

USHIO: Yeah! Masterpiece! Bang, bang, bang!

KARL: I don't know, can I add another colour?

NORIKO: No. Finished. You shouldn't think about the results. You cannot change the past.

KARL: Yeah . . . I don't know if I like it, then.

NORIKO: We finish the work, we don't think any more. After that the audience decide if it is good or bad.

It's a different way of working. Instead of spending ages trying to make a masterpiece, make something quickly and then at least if people don't like it, you haven't wasted too much of your time. I enjoyed the process but didn't like the end result. To me it looked like one of them pictures of a virus they show on the news when an epidemic breaks out, or the

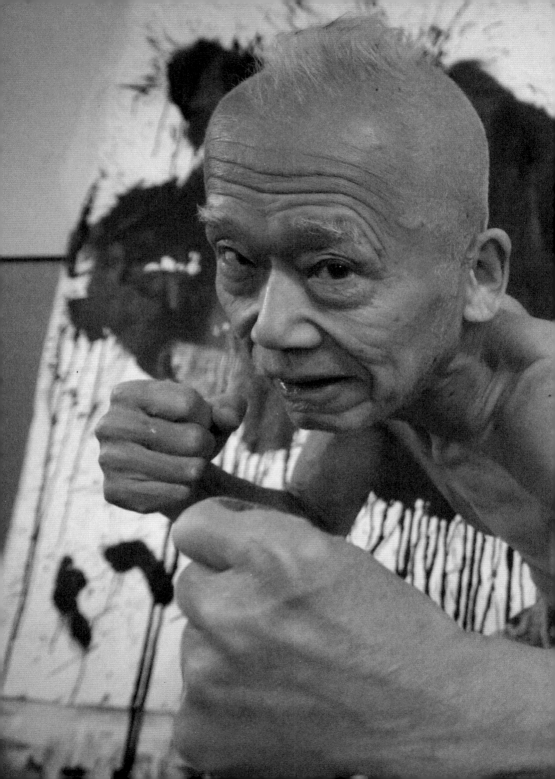

stains you get on hotel room walls in Spain where the last occupier had been kept busy killing mosquitoes. It was probably the most basic form of art, like the painted hand prints that kids make in their first year of school and then end up being stuck on the front of the fridge. They're always pretty crap. You never get someone putting someone else's kids' artwork on their fridge door, do you? It's because they look shit. I had made something but not something I was proud of. I could quite easily thump a piano with my fists and make a noise, but I doubt people would rush out to buy an album of it.

As the paint slowly dried on the canvas, I could also feel it drying on me and tightening my skin. I stood looking at what I had made while picking away at the paint on my arms. I used to like doing this at school when my hands got covered in Tipp-Ex. I got through quite a few bottles of correction fluid every month at school. The pages in my books were as brittle as poppadoms.

NORIKO: You can bring home . . . if you want?

KARL: I don't know . . . I don't know if it will go with the rest of the furniture.

NORIKO: You can just wrap it, keep it in loft for ten years.

KARL: I am not going to keep that.

NORIKO: If you didn't keep, you would regret later. So maybe ten years later, your idea go to look at it going to be different, so just keep it. Ten years later, you will be surprised – 'wow I made a big masterpiece'.

I couldn't take it home and shove it in the loft anyway as it's been converted into a bedroom. I'm sure the reason for more charity shops on the high streets these days is due to the fact that most people have converted their lofts, so they have less space to store crap.

Ushio strapped on some sponge and started smacking his arms and fists onto another canvas like Mr Miyagi's epileptic brother. He used just black paint. It didn't look too dissimilar to the one I had knocked out. It was funny to watch, as it's not every day you see a man in his 80s wearing nothing but shorts and goggles whacking a canvas to shit. Maybe it's more like performance art. I had a good day and enjoyed giving it a go, but just like the boxing I attempted when I was a kid, once was enough.

I WAS BEATEN BLACK AND BLUE . . .
AND PINK.

POLISHING A TURD

Art is something we like as it takes our mind off life's daily grind. We have so much going on in our heads that it's difficult to properly get away from it all. I find there are only a few things that help me clear my mind from the chaos: 1) cutting the lawn, 2) cleaning windows, 3) music, 4) rock climbing (I did it for the first time recently on a trip and when you are unclipping hooks from one rope to another, and your life depends on getting them in the correct order, it really makes you focus on the job in hand and you forget everything else), 5) standing in dog shit. No matter what is going on in your life, when you stand in some fresh dog shit and the smell hits you, everything has to stop while you find a stick to scrape the problem away from the tread in your trainers.

The only thing worse than having to do this is having to wipe it away from between your toes. I can still remember the feeling of this happening. I went to get some milk off the doorstep barefoot and our dog had defecated at the front door and I hadn't seen it. It made me gag instantly. I don't know if you've seen that film *127 Hours* where a man gets his arm trapped under a boulder and the only way he can escape is by cutting it off. If you have, the noises he made and the expression on his face were similar to me wiping that shit from between my toes. No one else was up yet, so I wiped it off my feet and went back to bed, the plan being to act like I hadn't seen it. Of course the only issue was that my bowl of cornflakes next to my bed and the milk already in the fridge and open were a giveaway, plus the fact that my footprint was in the turd, so a visit from Magnum P.I. wasn't necessary to work out I'd already seen it and decided to leave it.

Rightly so, I was in the shit yet again.

Today I was going to have to beat those demons and come face to face with dog dirt one more time, as I was having a day out with a couple of lads known as the Sprinkle Brigade, who since 2007 have been creating art using dog poo. Their names were Jeremy and Jeff. I met them at the site where the idea came about.

JEREMY: Well, we're called Sprinkle Brigade. We go around the city and we decorate the shit that people leave on the street. Because it's a problem. No one does anything about it. So we figured we'll do something to make it look a little bit more special to brighten up people's day.

JEFF: Yeah. Take something that people hate, and make them laugh a little bit.

KARL: I suppose there aren't many things left in life that get an immediate reaction like shit does.

JEFF: There's comedy in there, but for the most part you're right; it's disgusting and if we can take something that people loathe and make it something they laugh at, we think that's of value. We don't think the world is gonna pick up their dog shit. There's always gonna be people who leave it, and it's always gonna be something that we all hate.

JEREMY: We're very particular about the way we go about it. We don't just walk up to each piece and say 'oh, there's one right there, we gotta decorate it'. Everything is really thought out. There are three principles to it: having a great idea, finding the perfect piece that suits the idea, and then giving it a really great name.

The plan was to go shopping first and buy some props that would be added to the poo to bring it to life and make it art. On the way to the shop we came across the first small pile of dog dirt. They stood and chatted while not taking their eyes off it, just like Blake the art critic looked at the art in the Museum of Modern Art.

JEFF: It's a possibility but the size isn't there. We could do something with it but it's just . . . you know. It's not jumping out at me.

KARL: How long would you say that one has been there?

JEFF: I think it's newborn. That's a newbie.

KARL: Is that from this morning, then?

JEFF: It's got a brush of rain on it. Maybe like an hour of rain or something. So it could have come last night.

KARL: So that doesn't excite you?

JEREMY: I think it's a dud.

JEFF: If it's fresh and it has a tacky ordure, you can just go straight with the sprinkles. But in a case like this, I know that if I put the sprinkles on there, then it's not gonna stick. So, there is a little bit of a cheat we use, but it works.

JEREMY: It's called Spray Mount.

KARL: Oh right, like a type of spray glue. It's quite an expensive hobby this, then?

JEREMY: It gets a little pricey. Money is no object, though, when it comes to this.

KARL: Now the sprinkles are on it, do you take a photograph?

JEFF: I don't think we necessarily need to photograph this one, cos this is a standard, a basic hit. Unless it's like a cascade of shit, you know what I mean, like a real prize winner, then we might photograph it, cos it means something to us. But this one is just kind of routine. It just leaves a mark so when somebody comes around and sees it, they'll know the Sprinkle Brigade has been here.

At this point, I wasn't sure whether it was art just yet, but what I liked was that the sprinkles made it stand out on the pavement, which meant there was less chance of someone stepping in it. When I was a kid, standing in dog shit on the estate was something that happened around three to four times a week. I think I spent more time cleaning out the tread on my trainers than I spent cleaning my teeth. Thinking back, a popular toy back then that every kid had was stilts. It's likely they came into fashion as a way of avoiding getting shit on your shoes. Honestly, it was everywhere. The local park had 'Keep Off the Grass' signs, but I don't think this was an order, it was more of a warning, as it was like a minefield out there. Everyone goes on about Michael Jackson being the creator of the moonwalk, but he wasn't, everyone round our way was walking backwards like that scraping shit off their shoes.

KARL'S FACTS

Congo, a chimpanzee who made over 400 paintings, would scream if a painting was taken away from him before he was finished.

We went into a toy shop, and I got looking for props that could help turn dog muck into a piece of art. I followed Jeff and Jeremy around the place to get an idea of the sort of things they look for. Jeff picked up a plastic eagle.

KARL: So you'd just place that on the poo?

JEREMY: Yeah, kinda perched up on it like a wooden post.

KARL: Like a log?

JEREMY: Yeah . . . you know, like the big wooden logs that come up in the ocean. I'm really excited about that. I hope we can get a piece in a puddle, in the position that we want it. Like it's almost like, in the ocean. Really romanticise it.

The first thing that grabbed my eye was a small wooden TV which must have been for a doll's house.

JEFF: What are you thinking?

KARL: I'm thinking . . . shit coming out of the TV.

JEFF: Yeah . . .

KARL: And it would sort of be saying, you know, it's the shit on telly, like 'arghh, not this shit again'. We have a lot of repeats at home.

JEFF: Right. I think it's true, and I think it'd be funny for people and they can relate to it. I think it'd be cool. I think you have one there.

JEREMY: So we need to find a piece of poo that is basically severed in half perfectly so it fits right up against the TV, you think?

KARL: Right. So it actually looks like it's coming out. Let's buy that, then. Oh, look, toy butterflies. Maybe something coming from an ugly poo, like a caterpillar to a beautiful butterfly.

JEFF: I like the idea of butterflies. People think of them as a beautiful thing, so there's a contrast there which I think is kind of funny but . . .

KARL: It needs the ideal piece of excrement, though.

JEREMY: Yeah, unless it was one that looked like a cocoon and it was coming out of the cocoon, it might be too, you know . . .

JEFF: It might be too scientific.

KARL: It's not easy, is it?

JEREMY: No. I mean, we go back and forth for weeks on a few ideas, until we finally get it right. Even then you'll put in all the work and the time and do it and it'll be kind of anticlimactic.

JEFF: We always said it's like fishing. Some days you go out and then you might get scant or sometimes you might get something suitable to mount over the fireplace, so you just don't know.

I then saw a tub of Plasticine and an idea hit me with the title for the piece coming instantly. We paid for the few props we had picked up, and off we went onto the streets of New York, a city that's full of interesting things to do and yet here I was hunting down dog shit, the stuff I couldn't get away from when growing up.

KARL: Because you're around dog shit a lot, you wouldn't know what type of dog has left that shit, would you? You're not at that level?

JEFF: Well, that's a heated debate. But the truth of it is we've seen small dogs lay out a beast, and we've seen big dogs lay out something small. So I don't think there's a way to match the shit with the species.

I asked this question as I had a mate called Simon who had a dog that you could link to the stool, as it ate anything that was in front of him. If you stood in some crap and there was a toy soldier in it, you knew it came from his dog. I suppose at least there was some kind of perk to standing in it. At least you got a toy. It was like a very early stage of the Kinder Egg.

Jeremy and Jeff got out a map that they had designed showing all the hotspots where people very rarely picked up their dog's mess. I said their map was like a 'shat nav' system, but I don't think they use the word 'shat' in the States so they didn't know what I was going on about. To be honest, there was no need for a map as my nose could do the job. The place stank. Suddenly, everywhere I looked there were lumps of shite.

I SAID, SIT.

The place really did have a problem. New York is known as the city that never sleeps but round this part of town it was the city that never sweeps! One of the things that does my head in these days is when people walk into you cos they're not watching where they're going due to them reading an email or text on the move. Some people even read a book while walking from A to B. There was no way people could do anything but focus on where they were stepping in this neighbourhood.

It was annoying to think that there was a shovel hanging up in the Museum of Modern Art doing nothing. It was needed here.

KARL: And it's definitely all dog?

JEREMY: Well, there have been some instances when it was human. You know it's human if it's up close against the wall. Because it's physically impossible for a dog to press its ass against the wall.

KARL: So is that still game?

JEREMY: No, we stay away from that.

KARL: Fucking hell. What's going on?! People are shitting on the streets.

I think this will end up being a problem in the UK as we seem to have sorted the dog shit issue at home by having loads of bins especially made for dog waste, but I've been in situations when I really need to go to the loo and there's no public toilets around. I've been in loads of cafés and asked to use the loo, and they only let you use them if you buy something, which you don't always want to do. It used to cost a penny. That's where the saying 'I'm off to spend a penny'

POOTASSIUM.

comes from. Now it may as well be 'I'm off to buy a panini', as that's what you have to do. No wonder the country is becoming obese when you have to buy food to empty your bowels. I think human crap on the streets is going to be the new problem we'll be facing at home.

Jeremy pulled a banana skin from his bag and edged the skin up close to a dog turd, so it looked like a brown banana.

JEREMY: To be very honest, I think this one is grossing me out a little bit. Some ideas don't work. This one, I think, might be a little bit over the top for me. It could have been a great idea, but I think it's . . . disgusting. It's over the top.

JEFF: Don't be so sure.

KARL: But if you call it 'Pootassium', because a banana is full of potassium, I think it takes away the harshness.

JEFF: That's pretty good. I think Karl is right. Karl more than gets it . . . haha!

KARL: Are you getting enough pootassium?

JEREMY: Pootassium is really funny, it is really good. You saved it.

JEFF: I want to put that one up on Instagram.

I really wanted to get my idea started but was struggling to hunt down the right-shaped pieces I needed. No turd was the same, so I knew what I required must be out there. I even started to hang around a couple of dogs that looked like they were about to unload on the off chance they dropped off what I was looking for. I wouldn't like to be a dog as I wouldn't like to only be able to empty my guts when my owner takes me out. On top of that you have to do it while they stand there waiting. It puts me off when I go into the posh toilets in a restaurant where they have some bloke hanging about there waiting for you to come out and hand you a towel to dry your hands. I feel like I'm being timed. I always end up cutting it short.

I kept looking. Some were shaped like Twiglets, some like pretzels and others like walnuts. What I needed were a few loose pieces for my idea to work. As mad as this was, it felt like a lot more work than the boxing painting I had done with Ushio yesterday. While I was looking for the stools I required, Jeff and Jeremy had pulled out another prop. It was a pair of novelty 2015 New Year glasses and they were placing them on a dog poo that would act as a nose.

JEFF: Maybe. I mean it's a little thin. So we're gonna go right over the top here on this one. (*getting camera steady*) Then we'll take a photo of it this way. And we'll call it the 'Happy New Year Shit Nose'.

JEREMY: Mainly we use iPhone cameras because the nicer cameras usually pick up too much of the detail, and when we print those out, it looks disgusting.

KARL: That one should be called 'Happy Poo Year'.

JEFF: Happy Poo Year! Even better.

All my searching finally paid off. I found the droppings that would work for my piece at the back of a car park. Three small pieces, a few centimetres apart. I got out my Plasticine and rolled the first piece into a short stubby tail and stuck that down onto the tarmac a couple of centimetres away from one of the pieces of crap and then made another

slightly thicker piece. I then borrowed some eyes from Jeremy's craft box, which he carried with him. I stuck on the two eyes and stuck that down at the other end of the three pieces.

KARL: So, maybe the head coming out here. It's not absolutely right but I think you can tell what I'm trying to make.

JEREMY: All of a sudden it kinda flows. It's great. I think it's working.

KARL: Yeah?

JEREMY: Oh boy . . . oh, it's powerful.

KARL: So that's it. This one is called 'The Loch Mess Monster'.

The lads took photos of it. I'd got quite a bit of pleasure out of the day and was chuffed with what I'd created. Let me be clear here: it wasn't something that I'd want to stick on the fireplace, but as art made out of a turd goes, I think I succeeded. I didn't hang around to see what any passers-by thought of it, but I suppose as an artist you just put it out there and hope people like it.

As I left I'd been so busy looking at my art that I'd forgotten about my dangerous surroundings. I felt my foot slide. Oh shit.

BEAUTY FROM THE INSIDE

I'd been away for around a week and had been getting involved in some pretty odd art every day. So what came next didn't seem too bizarre at the time. I think I'd become a bit immune to it all. I knew it was going to be a challenging day, and what made it harder was that I wasn't allowed to eat for twenty-four hours, which is difficult as eating is what gets me through the hassles of the day. If something is annoying me, knowing that at some point soon I'll be eating makes it easier to deal with. America is the worst place to be when you're not able to eat, as you can't avoid it – food is constantly in your face on billboards and on TV. The rest of the crew were eating, so I had to just sit and watch, and it's never a quick activity in the States as the portions are massive. Food you didn't even order gets brought to the table. Even when you ask for the bill it comes with fries.

You hear about some artists who die for their art. Well, the one I was about to meet dosen't take it that far – she just gets sick. Literally. And the plan was for me to join her. But she didn't want any food in the sick so this was why I was not allowed to eat. I'm rubbish at being sick. Loads of things can make me gag, but it very rarely follows through to full-blown eruption. I guess it's like how some people are right-handed and others are left-handed; any badness tends to leave me via the other end rather than through the mouth. I'd honestly say that in my forty-three years of existence I think I've only been sick about nine or ten times. The last time was in 2010 during *An Idiot Abroad 2*, when I was staying in a cabin that stank of rotting fish while the boat rocked all over the shop. Another was during my first trip to India for *An Idiot Abroad 1*, where every hole in my body became an emergency exit after I'd eaten something dodgy. I was like a garden sprinkler! Before that I think it was mainly travel sickness if I had to sit in the back of a car.

Once when we were driving back to Manchester from a holiday in Wales, I couldn't sit in the front as my dad's mate was with us and he took that seat. It was a rainy day, so the heating had to be on to stop the windows steaming up, and my dad's mate's dogs were in the back with me and my mam, and they stank of damp. The night before, I'd been in the club house playing my mates at pool and drinking Britvic orange. I must have drunk about five pints of the stuff, so with that churning around in my belly, in the back of a hot car on the curved roads of Wales with damp dogs breathing in my face, we took a corner and 'Llllarrrrghhhhhllllllllllurggg' (that's not the name of the village in Wales, that's the noise I made). Five pints of Britsick down me dad's neck.

That was back around 1982. So I really didn't know how today was going to go down . . . or come up.

KARL'S FACTS

Neil Armstrong and Buzz Aldrin
left more than 100 items on the moon,
including a bag of vomit.

I met the artist in a studio. It was a totally white room with a couple of canvases on the floor, next to quite a few cartons of soya milk and bottles of food dye, which she would mix and then drink before heaving up onto the canvas. Her name was Millie Brown.

KARL: How did you come up with this, then, Millie?

MILLIE: Well, basically my art collective were all asked to go to Berlin and take over this gallery space there, and everyone was doing different performances or showing their work in this gallery, and I'd never done performance art before and I wanted to use my body to paint, and came up with the idea of painting from the inside out. I wanted to create a performance that was really raw and human and, like elements of being uncontrollable, so I had this idea I wanted to do a rainbow. I wanted every single colour in the rainbow. I had never made myself sick before and I didn't know if I could do it. I just got on stage and put my fingers down my throat, and did it. And I was like, either way, if it works or doesn't work it's gonna be an interesting performance.

KARL: So when did you last do this?

MILLIE: A couple of months ago in London. We were shooting an art film.

KARL: How was that?

MILLIE: It was good. I was shooting a film where it was like a Zar ritual, so a lot of the movements were me shaking my head around and around and around. It was an entire day, a good nine hours of me spinning round in circles having not eaten since the morning before.

KARL: What, while being sick?

MILLIE: Yeah, basically at the end of this Zar performance ritual I was sick. So it was a really long day of just sucking on sugar cubes to stop myself from fainting cos I was spinning around in circles for an entire day.

KARL: Was it worth all the hassle?

MILLIE: In the end, me actually being sick was cut from the film.

KARL: So it wasn't worth it, then?

MILLIE: I mean, it's always worth it, you know. Suffering for my art is part of what I do.

KARL: Why's that important?

MILLIE: I mean, it's not important to suffer necessarily, it just so happens that every performance that I do has an element of that suffering. I like to push my own mental and physical boundaries to get to that state of mind where it's kind of a pure creative place. I feel like

> by putting your body through some element of suffering or discomfort you are able to reach that state even more easily.
>
> KARL: Just doing as much as I've done today is pushing me . . . not having any food for twenty-four hours.
>
> MILLIE: Well, I think a lot of the performance is about the actual element before you actually perform. It's like a long kind of solitude performance that you do alone before you actually perform the piece.

As mad as the whole concept sounded, it had got my attention. If her thing was drawing with felt tip pens, let's face it, I wouldn't be visiting her. A lot of people think art has gone a bit mental these days. But I reckon it's our own fault. We're always looking for the next thing, and that pushes artists to come up with even madder ways of getting their work noticed.

Millie poured a pint of soya milk and added some purple food colouring. She got me to do the same. I went for red, and then I slowly drank it. For some reason I can't neck back any drink. My throat doesn't allow it. If I try, my throat goes into a sort of spasm where it locks for a few seconds, so I just took a few sips at a time.

Once Millie had drunk the full glass she crouched down and just splurted out a purple splat onto the canvas. It wasn't too messy and she didn't have to struggle to do it. It came out like soap out of a hand pump dispenser. It didn't run down her chin or cause her make-up to run. She then moved around the canvas and released the rest of the purple soya milk like it was on tap. She didn't have to give any force at all. I had a mate who could do this. Apparently it was because he drank so much fizzy pop. His stomach lining was knackered or something, so he could just force sick out on demand. He mainly used it as a defence mechanism; if anyone ever started on him he just threw up whatever he had been drinking, and it really confused them. He could double up as a fire extinguisher.

KARL: How do people react when they see you doing this?

MILLIE: Well, I think different pieces talk to different people, and we're all unique in different ways, so not everything is going to appeal to us. Some people hate my work and some people love it. There's not much of an in-between. I love creating art this way. A lot of my performances don't involve vomit at all, and I'm always doing new work, but I just love this form of painting. It really means something to me and it's something that I've done from the age of seventeen, so it's like a part of me, I guess.

KARL: So how do I do it?

MILLIE: Use two fingers and start touching the back of your throat, and just keep doing that movement back and forth until you start to gag, then you keep pushing and pushing until its starts to come up.

I've never met anyone who was so into being sick. Art is all about doing something you love, and she loves being sick. Most people have to stop doing what they love when they are ill, but Millie doesn't. In fact, she might create more than normal. I wiggled my two fingers about in the back of my throat, like I do when trying to grab a pound coin that has gone down the sofa. It was making me gag but nothing was coming up. It's funny, really, as during this trip, especially during the Times Square performance,

I found there was something inside me that made me want to perform, but my outside is normally the nervous bit. Yet here was a chance for my insides to show off, and they didn't want to know!

It was an odd experience to have Millie and the director and cameraman watch me trying to be sick. It's something that should be done in private.

KARL: You look like your weakest, don't you, when you're being sick?

MILLIE: I think that's the beautiful part about the performance – it's so vulnerable. It's something that you would never normally do in public, and it's strange cos when I'm actually sick, when I'm ill, I don't want anyone around me, yet making myself sick, I don't mind doing in front of hundreds of people. Somehow it's very different to me.

KARL: Yeah, this feels strange to me. Strange, plus I'm under pressure.

MILLIE: You know, it's not like a party trick, it's not about it coming out easily. I think when there's struggle that's what makes it human. This is raw and human, and it doesn't get more real. It can be disgusting, it can be beautiful, but it's human. So, however your body reacts to it, if you struggle, if you have snot down your face, that's all part of it.

I went from tickling my throat to scratching it like a scratchcard. And I was trying to force it out so much, it started to give me a bit of a headache. Millie said I should try bending over a bit more to help it out, but nothing would come. It's a bit of a worry, really, cos if I ate something poisonous that I had to get out of my system quickly, I'd struggle to do it. Maybe this is the problem that the old woman who swallowed a fly had; she couldn't sick it up so she had to swallow a spider to kill it.

I was doing little burps but nothing was coming back up. The director was asking me to keep going. Everyone was stood there gawping at me, but there was nothing they could do to help as I battled with my

stubborn gut. If nothing else, it proved that it was a kind of performance art as they couldn't take their eyes off me. I guess it's similar to people rubbernecking at an accident on the road. We enjoy watching sick people. I mean, a night doesn't go by when there isn't some sort of hospital drama on the telly. You've got *Casualty*, *Holby City*, *House*, *Quincy*, *St Elsewhere*, *The Young Doctors* – the list is endless. I'm convinced this is why the NHS are saying they've not got enough hospital beds to cope with the demand, it's cos all these TV dramas are using them!

Millie had now drunk another pint of soya milk. This time a beige-coloured vomit hit the canvas. She wasn't happy, though, as the first colour she had spewed up had not had time to dry. She would normally leave it for a day or two before she even thought about adding a new colour, but cos we were there, she added a second colour and it just all mixed into the first colour and ended up looking like, well, sick. She decided not to waste the canvas so used some kitchen roll to wipe everything off. I decided to stop trying as my head was now banging.

KARL: Cheers for showing me what you do. Sorry I couldn't do the business for you.

MILLIE: I think it's kind of better that you didn't, actually.

KARL: Why's that, then?

MILLIE: Because it adds that uncomfortable, raw, human, weird tension. For me it came out instantly, but you struggled. It's performance art and there are no rules to it, either. It's not like you failed because you couldn't vomit. The performance is what you make it, and I think that piece worked really well with the struggle that you added into it.

I was saying at the start how it would have been nice to have some art on my wall at home that had me in it, without it just being a straightforward photograph. This would have been ideal if I could have pulled it off. I'm not sure I'd want Millie's sick on my wall, but if the vomit actually came out of a family member or loved one it makes more sense. You could do it with the whole family. It would be especially good if you are from a bit of an ugly family and you don't want to have a photo on the wall reminding you how ugly you all are – just get everyone to be sick on the same canvas. Job done. Another thought: if someone is on their deathbed and they're ill, having their final spew on a canvas is a good way to remember them. It's no weirder than having their ashes on your mantelpiece, is it?

Once we'd cleaned up the art studio, we all went off to a diner where I had a foot-long hot dog and fries. Millie joined us but this time kept everything down. I gave myself a private show in my toilet that night. Like I said, with me, everything comes out the other end. It was like a Red Arrows display.

FINDING ART IN NATURE

I enjoyed this trip a lot. Even though I didn't like all of the finished art I was involved in, I did get something out of being part of it and seeing how much the people who made it got out of it. Jamie the director wanted me to show him what my favourite art was. At first I was thinking of maybe a painting I like, or a building or a piece of design, but then I recalled seeing something on the telly that I really wanted to observe in real life. Some would argue that it isn't really art, but to me it is. I'd say it's better than any of the performance art that humans do. We headed to Shapwick Nature Reserve in Somerset, where, with some luck, I would witness a murmuration. A murmuration is the name given when a flock of hundreds or even thousands of starlings fly about together before settling down in the reeds for the evening. I've watched them on the telly and I've clicked on loads of videos of them on YouTube, and they are one of the few things in life that give me goosebumps. I don't know what your body is telling you when you get goosebumps, but because it doesn't happen often I'm guessing it's when you're witnessing something special.

The reason I like it is that no one is still quite sure why they go through this motion. In a world where almost everything has been answered in life and yet they haven't come up with a solid answer to this activity, it makes it even more amazing. It's been said that maybe they do it to protect themselves like shoals of fish do, but I've never understood why fish do that. I've watched nature programmes where they all bunch together and a whale comes along and gets a right mouthful. Okay, it doesn't get them all, but it gets enough. I'm pretty sure if they all stayed alone the whale wouldn't bother chasing any of them as it wouldn't be worth his while. It's the equivalent of me grabbing a handful of nuts from a bowl. I wouldn't bother if there was only one.

KARL'S FACTS

Chains of schools of mullet spanning a whopping 100km have been spotted in the Caspian Sea.

The sea is another place I'll go looking at weird stuff on YouTube. It blows my mind the peculiar stuff you get in the oceans. Just when you think you've seen all there is to see, you find something else. I saw a fish called the sheepshead fish, which I thought was a joke that someone had made up as it's a fish with human teeth! When you're near wifi, just google 'sheepshead fish'. I've no idea who named it, as it looks bugger all like a sheep. It's a normal-looking fish but it has the teeth of Miley Cyrus. They could make dentures for old people with them. It's well weird.

It was a gamble dragging Jamie the director and a camera crew out to Somerset as there was no guarantee we would see a murmuration, and on top of that, there was a chance that even if we did, it might not be as amazing as it looked on the telly. This is the problem with TV coverage. It often shows the best version of something, and if you go and see the thing yourself it never lives up to it. Jamie the director said he wasn't convinced that it was art, which I thought was a joke when you think we started this trip looking at a bloody shovel in the Museum of Modern Art!

We set off from London at around 7 a.m. It was a damp, grey day with rain forecast. It took about five hours to get there due to the traffic. All the way, I was worrying as I really wanted it to be good and yet the whole thing depended on the starlings showing up and putting on a good show.

We got there and got booted up as it was wet and muddy. It felt like a million miles away from where I started my trip in New York. A nice quiet bit of countryside with clear air. I had no idea if the drizzle would mean the starlings would be a no-show. Surely a drop of rain wouldn't stop them; it's not Wimbledon. We made our way closer to the water – this is the place they tend to fly around as there are fewer predators hanging around. There wasn't a starling in the sky. Just one swan messing about in the water. We waited. And waited some more. It was like going to a Pete Doherty gig.

There was no guarantee it was going to happen. But that's nature for you. Most things in the world these days are on demand, but nature isn't one of them. I watch *Springwatch* live, and they always promise footage of all sorts of rare animals but never deliver, and end up filling the programme with live coverage of a box of baby owls.

I kept looking up thinking I could see a group of starlings in the distance, but it was just small clouds. The light was starting to go and so was my hope of seeing them. Due to us having another potential five-hour drive back to London, I could see Jamie the director was close to knocking it on the head and suggesting we should head back, when I saw a small dark patch in the sky. A bunch of starlings flew over, looking like a faint fingerprint. If I had to put a number on it I'd have said 200 starlings. We all legged it like kids who have just heard the chimes from an ice-cream van. It was hard to keep up, as there were trees all around so it wasn't easy to track them. We stopped and looked up, and even more were coming in from different directions. This was it. It was happening. It was unbelievable. In minutes, what looked like around 20,000 starlings, maybe more, were throwing all sorts of shapes, the sort you get in a lava lamp, but at high speed. Breaking off into three groups and heading off in different directions before turning and joining back together. Similar to a tornado hurtling through the countryside with the noise to match. I wasn't prepared for that. It reminded me of the first time I heard the crowd at Man United react to a goal from outside the ground when I was a kid. A noise that can only be produced by something in large numbers. A loud swooshing sound, mixed with the tweeting, as the starlings swooped into each other, but never collided.

The amount seemed to be growing all the time. How is this happening? Who's in charge and leading this madness? The best show on earth and yet we were the only ones witnessing it. For free. It was even better than when I've seen it on YouTube.

Blake the art critic said he would stand and look at a painting for an hour, which I couldn't understand, but I could easily watch this for longer. The only disappointing part was that I couldn't, as this show was over within twenty-five minutes, with no encore. One minute they were darting about the sky and next it was like someone had turned on a big vacuum that sucked them into the ground where they all lay to rest for the night. I've visited the Seven Wonders of the World and this shits all over them (actually, they probably would). I'd say it's definitely one of the things you have to see before you die. And it probably would be, if you were a worm.

Perfectionist
Caring
Stubborn
Funny
Hard - working
Loyal

THIS IS HOW Suzanne described me yesterday when I asked her to list my characteristics. I was pretty pleased with that review. I come across as quite a catch, and would happily have that stamped on my gravestone. I doubt I would have come up with a list as good as that on my own as I struggle bigging myself up. I've never got a job through an interview because of this, and have always relied on someone putting a word in, or I've worked for free for a few days to show them what I can offer. I'm like a toilet brush – not the most exciting thing to have in the home, but you'd be lost without it.

The thing is, I'm human and have more than these six aspects to my character.

I asked Suzanne to do a new list today, and I got this:

Rude
Disregard other people's feelings
Uncompromising
Shouty

You see, today started with a call to a furniture shop where I wanted to order two items. The delivery charge was £40 but the fella on the end of the phone wanted to charge me £80 as there were two items. I didn't see why he was charging me twice. He was coming to our address with the first item anyway, and the website suggested buying the items together, so why am I being charged twice?!

'That's the way it is,' he said.

'Okay, I'll order the two items and pay the delivery charge twice, but I want each item delivered on separate days, seeing as I'm paying twice.'

'Now you're just being silly,' he said.

'You're being a cheeky bastard!' I said.

He hung up. This is what got me the 'rude' and 'uncompromising' from Suzanne.

Later on, we went out for a walk before deciding to go for something to eat. The first place I suggested was shut, so that annoyed me, and then the second place was full, so by the time we got to the third place I was starving. Suzanne was on the phone trying her luck with the furniture company, seeing as I didn't get anywhere, so I picked a table that I thought was fine. Once she was off the phone she started moaning that the table was in the shade and it was too cold (even though I said she should have brought a coat with her)

so wanted to move to a sunny table. I got arsey and said it's like going out with bleeding Goldilocks. So now I was the 'shouty' one with 'disregard for her feelings'.

I'm always being told off for shouting. People think I'm joking if I say I'm not happy with something, and I find it's only when I shout that I'm taken seriously.

Suzanne said I even shout when I write as I do everything in capitals. She said her Valentine card messages look like ransom notes. But that's just because I've never got into doing joined-up writing. I think it's a selfish way to write. It might be faster for you to do it but you're taking up more time of the person who has to try and read it.

The other problem I have with it is it uses up more ink as the pen never leaves the paper.

Anyway, once I'd had a bellyful of food and ordered pudding I calmed down and apologised. Suzanne had also managed to talk the furniture bloke round so the 'cheeky bastard' was only going to charge us for one delivery. All's well that ends well.

I think a big part of your identity is how people see you rather than how you see yourself. Another way to get an idea of what you're really like is to look at your internet history. Sometimes I look at mine and wonder what I'm doing with my life. Currently my searches show I've been looking at pressure washers, I've watched the Um Bongo TV advert from the '80s as I used to like rapping along to it as a kid and I wanted to see if I could still remember it (I couldn't), I've been looking at images of sheepshead fish, I've been on my fantasy football league and watched another YouTube favourite of a gorilla on a BMX. I'm not sure what all that says about me.

A NEW HEAD OF HAIR

The plan during this trip was for me to look at myself and my identity, which began with me gozzing into a small test tube and rubbing a cotton bud-type stick on the inside of my cheek to collect some saliva to post off for a DNA test. Apparently my saliva knows more about me than I know about myself. From that, the experts can gather information on relatives I've not met and data about my ancestral origins, which is impressive, as the only thing it generally links me to is my pillow. Even though the duvet and pillows are thrown from the bed when Suzanne is changing the bedding, I still know which are my pillows due to the saliva stains. Yellow circles of goz cover seventy per cent of the pillows – it looks like giraffe skin. I don't know why I churn out so much. Science says we produce two to four pints every day, but I reckon I've got loads more than that. A few years back I sat in the garden and dribbled to see if it would eventually stop, but believe it or not I got bored before the supply came to an end. I reckon I could water the garden with myself.

Anyway, I read ages ago that humans share fifty per cent of the same DNA as a banana. I wasn't too fussed about the results of this test so I had two and a half bananas for breakfast to see if I could alter my DNA and be more banana than human when the results came back in.

If I had to describe myself, I wouldn't start with me being British, or white, or how old I am, I would begin with the fact that I am bald. I'd say it's my most distinguishing feature. I'm sure if people were talking about me but couldn't remember my name, they would say, 'You know him . . . that bald bloke off the telly.' It adds a bit of fun when I FaceTime Suzanne on my travels, as if we don't have much to talk about we'll kill time by having a game of 'Head or Knee'. I show her either the top of my head or the top of my knee and she has to guess if it's my head or knee. It's not as easy as it sounds.

I've been bald since I was about twenty-two, which means I've been bald for almost half of my life. I've said before that I don't know what to put it down to as my dad and granddad had a good head of hair, so I blame the power shower that my dad installed when I was younger – it was similar to the water cannons that police use in riots. But in all the time I've been bald I've never been tempted to wear a wig as I've not once seen a good one. You can spot them a mile off. They never sit properly on the head and the colour doesn't match. To me they're like having false cladding on the front of your house. Everyone knows it's not real, and on top of that, it looks shit.

Today I was going to see how shit I would look wearing false hair. I was meeting a man named Curtis at his salon in Atlanta who was going to fit me with a 'hair prosthetic'. When I got there I was taken off to a private room that was full of plastic sandwich bags full of hair and mannequin heads modelling different kinds of hair.

KARL: I mean, looking at that, that looks like real hair.

CURTIS: That's cos it's all real human hair.

KARL: When you say real hair, though, where's that from?

CURTIS: Asian women grow their beautiful black hair, then they go to the temples and have it shaved off. The hair is processed, stripped of its original colour and then recoloured in every shade from black to blonde.

KARL: But hang on, say if I'm wearing one of these and then I do a murder and they find the hair, she'll get done for it!

CURTIS: (laughs) Listen, they have proven that students react better to teachers who have hair than teachers who are bald.

They also found out that if two men are interviewed for the same job – one bald and one with hair – ninety-five per cent of the time they're gonna hire the guy with hair. It's not right. But it's the way it is in this society. Children are sometimes scared of bald men. And I've had teachers tell me the same thing as well.

KARL'S FACTS

During the Renaissance, it was fashionable for women to pluck their hairline to give them a higher forehead.

I sat down on a chair, and Curtis checked my hair shade before disappearing off into storage to get a 'hair prosthetic' to fit my head. At this point I thought it was merely going to be a bit of fun; he would pop it on my head, it would look like a wig, and we'd all have a laugh before shooting off to the next location. But that wasn't the case. He placed a pile of Asian women's hair in position and straight away I thought it made me look younger. It looked so real and wasn't too thick like most wigs normally are, and I could see my scalp through it which gave the impression of it being my own hair.

I had a look of James McAvoy about me. Long floppy hair with a centre parting. It was amazing how each time he tweaked it, it totally changed my look. He took the hairline back a little more and I switched from James McAvoy to Richard E Grant. It definitely improved my appearance. It immediately made me look friendlier.

I suppose this is the reason they never have those weird hairless cats on the front of Christmas cards. They don't look as cute as your normal bog-standard fluffy cat.

I THOUGHT GOOD HAIR SHOULD HAVE PLENTY OF BODY?

KARL: Have you ever had someone come back after having it done and say, 'You know what, I don't feel like me any more?' Do they ever say I wanna go back to being bald?

CURTIS: No. This is like a drug, it gets very addictive. And I warn my guys, don't get into this if you can't afford it. Once you see yourself looking better . . .

KARL: Roughly what would I be looking at price-wise?

CURTIS: About $3,500 a year. But remember, you're sleeping in this, you're showering in this, you're doing everything in this, Karl. We replace the adhesive once a month and the third time we just throw the piece away and get you a whole new one.

He wet the hair then and I was transformed into that Scouse comedian John Bishop. It was amazing how many different looks I could get. I was like Worzel Gummidge with his different heads. It annoyed me that I liked it as much as I did. I've become bored of seeing myself for the last twenty-odd years, but having hair back around my face gave me a reason to look in the mirror again. I know it's not important but it did give my head a new lease of life. I suppose hair is like garnish on a plate of food.

Most of the stuff people stick on there like celery or cress doesn't get eaten, it just brightens up the meal, and that is what hair does to the head.

Curtis said that if I was happy with the way it was looking now, I should definitely have it bonded to my head, as then it could be shaped properly. I didn't need any more convincing so went through to another room where a woman called Daphne got to work on it. She spread glue on my bonce like she was buttering bread. She slid the hair into place and after a few minutes gave the hair a tug. It was stuck down tight.

KARL: What is that stuff? Shitting hell, are you sure that can come off?

DAPHNE: It's not going anywhere. It has a twenty-four-hour curing period, so the more it cures the stronger it will get, so you don't have to worry about it coming off.

KARL: No, I'm not worried about it coming off. I'm worrying that it's not coming off.

DAPHNE: We can get it off, trust me.

I wasn't worried that it wouldn't come off cos I didn't like it, it was because I no longer looked like the photo on my passport, which could cause problems.

Daphne got out her scissors and started to trim it and blend it into my own hair, so you couldn't see the join from my hair to the hair that was growing on a Chinese woman's head just a few weeks ago. This hair was a lot better than mine ever was. I had now gone from a John Bishop to a Ewan McGregor. Within fifteen

GRIPPING STUFF.

minutes Daphne was done. And it looked well smart. It was really odd how she had cut it in a style that I used to have, without her knowing that's how I had it. It was like I'd got in a time machine and gone back twenty-five years. I couldn't help but look at myself in the mirror. It was the best hair I've ever had and it wasn't even my own! It was such a novelty to have something to play with and put my hands through. I can't do anything with the bit of hair I've got, it's pointless. It's like having curtains that don't fit a window; it holds no heat or the privacy of my head.

KARL: Me eyes look happier and everything.

CURTIS: I didn't notice your eyes before. It brings out your features.

KARL: Shit!

CURTIS: You look twenty-eight now. Shave that grey hair off your face and you'll look twenty-five.

KARL: My shirt looks shit now, though, you know what I mean?

CURTIS: See what it does to you? Now you're judging your shirt cos you love what you see from the neck up.

KARL: Most stuff below the hair, to be fair. Teeth look a bit shit as well now!

CURTIS: See, you're looking at every component of your body. That's why within six months I don't recognise guys. They've bleached their teeth, got contacts, lost thirty pounds! This is what this hair can do to someone!

It did make me feel younger, which is weird as I don't know why baldness represents being old. Sperm is as young as you can get and they're hairless. I was considering keeping it for as long as I could, so much so that I left the salon and went to get a passport photo in case my new hair did cause any confusion at passport control. The man who took my photo couldn't believe it was a toupee and said I looked more youthful with hair than I did on my old passport photo. My plan was to go shopping and pick up some hair products so I could make it look top notch before sending a photo to Suzanne. I bought a decent comb, shampoo and styling spray (£22 in total, having hair isn't cheap). I gave it a good wash and then took advantage of the hair dryer that was in the hotel. It normally annoys me when Suzanne uses a hair dryer at home, as it seems like such a waste of power when she could just use a towel. In our old house I used to get her to dry it in the living room so at least I got some benefit when it warmed the room up a bit.

As well as wanting my new rug to look smart for Suzanne, I also felt a bit of responsibility in looking after this hair as some woman in China had her head shaved for this. It's a bit like how you worry more about a hire car than your own vehicle. It made me wonder why we don't use hair from dead people to make these wigs, in the same way we use livers and kidneys. It would just involve ticking another box on a donor card. Why let it go to waste? Dead people are being buried with full heads of hair while living people are walking about bald.

I took a few photos of my new look, emailed them to Suzanne and then went to bed. I thought it would irritate me in the night as I can't even wear socks to bed normally, but it was fine, and it gave me another experience I hadn't had for a while, which was waking up with bed head. That's what makes this more than just a wig. It's stuck to me and is part of me.

My old mam and dad's neighbour used to throw his hairpiece on when my dad went and knocked on his door. Once, he put it on in such a rush it was on backwards. There would be no such problem with this 'hair prosthetic'.

I picked up my phone to see if Suzanne had replied while I had been asleep.

'I hate it. You look like a gormless thirty-five year-old!'

I called her up and put FaceTime on, and straight away she said, 'Why have you still got that on your head? It looks a mess!'

'So does yours when you've just got up!'

'You don't need to have false hair! You look poncey with that on!'

I wasn't happy. It's just as well that I don't have hair, as this is the style I would probably have and she didn't like it. It was hard to have a normal chat about anything else while I had this on my head as I was just looking at it and not paying her much attention. We couldn't even have a game of 'Head or Knee' to lighten the mood.

We finished talking and I just wanted to get it off my head. I'd enjoyed it the day before, but now Suzanne had said she didn't like it, what was the point? This trip was supposed to be about my identity, and yet I'm not really living my own life when I'm letting Suzanne control how my head appears. It's possible she wanted me to be confident with the way I already looked or perhaps she just didn't want me nicking her hair products. I didn't bring the matter back up when I got home so who knows?

I headed back to the salon and Daphne had some special solution to remove it.

I lost my hair for the second time in my life. The annoying thing is, Suzanne has haircuts all the time that I don't like but I can't just ask her to have it removed. Eventually I get used to her new style and I'm sure if I had just left it stuck on my head she would have come round to the idea.

'I DON'T KNOW WHY BALDNESS represents being OLD. SPERM is as young as you can get AND THEY'RE HAIRLESS.'

YOU ARE WHAT YOU WEAR

If I think of times when I have not felt myself, it's mainly been at formal gatherings. Like weddings. I'm with people I don't know, so Suzanne tells me to watch what I say. I'm at an event I don't want to be at, and wearing clothes I really don't feel comfortable in.

I think it's the clothes that are the biggest problem, as I'm only wearing the suit as it's what is expected of me. In my forty-three years of existence I've only worn a suit four times and I've never been happy while doing so. I hold myself differently when I'm wearing a suit, so in a way, even though I've made an effort to be there, I'm not really there as I don't feel myself. It might sound daft that a bit of cloth can have such a hold on me, but if I'm not comfortable then I can't relax. I've always been a fan of playing snooker, but would never be able to take it up professionally as I'd have to wear a suit. And why snooker players wear a bow tie I'll never understand. The only other people who wear them these days are clowns, so they may as well come out holding their cue while wearing a red nose, too.

After one occasion when I'd made a fuss about not wanting to wear a suit, Suzanne got me to buy a quite expensive one, you know, made to measure, to see if that made any difference. But I found that suit just as frustrating as it had false pockets. Not only was the clothing making me feel false, so was the suit itself! The pockets were just there for show, they couldn't actually be used, as the bloke who made it said it would ruin the way the suit hung if I put things in the pockets! How stupid is that? What annoys me is that this didn't annoy Suzanne, yet when I bought a jumper that had a bit of a shirt built in, she laughed at it and said it was tacky. I like it, as it gives the impression of smartness but I don't get as hot wearing it. Basically it's just a shirt collar sewn into the V-neck of the jumper. You'd never know, and it didn't take anything away, unlike the suit with the false pockets. That to me is clever clothing. It looks smart and it's two in one. I don't know why they haven't taken it further and made trousers with built-in underpants.

I've never understood why snooker players wear suits, and it also seems an odd choice for James Bond, considering his line of work. On a daily basis he's getting into fights and rolling around in gravel and dirt. His dry-cleaning bill must be mental. Plus he's always hopping into bed with different women, so a lot of valuable time is taken up removing jacket, waistcoat, tie, shirt and so on. My idea of trousers with built-in undies would be ideal for Bond. But the oddest thing for me with James Bond's choice of clothing is his shoes. Most of his chases would be a lot shorter if he went for a decent pair of trainers. Viewers complained that the latest film *Spectre* was way too long, but if he had worn trainers I guarantee it would have shaved half an hour off the running time.

So, it was footwear that I was looking at next. I visited a place called Matehuala in Mexico where they have a unique fashion for the feet. I met Fernando in a local shoe shop, but saw his shoes before I could see him. You see, the fashion that's popular in these parts are pointy boots. Not your bog-standard pointy boot – the points on Fernando's shoes were around 50 cm long and are worn by men who are involved in the local tribal electronic dance culture.

KARL: This is a look that hasn't reached England.

FERNANDO: For us it's an honour that you come to learn about our culture and you take it back to your country with you. It's an extravagant fashion, a way of getting attention – we use it more than anything for our dancing.

KARL: When I came in, what did you think about how I looked? What impression do you get from me?

FERNANDO: You are not colourful. Boring, boring colours. When you came in, we see someone serious and quiet and not energetic. Once you put on the boots, they will turn you into a happy person who can dance. They will cheer up your life and other people.

It wasn't anything I hadn't heard before. Suzanne is always telling me I dress down too much. I think it's because I prefer to disappear into a crowd, I don't want to stand out. I prefer people not to know too much about me until they get to know me. I would never wear a football top or a T-shirt with a band name on it, as that's all personal information. Same goes for tattoos. People used to just have images of a British bulldog or a skull and crossbones, but now they have their whole family tree down their arms and legs. No wonder identity fraud is on the increase when people put so much information about themselves on show. These people need to be shredded instead of buried when they die.

Fernando gave me a pair of boots in my size. They were probably the fanciest footwear my feet have ever worn. Covered in a type of purple glitter with a point that was close to a foot long. As I leaned over to slip them on I almost lost an eye. I walked up and down in the shop and they felt strange. The long point really altered the way I walked. I had to concentrate and be more aware of the space around me. It was similar to walking upstairs with a ladder, or towing a caravan by car; suddenly I had more to think about.

KARL: At home where I'm from, if you're wearing a Man U shirt, you might get a bit of grief. Do you get grief for wearing these boots?

FERNANDO: There are people who don't like them, yeah. You can have a fight cos of it. At dances, a lot of jealous people don't have boots and you're showing off and they try and break them or kick them and you get up and fight but you take them off and use them as a tool, a defence weapon. Haha!

A lot of clothes that are designed to make a fashion statement never look very comfortable, but these were okay, which was good news, cos if my feet aren't happy, I'm not happy. I reckon if I'd have been around back in caveman days I would have invented shoes way before worrying about inventing fire, as it can't have been easy walking around barefoot on all the rocks and pebbles.

When I was a kid we had a dog that chewed its way through five or six pairs of my school shoes, so my dad found a pair that were dog proof and got his mate Alf, who was a cobbler, to pimp them up with extra thick soles. They were so torturing that I blame my bad exam results on them, as I couldn't think straight when wearing those things. The sharp hard edge cut into my ankles, and they crushed my toes to the point that today they look like a bunch of penguins huddled together trying to keep warm. I left the shoes out for the dog, hoping that he'd rip them apart, but there was never a mark on them. I'd have to have had King Kong as a pet to destroy them. I hated those clogs so much that I decided to get rid of them by popping them on Guy Fawkes at the local bonfire. The next day on the way to school, I passed the site where the fire had taken place to find everything burnt to a cinder apart from those bloody shoes. They were indestructible. They could have been used by shoe bombers and offer repeated use! Since then, I've treated my feet like a dog that's been a victim of animal cruelty. I try to spoil them as much as I can. I've just got underfloor heating and they've never been happier. I don't even have to wear slippers or socks to keep them warm any more, they're free-range.

KARL'S FACTS

Pointy shoes were fashionable in 14th Century Poland. The longest had chains attached to the tips so the wearer could lift them and avoid falling over.

I met Antonio who creates these shoes in the back of the shop. He showed me how he took a normal pair of boots and added the point by shaping flexible foam and gluing it onto the front of the boot before covering it in material. When the craze first started he was making around 500 pairs a year. The plan was for me to come up with a design for a pair of my own boots that I would wear to a dance event later that day.

KARL: How crazy can you go with these? What's the maddest pair of shoes you've ever made?

ANTONIO: The craziest were 1.9 metres.

KARL: So is it all about length? No other tricks to make them more impressive?

ANTONIO: We add colours and lights . . .

KARL: Lights?

FERNANDO: You can put baubles or bells, a candle, anything . . . depends on your creativity. You can put fireworks on them, sparklers, spray water . . .

KARL: Water?!

ANTONIO: Yeah, you can put pipe on it, hose. Mexicans are creative, you can do anything.

The cobbler got to work making a pair of boots with a long point for me to wear, while me and Fernando went shopping to buy props to make them personal to me. I kept the pair of purple glittery boots on so I could get used to the feel of having such a long shoe on my foot and to see what reaction I'd get on the street. On the whole people just smiled, a few took photos, and one couple cheered.

As comfy as the boots were, they're not for everyday use. It was a bit of a pain getting in the car wearing them. I also found it tricky going up and down narrow aisles in shops without catching them on things, and

WHAT'S THE POINT?!

they're not the shoes to wear when trying to use a urinal. But I liked the way they kept people at a distance. Quite handy in a highly populated country like Mexico. They could come in handy at Christmas time on Oxford Street.

We nipped into a few toy shops and hardware stores where I bought a battery-powered strip of lights, twelve feet of piping and a bag of party horns, the type that unroll when you blow. My plan was to attach them to the tips of the boots, run the pipe along the side of the boot, up my trouser leg, up my shirt and through my collar to my mouth, so I could blow into it and make the party horn fan out as I dance.

Fernando showed me a few basic dance moves I could do later that evening. It was difficult to do anything too complicated as I kept tripping myself up, but even simple moves looked quite impressive as the tips of the boots swayed around. And considering I'd had them on for an hour my feet still felt good. As I've said, if they weren't comfortable I'd have probably been in a bit of a mood. There is definitely a link between people's behaviour and the shoes they wear. If your feet are happy, you'll be happy. Gandhi, Mother Teresa and the Dalai Lama: happy people who all wore flip flops. That's no coincidence. Instead of sending missiles into countries we can't agree with, we should just send in boxes of flip flops to calm things down.

When we got back to the shoe shop Antonio had almost completed my boots.

They were impressive and had a metre-long point. We just had to add the strip of lights and party horns before heading off to the venue where the dance competition was taking place.

When we got there I met a few of Fernando's mates who I would be dancing with. They went through their routine and asked me to copy them, but it was too much for me so I said I'd just make stuff up on the spot. I prefer to dance this way anyway, as I don't enjoy it otherwise. If I'm having to concentrate on where my feet and arms should be it takes away the fun of dancing. That's why I'd never do *Strictly Come Dancing*. I am fond of a dance, though, and I suppose that's another part of my identity; it's like another me comes out when I hear music.

I didn't feel nervous about dancing in front of the locals, as even if my moves weren't too clever I knew my shoes would keep the crowd happy. Other groups of lads turned up and did their dancing wearing their pointy boots, too. Some were the same length as ours, a couple were longer, but nobody else had the lights or party horns. We got on the stage and went for it. As my lights came on, the crowd cheered, and I danced about throwing my legs all over the place, being careful not to get tangled up with the others. The long points whipped around as I jumped up and down. The lights made it look like the lightsaber fight scene in *Star Wars*. Our boots collided a little and we crashed into one another like giraffes cracking necks when they fight, but it all came across as planned. Just when I thought I had peaked too early, Fernando's shoes let out a bang and an inferno erupted from the tips of his boots! He'd had bloody fireworks attached to the end of his! The music ended and the crowd gave us a round of applause.

It had been a good day. Fernando was proud of my efforts and I had enjoyed the experience. But to be honest, taking off the shoes was the best bit of the day as my feet were free again.

TRYING OUT A NEW VOICE

Some say I'm a bit miserable and down on everything, but I think part of that is my accent. And because that's how people perceive me, I have become a bit negative and down on things as a result. So I'd say my accent is a big part of who I am. Nowadays Suzanne deals with a lot of things that need sorting on the phone as my accent isn't very good at hiding my contempt when I'm not happy with somebody or something, and it never really ends well. It's not because I swear. She says it's the tone of my voice that comes across like I'm not impressed. She says even when I say I'm happy about something, it sounds like I'm being sarcastic. I know what she means, but she has to remember that it's even worse for me, as my thoughts sound this way to me, too. I don't read many books, which I put down to the fact that I hear my voice in my head reading the lines and it bores me as I sound disinterested. I think maybe a lot of people have the same problem, and this is why audiobooks are popular these days. It's better to have someone with a good voice reading it to you.

When I first moved down to London it took quite some time for work colleagues to get used to me and my tone. They'd be concerned, thinking I was angry because I had a different tone to everyone else, and they took it as me having a problem. I didn't blame them, though, as we all make snap judgements. First, we judge people on the way they look, and then on the way they speak. I'm guilty of it, too. I take a lot of flights when doing these trips, and I've found I have more trust in a posh-speaking pilot than I do when I've been on an EasyJet flight and hear, say, a Scouser or a Brummie come on the Tannoy. It's nonsense, as it's just me being judgemental. For some reason my brain has more confidence in someone who is well-spoken. It's not cos I can't understand what they're saying – I've met posh people with no accent who I couldn't understand at all. I had a doctor for a short time whose accent was so posh I never understood a bloody word he said, and on top of that I couldn't read a word of his writing on his prescriptions either. Thinking about it, he was in totally the wrong job. I'm surprised he was never snapped up by MI5 as the enemy could never get any top secrets out of him, even if he did speak!

But I do think your accent can dictate your life a little bit. I'm one hundred per cent sure that his futuristic-sounding computer voice helps Stephen Hawking when he's telling people about space and time and black holes, as it suits the topic. I could see him fitting in at the post office, too, telling customers which checkout window to go to. I figure he would struggle on a sex chat line, though, as you need the ups and downs in tone to help you along or hold you back, if you know what I mean.

KARL'S FACTS

The man with the deepest voice can hum eight octaves below the lowest G on a piano. So low that humans can't hear it.

For this part of my trip looking at identity, I was headed to the mountains of San Pedro Sochiapam in Oaxaca, Mexico, to visit a small community who use the Chinantec whistling language. Its main purpose, according to linguists, is to help farmers who are separated by long distances over the fields and deep valleys to communicate with each other, as the mobile phone signal in these parts isn't great. I met a young lad called Jose who spends his days collecting corn in the local fields. Now it's going to be difficult to explain all this on paper, but his name in the whistle language sounded like the hook from the Dexys Midnight Runners song 'Come On Eileen', which made it easier for me to remember.

He told me how my name was whistled, but it was hard for me to take in as all the whistling was driving his three pet dogs wild, so I suggested a whistle to him for my name. I went for a version of the 'Ooh Danone' jingle from the yoghurt advert, as that was easy for me to recognise.

At first I felt like it was a bit of a wind-up. Then Jose managed to call his friend Arturo down from the hills after whistling a few words. I gather that people on Twitter call their messages 'tweets', but this was real tweeting. The intention was for me to help them both the following day to collect the corn from the fields, so I recorded some phrases on my phone that I hoped would come in useful. I was looking forward to the challenge at this point as I haven't learned any other languages. People I know are always surprised that with all the travelling I do I haven't picked anything up, but it doesn't work like that, does it? I've probably taken about 300 flights over the years but I can't fly a plane, can I?!

Jose and his mate Arturo gave me the following whistling commands:

What I liked about this form of communication was that it was simple. They didn't have any whistles for long complicated words. I don't know why we introduced words to our language that can be a struggle to

even pronounce, never mind understand. I went through a period when I was first starting to write books of reading the dictionary when I was on the toilet to try and expand my vocabulary. It's quite a good toilet book, as you can pick it up and put it down fairly easily without having to remember where you left off. If I had to review it, I'd say I found it rather wordy on the whole, but at least if there are any words you don't understand, the explanations are right there for you. The only problem is that you can never finish reading it, as they're continually adding new words. A quarter of the way through, I read online that something like fourteen new words a day are being invented, so it's a book that will never end. And they won't just add the new words at the end of the new edition; they have to be in the right order, so you have to start from scratch again. I knocked it on the head as it's not really a book you want to read more than once.

I got back to my hotel room and spent an hour trying to learn the phrases I'd recorded on my phone. It didn't occur to me at the time, but if there were any locals in the rooms next door they must have been wondering what I was up to when I was continuously whistling the command of 'Bring me the machete'!

When I went to bed I had the phrases on loop through my headphones, as I've heard you can still learn while you're asleep. I don't know how true that really is, as I spent most of my history lessons at school asleep and couldn't tell you a thing about what the Tudors got up to.

I woke up early to the sound of whistling, not from my phone but from the birds outside. It made me wonder if the locals find that sound as relaxing as we do, or whether it just sounds like people chatting non-stop.

I got to the farmland, and my efforts paid off as I managed to track down Jose by whistling the command for his name along with 'Where are you?' I could hear a reply of 'Come here' so kept whistling 'Where are you?' and followed where his reply was coming from. I eventually located him hidden in the overgrown corn fields. He handed me a machete and showed me how to cut the corn from the stalk. He tried to teach me how to whistle the word 'help', in case there was an emergency, but I told him that I wouldn't be whistling if I got an injury, I'd just be screaming 'Help!' I understand that normal chat might get lost through the valleys, but surely if I start screaming my tripe out after cutting a finger off, the sound would travel and it should be obvious that something is wrong. I doubt it would be easy to whistle if I was in agony, anyway. Whistling isn't something you normally do in times of stress. I associate it with calmness and happiness. I used to do it in the past to put people at ease. If I was walking on a quiet road late at night and there was a woman in front of me, I'd whistle a tune as a way of saying 'I'm letting you know I'm here and I mean no harm'. I'd whistle a nursery rhyme like 'Humpty Dumpty' or 'Three Blind Mice' until Suzanne told me if she heard that behind her on a dark quiet road she'd be terrified, and she advised me to stop doing it. (It's becoming quite clear to me how controlling that woman is. I can't have the wig I liked and she doesn't let me bloody whistle.)

I went off deep into the field and started to chop away at the corn. As I was cutting I could hear Jose and Arturo chatting away like a pair of Clangers but had no idea what they were talking about. It reminded me of my holidays in Wales where the locals used to switch from English to Welsh whenever I entered the local shop and I became a bit paranoid that they were talking about me. Jose and Arturo might not even have been talking to each other, they may just have been whistling a local Mexican hit for all I know. It was a pleasant sound to listen to, though, and would be an ideal language for bin men to use when doing their early morning collections, as it's a lot less intrusive on the ears then them yelling at each other.

THE CORNS ON MY FEET AFTER WEARING THE POINTY BOOTS WERE JUST AS BIG AS THESE.

I carried on for a few hours collecting the corn and chopping away while thinking about the benefits to this whistling language. It's a tough one to learn, but what I like about it is the way you don't have to work at getting the accent right.

When I did French at school the teacher always said I sounded like an English person speaking French, which was a daft thing to say, cos that's what I was. Another advantage of this language is that you can't eat while doing it, so parents wouldn't have to tell their kids to stop talking when they have a mouthful of food. Also, it might make people look after their teeth more, as without them it's pretty difficult to whistle. And thinking about it, it could also save your teeth, as I remember going to a Manchester v. Liverpool football game and the only seat I could get was with the Liverpool fans. Me and my mate were scared to open our mouths, cos if the Liverpool fans around us heard our accents we could have had our teeth knocked out. Yet with whistling everyone sounds the same, no matter where you are from. You could say it's like a fart in that respect – you can't hear a fart and tell which country the arse that released it is from.

I eventually called it a day on the whistling, as I found that, like in my French class, I could whistle a few commands but couldn't understand the replies. I got that confused at one point I think I may even have been trying to take commands from a bird.

BEING SOMEONE ELSE

Next, I was to have a day off from myself. I wasn't looking forward to this at all, but then that's probably because 'I' wasn't going to be as involved in this part of my trip. What is 'me' meant to do while I'm having a go at being someone else? The closest I've come to changing myself a little bit was when I was a kid and told everyone in the house that I wanted to be called Brett. Everyone was very good and went along with it. The problem was, I didn't. I kept forgetting, so even though they were calling me Brett, I was ignoring them. If I couldn't cope with a name change all them years ago, how was I going to cope with a total identity change when I've been used to being me for forty-three years?!

To help me get away from myself, I went to Vegas. It's a place that many people go to when they want a break from themselves. I've been here a few times before, and the person I've most wanted to become during those visits is pretty much anybody who isn't in Vegas. I can't stand the place. Everything about it feels false to me – the false Big Ben, false London Eye, Eiffel Tower, Pyramid, the false Sphinx and many, many false Elvises.

The plan was for me to become a look-alike for the evening, but I had no idea which famous person I could pull off. When I had my new hair stuck on my head, the options would have been endless but my bald head limits the possibilities. I googled to see if anyone had ever linked my face with a known actor or singer to give me a few ideas, but I only found photos of people who were saying *they* looked like me, even though none of them really did.

ELVIS HAS NOW LEFT THE BUILDING . . . VIA THE RAMP.

The main link seemed to be with anyone or anything bald and wrinkly. I may as well have a go at impersonating a bollock!

To help me get my wrinkly forehead around the whole look-alikey idea, I was meeting a man called David who spent the majority of his time being George Clooney. He was in Vegas on business where he had been booked to attend an event. He got into this line of work after his mam entered him in a look-alike competition in *People* magazine. Although he didn't win, he did make it into the top ten so he decided to turn it into a living.

KARL: You're lucky, aren't you? George Clooney is a good-looking fella and not a bad man to be likened to. I suppose that made it easier for your mam to tell you to enter.

DAVID: She calls me George to this day now, she really does. She loves showing the pictures that I send her of the events I do to her friends. She gets a big kick out of it. I give her credit cos without her none of this would've happened.

KARL: How much does being a look-alikey take over your life? What if you wanted to shave your head?

DAVID: It's funny you should say that. My son got this cool haircut about a month ago – kinda short sides and flipped-back front. I could never do that cos I never know when I'm going to get that call for my next event.

KARL: What if it's the other way then? What happens if George Clooney shaves his head?

DAVID: If he does it, I have no problem doing that.

KARL: The thing is, though, it's not like you're putting make-up or wigs on, so it must get in the way of everyday life.

DAVID: Yeah, I've been out and about having a burrito in a restaurant, wearing a cap and glasses cos I feel like it, and then I look like I'm George Clooney in disguise. People come up to me all the time when I'm in a hat and sunglasses.

KARL: Isn't that annoying? All the hassle without the perks of being the real George?

DAVID: No, it's flattering. There are worse people to look like, obviously.

That's the thing with being a look-alikey, it's easier to accept if it's a good-looking person. I once upset one of Suzanne's mates when we were out for some food. I said, 'You look like that horse-racing expert.' Everyone around the table glared at me as Suzanne's friend hates being compared to Clare Balding. I don't know why, as she's definitely not the worst person in the world to look like. I could have meant the other horse-racing expert, John McCririck.

KARL'S FACTS

Given the limitations of genetic diversity, it is likely that everyone on the planet has a doppelgänger somewhere.

KARL: So what are the rules, then? What do you do if people think you're George?

DAVID: You feel a certain responsibility to stay in character. That's what I was hired to do so I play with that.

At first I thought it was a bit odd to lead people on, but as long as he wasn't being rude to anyone I don't see the harm in it. If it means people walk away thinking they've just met George Clooney and that he was a nice bloke, then everyone's happy.

To me, the whole fame thing is nonsense, anyway. I don't know why people are so obsessed with it. I really like watching Alan Partridge, but if I saw Steve Coogan walking down the street I wouldn't want a photo with him just because I like his work. I was really happy with the work my builder Lucas had done on my front wall, but I didn't ask for a photo with him.

Someone once ran up to me and said, 'Stupid people shouldn't be famous!' before running off. It made me wonder – why can't stupid people be famous? I wouldn't mind if he had just said, 'I hate your programmes!' or 'You're not fit to be on TV!', but it was like he was holding fame up as being something special. Just because you are well known, it doesn't mean you're anything amazing. I'm known by a small few cos I'm on the TV, presenting a few half-arsed travel programmes that are there to kill forty-five minutes of your time if you've got nothing else to do. There are more impressive things being done by people who aren't famous, so does that mean they're not amazing just because they're not known by the masses?

I don't think being famous should be so highly regarded. Luckily, I'm hidden away on a satellite channel, so the most I get is, 'Aren't you that bald bloke off the telly?' I say, 'No. You're thinking of Ross Kemp.' My favourite thing that happened was when I turned up at HMV recently and I walked over to an employee who was busy sorting some CDs out and said, 'Alrite, I'm here for the DVD signing,' and he said, 'Okay, grab a DVD and join the queue on the second floor.' Even my own mam doesn't always recognise me. She phoned me up once and said she had just seen me on the telly. Turned out it wasn't me it was just a random bald bloke!

David went off to do his Clooney appearance so I went along to meet a look-alikey agent called Matt, who I was hoping could suggest someone I might be able to impersonate. As well as being an agent, Matt was also an Elvis look-alikey. He was at his office with his make-up artist Sean.

MATT: Do you think it will be easier to be someone else?

KARL: I don't think it will be easy at all. I don't think I can get away from me. It will be one of the hardest things I've had to do during this trip.

MATT: But don't we all wear a mask? I mean, really, are you *really* you?

KARL: That's what I've been wondering. How often are you allowed to be yourself, anyway? If you're going for a job interview you behave in a certain way. I suppose the only place I am really me is in here. (*points to head*)

SEAN: This is deep, and very true.

MATT: Would you want to try on some masks in order to find another you?

KARL: When I walked in and you saw me for the first time, did you think you're a dead ringer for . . . whoever?

SEAN: I kinda did . . .

KARL: Who?

SEAN: J. Lo.

KARL: Seriously, though, who do you think? Cos this is the problem. I haven't got strong features. I've got a very round nothingy face.

SEAN: Sometimes you can create features with make-up.

KARL: Look at this photo. I got my hair back a few days ago. Look how different I looked.

SEAN: Oh wow, you know who you could be right there? At a quick glance? Ricky Martin.

KARL: Can we do Ricky Martin? Mind you, hang on, though. That's nice of you to say, but would anyone else know who I was? Ricky Martin hasn't had a song out for years!

SEAN: That is a problem with Ricky Martin.

MATT: You could be Elton John.

KARL: Come off it! How can you go from Ricky Martin to bloody Elton John!

MATT: The younger Elton John.

KARL: Don't try and backtrack. There's not a good . . . he didn't look that great when he was younger. I like his music, though – this isn't a diss to Elton John.

SEAN: You're way prettier than him . . . but with the glasses, outfit and hair.

Sean said it was my face shape that lent itself to being Elton. My idea to dress as a bollock seemed more appealing. He brought a collection of Elton John-style clothes from the late '70s/early '80s – sparkly suit, red feather boa thing for around my neck, make-up and a bald wig. He finished off by applying some black paint to put a gap in my front teeth and putting on the glasses.

SEAN: Whoa, back up, Elton!

KARL: It's weird for me to say it, but I'm still seeing me in there.

MATT: I see me, every time I do Elvis. I think the real test is what other people see.

> KARL: When you're being Elvis, how much Matt is there, percentage-wise?
>
> MATT: I would say eighty per cent Matt, twenty per cent Elvis. I might look eighty per cent Elvis, but what's coming from the inside is eighty per cent me.

I looked ridiculous. I stuck with it, though, as the clock was ticking and if I hadn't agreed to be Elton John, I had no idea what other round-headed people were on Sean's list. He could've dressed me up and sent me out onto the streets of Vegas as Humpty bloody Dumpty. I had actually been hoping they might have done me up as someone decent like Bruce Willis or Vin Diesel.

Sean told me to try to be more flamboyant, but that isn't me. Even though I was dressed like Elton, I still felt like me. Style can't change you that much. It always annoys me when Suzanne asks what pasta I want. There are loads of shapes – penne, tagliatelle, spaghetti, ravioli – but in the end it's all pasta and I'm happy with any of it. Who picks their food by what shape it is?!

I couldn't imagine anyone wanting a photo with me looking like this.

HELL-TON JOHN.

> KARL: Give me a sum, an amount of money you want me to earn tonight.
>
> MATT: I think a respectable sum would be $100.

KARL: Seriously?! That's about £70! I can make £70 an hour from looking like this? That's good going, innit. What will people expect from me for that?

MATT: They are gonna come up to you and they're gonna get their picture with you.

KARL: And do I say 'It's going to cost you' before or after?

MATT: You can say that if you want, or you can take the picture and it's expected that they will probably tip you. If they don't then, yeah, you're gonna have to say, 'Can you donate to my college fund?'

I headed off to Fremont Street, which is similar to London's Leicester Square, full of tourists roaming around even though there isn't actually anything to see. The lights seem to attract them like moths. I'm always wary of places that put lights on everything. It's like icing on a wedding cake, trying to make something look better than it is. I looked around to check if there were any other Elton John look-alikes.

There were loads of street entertainers. There was a long-haired man in shades wearing a G-string and playing a guitar, some naked ladies who had been painted in stars and stripes, a few American superheroes like the Hulk and Captain America, feathered-up dancing girls, a bunch of break dancers, and some lads playing drums. I understand why people used to come here years ago when Elvis was playing live and gambling wasn't allowed anywhere else, but now we have the internet, this place shouldn't exist. You can do all that in the comfort of your own home. Just yesterday I was looking on the internet at snakes wearing hats. Who needs Vegas?!

I did try my best to begin with, saying 'Welcome to Vegas' to people passing by, but I don't think they even noticed me. They just drifted by like they were in a trance, hypnotised by the flashing lights and noise. Not one stopped to have a photo. But then again, why would they? What I liked about David, the George Clooney look-alike, was the way he didn't have to wear a daft costume. He just looked like George. Like I said, I wanted to be Bruce Willis from *Die Hard*, but to me, this was more *Try Hard*. Way too much effort for a crap result.

I think inanimate objects that look like people are more interesting. Years ago, my brother called everyone upstairs to the toilet when he had done a number two that looked like a donkey with a hat on. You had to squint to see it, but it was there. I also like the look-alikey cats you get on the internet. Hitler cat, Charlie Chaplin cat and one that looks like Tom Selleck from

WHOEVER SAID THIS LOOKS LIKE ME OTTER BE ASHAMED OF THEMSELVES.

Magnum P.I. They're not trying to look like them, they just do. I've just googled to see if there are animals that look like me and someone had posted this. I don't know what animal it is, but to be fair, it looks more like me than I looked like Elton.

I'd been there over an hour and I can honestly say I've had more fun waiting for a bus. Even though the whole point of this experience was about trying to be someone else, I felt more like myself than I had done since the start of the trip. I suppose it's when you're not happy that the real you comes out.

I was only acknowledged twice, once by a bunch of young drunk lads who asked if I knew where the nearest 'boobie bar' was (seeing me dressed like a tit obviously wasn't enough). And once by a couple who said, 'Karl, what are you doing here?!' So much for having a night off from myself.

You might remember that I ate two and a half bananas for breakfast before doing the DNA test at the start of this trip to see if I could make myself more banana than human. Well, I got the results and sadly there was no mention of me being part banana. But I did find out that I was fifty-one per cent British, thirty-three per cent Irish and six per cent Eastern European. That made up ninety per cent, but I still don't know about the other ten per cent. Maybe it was banana after all but they were too confused to list it.

I've no idea how they work all this out just from a sample of my saliva. I mean, how was I six per cent Eastern European? Was there a chance I could have had some meat stuck in my teeth from my tea the night before? A little bit of Polish sausage mixed into my saliva maybe?

They also found a link to a Scandinavian woman whose DNA was similar to mine, which meant she could be a distant cousin. The director asked me if I wanted to make contact with her but I really didn't want to. I've plenty of cousins already who I don't bother seeing, so there was no point in getting in touch with this one. It would just be another person who'd get stroppy if I didn't send a Christmas card. It's funny how you might not speak all year and yet if you don't send a card, people will moan at you! I think this is why some people have their brothers', sisters' and cousins' names tattooed on their arm – it's not out of love, it's just handy having a list of names that they can tick off when doing their Christmas cards.

For me, the people you live next door to can play a bigger part in your life than some family members do. If I got in touch with this Scandinavian woman, what's the best that could happen? I'd prefer to meet a total stranger, as they don't expect as much and there's less chance of them demanding money or a kidney. I don't think I'm alone on this. It's why social media is so popular; it's safer talking to strangers where there are no ties. Years ago there was a programme called *This is Your Life* where Michael Aspel would surprise a celebrity, take them back to a studio and look back at their life with all their family members there. It had to be a surprise as no one would agree to it otherwise!

They've stopped doing it now, as quite a few people told Michael to piss off. Instead we have *Who Do You Think You Are?* Everyone seems happy to take part as there's no chance of your dead relatives calling you up and bawling at you for not sending a Christmas card. Mind you, even that programme annoys me. You get some celebs bursting into tears after finding out about a great-great-great-granddad who died from TB. They didn't even know them five minutes ago and now they're having a breakdown over it. A lot of these people probably wouldn't bother keeping in touch with family members who are living, so don't be worrying about the dead ones.

I'm not interested in my distant past. Maybe if they could go way, way back and link me to a jellyfish or a bowl of bacteria, that would blow my mind, but other than that I'm not too fussed. The most interesting thing to come out of the test for me is that I'm only fifty-one per cent British! I couldn't believe that. I've never been really good at anything. Even my DNA is shit at being British.

DRESSING UP AS A WOMAN

For the next part of my trip I was going to see someone called Rob. He was wearing a pair of dark glasses and a wig. Not the good sort of wig that I wore earlier in my trip, this one was like plastic flowers – you know what they're trying to be but you know they're not real. It was fine, though, as Rob knew that I knew his hair wasn't real, and I was aware that his name wasn't Rob either. He was in disguise, which was fine, as I was actually there to meet Sherry, one of the many female characters that he enjoys dressing up as.

KARL: What do you class it as? Is it crossdressing?

ROB: Technically I would class myself as a female impersonator. I started out as a crossdresser but I wasn't happy with my looks. So rather than just putting on girls' knickers and a set of breasts, I took it to the extreme which requires wearing a mask and a body suit.

KARL: What is it all about, though? Is it a gay thing?

ROB: Oh, okay, well, that's what I thought when I started crossdressing seventeen years ago. I thought, oh God, I must be turning gay if I'm having fantasies about being a woman. I must be gay. In fact, now I know that the percentage of actual gays in the trans community is the same as in the regular population – seven per cent or something like that.

KARL: Do you remember the first time and the first garment you put on?

ROB: The first thing was actually ladies' jeans. I wanted to see if I could get them on, and they were very tight and I managed to get them on. And then I tried on some other gear.

KARL: They always look a bit uncomfortable to me, tight jeans. You see, for me clothing is all about comfort.

ROB: Me, too. I have always been about comfort until I started wearing women's gear. Then it's all about uncomfort. You look more girlie the more uncomfortable you are.

KARL: So there is a big difference, then. You're not being a frumpy woman, you're going from comfy guy to sharp-dressed woman.

ROB: If I don't look hot, I'm not satisfied.

We walked quietly upstairs to the bathroom, so as not to wake his daughter. His rubber body suit lay wrinkled in the bath looking like a cross between a plate of shrivelled antipasti and my auntie Nora. Rob dragged a heavy-looking box from the corner and opened it up. It was a body suit that had been ordered and delivered to his house for me to wear. He was as excited as a kid opening his Christmas presents. I didn't notice if it came with a manual (or womanual), but he unpacked it and laid everything out to make sure all the parts were there, just like he was unpacking an IKEA table. Except this time, it was okay to have a couple of nuts missing. The body parts looked pretty realistic.

KARL: They're very detailed. They must use a model?

ROB: The makers told me the body suit is a combination of two women, a Brazilian and an Italian. When I got my first suit and put it on, it changed my life. All the thoughts I'd had about getting surgery, being female and having breasts stopped as soon I saw myself in the mirror as a woman. The whole fantasy I had about being a woman disappeared. I'm satisfied just looking like one.

I left Rob to put his body suit on. I took advantage of the break and had a quick pee before I put my own suit on. Rob had told me the suits come with a catheter, which meant I could pee in the suit and it would leave via the rubber woman's parts, but I wasn't up for that. I was prepared for the general public to take the piss when we left his house dressed up as females, but I didn't like the idea of the suit taking the piss.

Rob called us into the bathroom, and he was in his naked body suit, breasts and bits on full show. He hadn't put on the mask yet, as he said he would get too warm, so he was still wearing the dark glasses and wig disguise. It was a unique look. Not one that is covered in the classic board game, Guess Who?

The smell of body odour and rubber that had been in the bathroom before had now been replaced with the smell of the talc that Rob had used to ease the suit on. I was thinking that the smell of talc has never changed over the years but the reasons people use it have, as I poured it into my false arse and thighs. It wasn't an easy thing to slip into, and I worked up quite a sweat as I pulled and wriggled my way into the suit. Suzanne takes about as long as this to get ready in our bathroom. I'm starting to wonder who I'm living with!

I had a quick glance at the false arse and thighs I was now wearing in the mirror, and the arse didn't look too dissimilar to my own. Considering they had to use two different arses from Italy and Brazil to get the perfect look, it gave me pride in my own buttocks. They could have just taken a mould from me. Most people who have seen my programmes tend to call me an arse anyway, so I may as well be a 'professional arse' and be a model for these suits. If I manufactured these suits, I would try selling them to cyclists as the padded arse cheeks would be comfy for them and reduce the risk of getting hit by cars. I'm pretty sure a bare arse would get noticed by motorists.

KARL'S FACTS

A man fell on a high-pressure air valve that got lodged in his bum and inflated him to twice his size. It took three days to fart and burp out the excess air.

As much as the arse looked like my own, the front part of the suit did not. I was as flat and smooth as Action Man. My bits were extremely comfy, though, tucked away like they were hibernating and safe from any harm. It was nice to have a bit of a vacation from my testicles. Men reading this will understand how delicate you have to be with them, but for woman readers I'm just letting you know the slightest tap can be crippling. It's weird, as sometimes you can knock them and you think, oh God, this is gonna hurt, and then nothing happens. Other times the lightest tap will have a man in absolute agony. You never know which way it's going to go. It's like when a kid falls over and there are a few moments when you're thinking, is it just going to get up and carry on playing or is it going to start screaming its tripe out?

Even though my bits were safe and sound and out of sight, I wasn't getting much else from the experience at this point.

KARL: Thing is, Rob, it looks real, but I don't feel less manly. Just cos those bits are gone, I don't feel any differently to how I normally do.

ROB: Some crossdressers and trans don't want to wear this. They don't care about looking like it has gone. They want them gone.

KARL: That's a dangerous game, though, isn't it? It's not like you're just shaving your head – it doesn't grow back!

ROB: Well . . . they feel like they are women.

KARL: Yeah, but how do they know for sure? It's a one-way ticket! I wouldn't even have a tattoo, never mind have my knob and testicles off. I tell you what, though, I think the female body is better-looking than the man's – all the bits, it's not great down there, it doesn't look amazing. But with this suit on, it's a nice clean look, no lumps and bumps.

ROB: That's the way straight men think. They find women attractive.

As much as I don't like looking at my bits, I wouldn't get rid. They can do my head in when they get in the way, and I hate drying them. It's such a boring activity. I've thought about getting one of those Dyson hand dryers fitted to the wall in the bathroom so I could just dangle them in there . . . job done in seconds. Still, I don't know how you can possibly say you're one hundred per cent certain that you want your tackle removed. I mean, just because you wear a colostomy bag, you don't go and get rid of your toilet, do you?! It's a big gamble. I've heard some people say they feel like they're a woman trapped in a man's body, but I don't get that as I don't think I feel like a man or a woman. I know I'm a man as science has called me one but I don't think I feel like one as I don't know how it feels to be a woman.

KARL: So how old are you?

ROB: Seventy-two.

KARL: And how much younger do you feel once you're all dressed up?

ROB: Most people mistake me for a twenty-something/thirty-something woman. When I tell them how old I am, they can't believe it. Sometimes I can't believe it.

KARL: Is there a woman in your life at the minute?

ROB: No.

KARL: When was the last time a woman was in your life?

ROB: A couple of years ago, though I had a hard time doing this and dating women. I had to tell my family cos I was scared I was going to get caught, but no one else knows that I do this. I'm a crossdresser, we do it in private.

KARL: Would it have that much of an impact?

ROB: Some people's lives are destroyed when they come out.

That surprised me as it's not such an odd thing to be doing. I'm not sure if it's because I've travelled a lot or I've seen too much odd stuff on the internet or what, but I didn't understand why this would be such a big deal. There are worse things I've heard about. I've read that there are fellas who like being breast fed. That's weird. To me this was not that different to the blokes who dress up in battle gear and re-enact some old war on a Bank Holiday Monday. A lot of people get off their tits

I FELT A TIT AT THIS POINT.

on drugs in their spare time; Rob just puts a pair on.

I'd now managed to get the other part of the suit on, which was an all-in-one armless jumpsuit with breasts. It felt like the time I had to get into a wet suit when I did shark diving for *An Idiot Abroad*. That also took some balls.

The breasts didn't look too clever at first. They were like little pork pies stuck on my chest until Rob inserted the silicone fillers. They looked and felt nice for a while, but soon became a bit of an extra weight. This is what would put me off having the proper op, even if I felt I was a woman trapped in a man's body. I never take hand luggage on flights as I don't like carrying unnecessary baggage. They're like binoculars in a way. They give your eyes something to look at but are a pain to carry.

I was still confused as to what Rob got out of it.

ROB: There are transgender people who are women stuck in a male body. There are some who don't want to be a woman but would like to express that part of themselves, and there are others like myself who just want to look like a woman. I lived as a regular guy for fifty years, and in that time it never occurred to me to try on women's clothes. Why would a straight guy try on women's clothes?

KARL: It depends what sort of women's clothes. A lot of women's clothes are similar to fellas' clothes nowadays.

ROB: Yes, and the crossdressers resent that cos women can crossdress and no one says a thing about it, and yet men wear a womanly pair of jeans and shoes and a bit of make-up, and all of a sudden 'you are gay'.

KARL: Do you resent needing this in your life? Is there a bit of you that wishes you didn't have to do this?

ROB: There is a definite conflict cos I can't tell anyone about this. If I was really serious about a woman, I would have to tell her cos it's such a big part of my life. It's a two-sided sword for me, cos my daughter who I live with is not into this at all and I have the guilt of dealing with that. Also, to be honest, sometimes it seems a little funny to be a man dressing up as a woman – what am I doing playing dress-up? I should be watching more football on the telly.

KARL: That's funny that you know it's a bit of a weird thing to do but you still want to do it, like it's a big part of you and your identity. If someone said, you can't do this any more, Rob, you have to stop, it's upsetting your daughter, could you stop it now?

ROB: You know, probably not. I think it's a compulsion, the only one I ever had, something I just can't stop doing.

I picked one of the masks and slipped it on. It covered my whole head and tied up with laces around the back.

KARL: That is weird. Wow.

ROB: You see! What happened to Karl? He's gone! Karl's gone!

KARL: This is probably the furthest I've ever gone away from myself even though I'm still here. You know what I mean?

ROB: No. (*laughing*)

KARL: I'm looking at myself . . . but that's not me.

ROB: Exactly.

It was strange. Like Rob said, Karl had gone. Even though I was stood there, what I saw in the mirror was far from what I normally see. Even in my dreams I'm always me. I don't wake up and think, who was that I was being? And when I was dressed as Elton John the night before I could still see me. This was different.

We went into Rob's bedroom where there was a huge collection of women's clothes piled up on the floor. It looked like a New Year's sale at Next. To get into the part, I decided that from this point on I would be Karla, not Karl. I was thinking about what kind of a look I'd go for if I had been born a woman.

KARL: Normally, as Karl, I don't care about clothing too much. It's just there to do a job. Suddenly, as a woman, I want to make a bit more of an effort.

ROB: Now you're getting it, what the fun of this is. There's no fun being a guy, putting on the same clothes every day. It makes no sense.

KARL: I wear the same stuff day in, day out.

ROB: But with women there's no end. I've been doing this for, like, seventeen years and I haven't figured it out at all. There's so many combinations.

I spent just over an hour trying on various clothes, which is something I've never done before. I look at menus in restaurants longer than I spend selecting clothes. The thing that takes the longest when I get dressed is finding a pair of matching socks.

Suzanne says she would happily pair them up for me after washing, but I like to see how fast I can find a pair. I treat this daily job as a bit of brain training.

Even though this was a new identity, I still went for fairly normal clothing, but with a tad more colour. I selected a light purple fitted V-neck jumper with a red loose skirt and a small black bag. I'd say I had the image of a respectable forty-five-year-old woman. I looked older than I was as Karl but more intelligent. I could easily pass for a BBC breakfast news presenter. I certainly looked more above board than some of the weather presenters. They always look like they're going out on the piss the minute they've finished telling us about the isobars and westerly wind, the way some of them are made up.

The idea was for us both to go for a walk by the beach, so I picked some flat sensible shoes. I popped the mask on and finished off the look with a medium-length blonde wig. I actually wanted a black bob, as I've always liked Catherine Zeta-Jones's hair in the film *Chicago*, but Rob didn't think it would work, as it would be too short at the back and would expose the laces of the mask. The blonde wig wasn't too bad; it gave me a look of Joanna Lumley, which was an improvement on Elton John.

Rob got dressed and settled on some very short denim shorts, a low tight cropped top (no bra) that showed off the stomach (and nipples), with high heels and long dark hair. We looked in the mirror before leaving for the beach and we looked the spitting image of an album cover for Abba. Never has the phrase 'getting dolled up' been more appropriate.

KARLA: Do you use Facebook and Twitter? Cos that's how most people become someone else.

SHERRY: Yes, that's what most crossdressers do. They have their female identity on a separate page, too. It's funny, Sherry has over one thousand friends on Facebook, yet I only have thirty.

At that point a young kid came up and stared at us.

KID: What's the matter with your face?

SHERRY: What's the matter with my face?

KID: Yeah, it doesn't look real . . . it looks gross.

SHERRY: Oh, okay. But if it was our real face it would be worse!

By now I was quite comfortable wearing the clothes and didn't feel any different to how I normally feel. During this adventure I've found that no matter what I wear, or who I'm made to look like, it doesn't really change anything. It was still nice to have a walk by the beach on the pier with Sherry as the sun went down. It was a lot more relaxing than when I was on noisy tacky Fremont Street in Vegas the night before dressed as Elton John. And that's what I discovered from this experience: I'm quite happy being anyone, as long as I'm in a place that I like with people I can get on with.

I FIND THAT opportunities to help people these days are few and far between. I give to charity shops, which I suppose goes towards helping someone somewhere. In fact the local charity shop has had so much of our stuff that at one point I could have moved in and felt quite at home. But I don't mean that sort of help, I'm talking about direct help.

Years ago a neighbour might have knocked on your door to borrow some milk or sugar, but petrol stations sell everything you need and are open twenty-four hours now. I don't find myself holding doors for people as much since the invention of electronic doors. I also can't remember the last time someone asked me the time as everyone carries mobile phones nowadays. And thanks to sat nav it's rare for someone to pull up in their car to ask for directions. Though to be honest, I'm glad this one has gone as nine times out of ten I've not been able to help – even if they ask directions to the street I actually live on I still find it hard to explain how to get there. Whenever I used to see a story in the local paper about a missing person I'd wonder if it was someone I gave directions to. The problem is I can't remember street names. It's as if my brain doesn't want to use valuable space for information that I don't really need to know. I'm sure I go through most things on autopilot. I just tried to guess what colour my underpants are – I would have put money on them being light blue but they're black. In some ways I should just be thankful that my brain remembered to put a pair on at all.

When it comes to giving directions I can just about manage if there are shops or landmarks, so I can say, 'Turn right at Blockbuster and then take a left at the curry house,' but seeing as Starbucks has taken over every corner shop these days, it's impossible to give someone directions using this method. My dad on the other hand is brilliant at it as he used to be a black cab driver. I used to feel sorry for anyone who asked directions from him though as it was difficult to keep up with him yelling 'Left, right, straight on, second left, right, right, left' like some sort of deranged commander leading his army round a maze. They'd often drive off looking more lost than they were before.

I used to get lost all the time too, especially if a familiar road was closed for roadworks. It was quicker for me to just park up and wait for the works to be completed rather than try to find a new route. To give you an idea of how bad I am with finding my way about I'll go right back to the early days of meeting Suzanne. Even though me and Suzanne aren't married, we say our anniversary is 17 July. We had known each other for a couple of weeks, but this was the date that I was invited round to hers to watch the World Cup final between Brazil and Italy in 1994. She was living in West Didsbury, which was only about four miles from where I was living at the time. I remember rushing home from work and having a quick wash before setting off with only a street name and house number on a piece of paper. I thought I had a rough idea of where she lived as I'd been to a curry house in West Didsbury quite a lot which was also close to where my auntie lives. I set off from home at around 6.30 p.m. and found myself still driving round in circles at 9.30 p.m. You have to remember that this was well before mobile phones and I didn't have a number for her so I just kept steering up and down the same roads, taking every left and right. I felt like I was Pac-Man. If you're familiar with the game of Pac-Man you'll know he was chased by ghosts; well, as I was trying to find my way to Suzanne's gaff I was being chased by prostitutes. It was a bit of a rough area at the time and with me driving round in circles and slowing down to read street names they must have all thought I was on the look-out for some action. It didn't help that they kept crossing the road and moving around as I was trying to use them as landmarks.

It got close to 10 p.m. so I gave up the search and decided to try and make my way home. It was at this point that I happened to drive past the street! I must have driven past it eight or nine times that evening but hadn't seen the street sign. I knocked on Suzanne's door and she asked 'Where the bloody hell have you been?!' for the first time in our relationship (she's said it many times since) and gave me some burnt food (I've eaten this many times since too – I tend to know my tea will be ready soon when I hear the smoke alarm going off). The World Cup final was over. Brazil had won on penalties.

HELPING OTHERS

Anyway, I went off track a bit there. This all started by me telling you that I don't get to help people out very much these days, which is a shame as it's an important value in life. It was values and ways to live your life that I was exploring next.

I started this trip with a man who spends most of his free time helping strangers. He is part of a group known as the Real Life Superheroes. His name is Mr Xtreme. After being bullied at school and attacked by a group of gang members, he decided that it was about time that someone took a stand before more innocent folk were hurt. This was when Mr Xtreme was born. He now spends his evenings pacing up and down the crime-ridden streets of San Diego, dressed as a superhero, hell-bent on breaking up fights and maintaining order. He's been doing this for over ten years.

When I met him he wasn't in his superhero costume just yet, but was wearing a disguise of dark shades and cap as he still wanted to protect his identity for the safety of his friends and family. The plan was for me to join him on his patrol later that evening. He was a very serious bloke. I don't think I saw him smile the whole time I was with him. When I think about it, most superheroes are like this. They're generally troubled individuals. It always seems to be the baddies who have more of a laugh in the movies.

KARL: I haven't been here long but San Diego seems like quite a nice place.

MR XTREME: Yeah, we have a very nice city, nice weather, a lot of great tourist attractions, but don't let the look fool you. I mean, just like any major city there's crime, there's violence, there's people that are in a state of despair. And that's why I'm out there.

KARL: So what do I need to know before we hit the streets?

MR XTREME: First of all you gotta make your voice assertive and straight to the point. Back off! Stand back! Stop! You know, don't make it like a question. You gotta use commands. You gotta tell them to back off and you gotta insist on your personal space. Because otherwise they're not gonna take you seriously and then they're gonna think you're weak and then they're gonna say, 'Oh yeah? Oh yeah?', you know? No smiling, because if you smile at them they're gonna think that you're disrespecting them and if you disrespect them that's gonna motivate them even more to attack you. So you gotta be calm, firm, straight-faced.

His deep American accent suited the authoritative commands that he yelled out. I struggle to do the serious hard voice thing as when I get annoyed or angry my voice tends to go higher. The longer the sentence, the higher-pitched my voice gets, so I end up sounding like I'm singing a song by Queen.

LOOKS ARMLESS.

Mr Xtreme then went through some self-defence moves with me, which included punches to the nose, elbow to the face and eye gouging, which he performed on a dummy named Bob that he had in his back garden. Bob was just a rubber head and torso. I don't know if that was the shape Bob was in when Mr Xtreme bought it or if he had bitten the limbs off with his teeth during an intense training session. After just fifteen minutes I was absolutely knackered. He had worked me pretty hard and I was sweating like a pig. I very rarely work up such a sweat through exercise. My main weekly workout is usually Suzanne asking me to mash the potatoes. But I now felt pumped up and ready to handle any legless/ armless thug who may be on the streets of San Diego.

KARL'S  FACTS

There was an American comic book superhero called 'normalman'. He was the only person without superpowers on a planet full of superheroes.

If you're going to be a superhero, you have to look the part so it was time to go and get myself suited and booted ready for the evening ahead. We went to a local costume shop where I met one of the other local superheroes who was part of the Xtreme Justice League that Mr Xtreme had set up. He was known as the Midnight Highwayman. He was dressed all in black, in a coat fastened right to the top, which covered his mouth. Round goggles covered his eyes and a tricorn hat similar to the kind that pirates wore was balanced on his head. He also had leather gloves and boots on his feet. Everything was black apart from the red-and-white Xtreme Justice League badge that was sewn onto the arm of his coat. It was a really sunny day so his heavy black material was absorbing more sun than a solar panel. He must have been suffering as after a few minutes he undid a few of the buttons on his jacket and I felt the warm air hit me. It was as if he'd opened an oven door. Honestly, I could have dried washing in the hot air that he emitted. Rather than Midnight Highwayman, I think Radiator Man would have been more suitable.

As well as all that clobber he also had a utility belt around his waist that contained everything from medical supplies, pens, paper, handcuffs, paperclips, batteries, string and menus for takeaway pizzas. Every pouch was

IT'S MY WAY OR THE HIGHWAY . . . MAN.

filled with gubbins. He did look quite intimidating though. If anything he looked more like a baddy, but this tends to be the way superheroes have gone in the last twenty years. If you look at Batman in the '60s he wore a calming shade of grey – what Farrow & Ball call Pavilion Grey – whereas these days Batman is fashioning a black rubber jumpsuit that must weigh a ton. It doesn't make sense to wear such material when you've got to be chasing people around, as surely you'd pass out? It would be like Mo Farah trying to do the 1,500 metres in a bondage outfit.

KARL: What was your reason for joining the Xtreme Justice League?

MIDNIGHT HIGHWAYMAN: I have always been the kind of person who likes to step in and help people, and I have got a background in security – semi-law enforcement you could say – and some medical training so this is kind of natural, to want to get out there and put that to a good use.

If truth be told I can't say I'm the sort of person who likes to step in and help. There used to be a lad at school who had epileptic fits. It was bright colours and patterns that triggered him off. The '80s weren't a good time for him as everything was brightly coloured back then. If someone was eating a tube of Smarties while playing with a Rubik's Cube, that would be it, he'd be flipping about on the floor. If he had a seizure when he was out shopping, a crowd would circle and start clapping thinking he was a breakdancer. Having epilepsy in the '80s was not easy.

I used to hate sitting next to him in lessons. I couldn't relax, as there was an unwritten rule that whoever was close to him had to step in and help protect his head and move any sharp objects if he started to have one of his fits. The toughest part was trying to grab his tongue so he didn't swallow it. I only attempted this once or twice and it was impossible. My hands got covered in so much saliva I looked like I'd helped to deliver a calf.

I would always prefer to leave situations like this to someone else, but of course if there isn't anybody else around then I'll step in. A few years ago I was closing the curtains in the bedroom and heard a load of banging going on outside. I pushed my face up against the window and it was a neighbour who appeared to be trying to break into his own house. He kicked the door so hard he fell backwards into the road and his bag of takeaway curry went all over him. He just lay there comatose, obviously pissed up. Curtains were twitching on the street but after a few minutes nobody had gone out to help. I couldn't leave him there, as quite a lot of taxis used the road as a cut-through and it wasn't particularly well lit either, so he could have ended up being squashed. I nipped outside in my joggers and flip-flops. He was well and truly out of it. I fished his keys out of his coat pocket, opened his front door, lifted him up to his feet, shuffled him into his front room and plonked him down. I went back home with chicken tikka masala all over my chest looking like I'd just played the lead role in the film *Carrie*. The next day I knocked on his door to check he was okay and he apologised for causing trouble and gave me some frozen minced beef as a gift.

KARL: So how do you put together a costume?

MR XTREME: A lot of people like to pick a theme: patriotism, a favourite hero, an aspect of their personality, or favourite colour. I would say my recommendation is get a cape. At least if you have a cape, you can be quickly identified as a superhero.

I've never understood capes. They don't offer much warmth, it's not a coat, it's not a scarf, and there are no pockets. I really don't know why a superhero would choose such a garment. While someone is being mugged or attacked valuable time is being taken up fastening the useless thing around their neck. I've never been a fan of clothes that drape around you as they end up getting caught in car doors or lifts. I think this comes from the time that I almost strangled myself with my paper-round bag. I'll explain. I used to love my paper round but my mam hated me doing it in the winter when the weather was really bad. I woke up one morning to find she had locked the front door and hidden the keys so I wouldn't go out on my round. But I didn't let that stop me. I put the bag over my head and on my shoulder and climbed out of the bathroom window where I thought I'd be able to descend onto the porch roof. It was all going to plan until my bag strap got caught on the window hook. I couldn't set it free as I needed both hands to hold my weight and I couldn't quite reach the porch roof with my feet. No matter how much I tried, it would not come free. I was left hanging there like the bus on the edge of the cliff at the end of *The Italian Job*.

After about forty minutes my dad came home from working the night in his black cab and shouted directions at me: 'What you need to do is go up, left, right, left, up, left.' As I've already mentioned, I could never follow his directions so eventually he went inside and unhooked me. Since then I've never worn draping clothes.

As I wandered around the costume shop I thought about what my character should be based on. I was thinking about some kind of insect, as humans are rubbish in comparison to some of the powers they have. I've already raved about how good octopuses are, but when you get a spare minute make sure you look up the 'mimic octopus' on YouTube. That has proper superhero skills. It can basically shape-shift. It can make itself look like anything. I'd say it's the most remarkable thing I've ever seen. There's a clip of one where it looks like the spitting image of a lump of coral and then you see it change back to an octopus and swim off. How nature created this skill I will never understand. There's not much footage of them but that's probably because they're hard to find. I don't know if the octopus knows it has this gift. Maybe it sits on a rock and wonders why female octopuses are ignoring it, not realising it's because it's sat there looking like a rock.

Mr Xtreme came up with the idea of me being 'Ant Man'. Ants are strong and hard-working. They don't sleep much either, which would make them good superheroes as they'd always be ready for action. On an average day a single worker ant takes around 250 naps, but each nap only lasts just over a minute so that works out at four hours and ten minutes of sleep a day. I wonder if us humans could get by using this technique. If we could, we'd no longer need bedrooms. We could just kip on a park bench, or have a quick snooze while waiting for the traffic lights to change.

We got to work looking for an ant-like outfit. First, I came across some goggles that also covered the nose area and easily passed for an ant face. I wanted a black bodysuit, but Sue who was in charge of the shop said she was all out of black bodysuits and only had bright red in stock. Mr Xtreme suggested I become the 'Red Ant Man'. Problem sorted. Mr Xtreme found a red top hat. Again, a bit like the cape, I'm not sure a top hat is an ideal piece of clothing for fighting in. I think only a tiara could top it for being more inappropriate. What was he going to suggest for footwear – bloody flip flops?! I added some small feeler-type things to the top of the hat and grabbed a black belt and gloves and finally a pair of boots. As I was trying on the knee-high leather boots for size I suddenly got cramp in my leg. I had a proper painful muscle spasm, which must have been caused by not drinking enough water during the vigorous training earlier that day. Mr Xtreme and the Midnight Highwayman stood there looking down on me – I resembled an ant that had been sprayed with Raid.

Sue appeared in seconds with a jar of mustard and a spoon and told me to swallow a mouthful, as it would stop the cramp. And amazingly it actually worked. Almost instantly the cramp was gone. I think the Midnight Highwayman took note of this and has no doubt since added a jar of the stuff to his utility belt. Once the boots were on I checked myself out in the mirror. It all seemed to go together quite nicely but the bodysuit was more revealing than I thought it would be. I don't want to get vulgar but let's just say I think rather than trying to base my look on the ant, maybe I should have gone for the worm!

> MR XTREME: You got to understand, it is not all about the costume. The confidence comes from within, from experience, from training. The costume is like a symbol of that confidence, of that dedication. It isn't going to make you a warrior or a superhero. You can try on ten more costumes, but once you get out on the street you are still going to feel the same. It is what is coming from within ya. I honestly think this is not bad, you are a good Ant Man. I think it looks pretty cool.

We agreed to meet in an hour, so I nipped off and had some early tea as there would be no time for food once we started our patrol. I stopped off in a quiet little café and had some noodles. To my surprise the cape actually came in quite handy. I may have mentioned before how I'm quite a messy eater and normally have to go topless when eating Sunday dinner (obviously not when I'm in a Harvester) as I end up dropping a bit of chicken onto my plate causing gravy to splash all over my T-shirt. Well, I swizzed my cape round the front and used it as a bib to stop the noodle juice from splashing on the front of my red Spandex. It did have a use after all.

As the sun set on San Diego I met with Mr Xtreme on top of a tall building so we could survey the whole of the city. It was a Friday night so the streets were starting to get fairly busy. Mr Xtreme was in his suit now. There was a big difference between our two costumes. He looked like a proper superhero, whereas I looked like one of the members of Hot Gossip, the '80s dance group.

He wore a proper soldier's helmet and bright green protection gear like the sort ice hockey players wear: ski goggles, yellow-and-black combat trousers and shin guards. To finish it off he wore a wide, long purple cape that he could wrap all the way round his body like a hairdresser's gown. To give you an idea of the look, imagine a Teenage Mutant Ninja Turtle at the barber's.

I met with all the other superheroes who had signed up to the Xtreme Justice League. Mr Xtreme divided them into two groups and did a quick check of everybody's radios before allocating the routes he wanted

them to patrol. The other superheroes were called Emerald, Fallen Boy, Green Knight, Freedom Fighter, Grimm and Dixy, and were all kitted out with impressive outfits. Midnight Highwayman remained in his car as he suffers with a bad back so can no longer do the twelve-mile hike around the city. Maybe this is why he's known as Highwayman, cos he drives the highways. His motor was stacked full of snacks and bottles of water which were there to hand out to homeless people.

KARL: Who pays for all this – the water and the snacks?

EMERALD: We do. But on our website we have a PayPal donation so people can donate and get a tax-deductible receipt. But most of it comes out of our pocket. There's something about helping other people that does something for your soul.

KARL: How long have you been doing this?

EMERALD: I've been with the team since 2012.

KARL: What got you into it?

EMERALD: My son was part of the XJL and he was in an automobile accident and the team came up around me afterward. It was a fatality accident. So, they became my team.

I was given a carrier bag containing a few bottles of water and granola bars to hand out to those in need. This ruined my superhero look, as it's rare that you see Superman doing a food shop. We started our patrol. It wasn't long before people wanted to have selfies with us. I'm not sure if they realised we were there to keep the streets safe, or if they just thought we were on a stag do. To be honest though, I think if real superheroes existed most of their day would be taken up having selfies with people. Could you imagine the hassle they would get? Every newspaper would be chasing them around trying to find out their real identity. It was bad enough for the Stig off *Top Gear*.

Even though the streets were busy everyone had been fairly well behaved. Who knows if that had anything to do with our presence or not. I strolled up and down the streets like those prostitutes hanging around Suzanne's house all those years ago, except in this bodysuit I think I was showing off more than they were.

As we turned a corner at Starbucks (of course) we could hear a man yelling. He was wandering around in the middle of the road. Other people were just laughing at him and taking videos on their phone. Mr Xtreme stepped in.

MR XTREME: Hey, get outta the street! Get outta the street! You're gonna get hit.

MAN: I don't need you to fucking tell me!

MR XTREME: You're gonna get hit, sir!

MAN: I don't need you to hold my hand! I'm not a goddamn child. I'm four times the IQ of you or anybody on this block. I know exactly what I'm doing! So leave me the hell alone, please. Goddamnit!

I didn't offer him a granola bar as he seemed nuts enough. As I was stood there with my carrier bag looking a bit helpless, a few pissed-up onlookers got bored of watching the mad man and started taking photos of my crotch!

'Oi! Nothing to see here!' I said. 'Too right,' said one lady.

Cheeky cow. Did this ever happen to Spider-Man?! Mr Xtreme got out his mobile. For one second I thought he was going to join in and start taking photos of my crotch too, but it was to call the police.

MR XTREME: Hello, San Diego Police? Yeah, I just wanna report that there's an elderly man, I'd say in his sixties, just walking in and out of traffic on Fifth Avenue and Broadway. He's white. Estimate maybe five, five feet ten. I'd say medium build. He's wearing a camouflage jacket and a black baseball cap. Blue shirt, black jeans. I don't see any weapons. It looks like he's possibly mentally distraught or maybe on drugs or something . . . Okay. No problem.

KARL: Do the police mind you being out on the street?

MR XTREME: Oh, they love us being out here. Oh yeah.

KARL: I suppose it's an extra pair of eyes.

MR XTREME: Eyes and ears. That's what it's about, eyes and ears for the police.

We hung around for the police to turn up and take care of the roaming drunk. At the start of the day I thought the whole thing was a bit of a waste of time, but to be fair Mr Xtreme was the only person who went out of his way to make sure the guy didn't get himself badly injured. The police did eventually turn up and put him in the back of the police car. All in a night's work for Mr Xtreme and I doubt he got any minced beef for his trouble either.

'If real SUPERHEROES existed, most of their DAY would be taken up having SELFIES with people'.

BEING KIND TO ANIMALS

Whenever I do interviews, I am always asked if I have ever been approached to appear on *I'm A Celebrity . . . Get Me Out of Here!* I don't know why they need to ask this question, as I'm pretty sure anyone who's ever been on telly has been asked to go on it. You only have had to be on TV for five minutes to qualify for that show. It wouldn't surprise me if in the next series you'll see some criminal who's been featured on *Crimewatch*. The problem is, the longer that programme runs, the more unknown people get asked to take part. It's the same issue the Queen has to deal with every year when it comes to handing out OBEs. All the proper good people have already been awarded so she ends up handing them out to some bloke who once thought about standing up for a pregnant woman on a bus.

So yes, I've been asked to fly down under to take part but I'd never agree to it. Going all that way, being stuck with a load of strangers in a tight space, listening to them burp and fart for hours on end while eating crap food isn't my idea of fun. Then I'd have to go through it all again on the return flight home. (That's a proper shite joke, that.) No, the main reason I would never go on *I'm A Celebrity . . .* is I don't think it's right how cockroaches, spiders and other insects end up getting injured and killed on the show. I'm pretty sure some of those creatures have done more good for the planet than many of the contestants and yet they end up getting stressed, crushed and eaten. I couldn't be doing with it.

Little bugs have always fascinated me. I think I get this off my mam as I used to see her putting creatures out of the house all the time rather than killing them. Since me and my brother and sister have left home, she doesn't even bother letting them out any more, she ends up keeping many of them as rent-free tenants for company. I think I've mentioned before how she once kept a spider in the house and dabbed a small dot of Tipp-Ex on its back so that its dark body stood out against the carpet, which then prevented it from being accidentally vacced up. I doubt the spider appreciated it, having to walk about the house looking like a bloody domino, but she's daft like that. She thinks she's helping things out when she's probably causing damage. She's got squirrels in her garden at the minute that she's feeding ginger nut biscuits to. They do seem to enjoy eating them but will no doubt be suffering with Type 2 diabetes within a year.

My dad, on the other hand, wouldn't do such a thing. Not because he's worried that the squirrels could end up with a high sugar intake, but because he doesn't want to share his biscuits. He doesn't think twice about killing things. The only reason he still buys a newspaper is because it's difficult to swat a wasp with an iPad. Normally when you flick through a newspaper you'll find the odd flyer. With my dad's paper you'll find flyers and non-flyers (i.e. dead flies). Seriously, it contains more species of insect than the Natural History Museum. He says the flies are attracted to the newspaper as it's always full of shit.

I'd say I'm more like my mam when it comes to saving creatures. I've driven Suzanne up the wall due to the lengths I'll go to trying to protect them. Recently I gave her a lift to the gym and I noticed a spider in the passenger wing mirror that was clinging on for dear life. I couldn't concentrate on my driving as I was worried for it, so I pulled over and placed it on a nearby shrub. Maybe my driving instructor was a fan of spiders too as he always told me I should check my mirrors before pulling away.

Sometimes me interfering does not always go so well. Daddy longlegs are tricky things to shift without injuring. They must be up there as one of the most delicate insects that have ever existed. They seem to detach their legs easier than Heather Mills can. It's weird, as they don't even seem to notice. You'll have one in your hand and then they'll fly off leaving a leg behind. They lose their legs like us humans lose umbrellas.

I was looking forward to the day ahead in a place called Monterey on California's rugged coast, where I was to help a Buddhist monk free some creatures. According to Buddhists there is no fundamental difference between a human and a non-human animal, therefore if humans are important then so are other animals. It's because of this attitude towards nature that I've always thought of myself as a bit of a Buddhist. They have that skill where they can remove all thoughts from their heads by using meditation, which I'm also good at. Just ask Suzanne: she's always saying that I'm thoughtless.

KARL'S FACTS

According to neuroscientific recordings of brain waves, Matthieu Ricard, a Buddhist monk, is literally the happiest person ever tested.

The monk's name was Rinpoche. A Tibetan fella dressed in the typical orange-and-brown Buddhist robes. He was a happy calm man who had a constant smile and soft voice. He had brought along a couple of tubs of creatures that he had bought from a shop, which I presumed were either for feeding to exotic pets or for use as fishing bait, but the plan was to free them back into the wild.

RINPOCHE: Every month I buy worms, frogs, snails, different animals, and release them. I want happiness and creature want happiness. I need long life, creature needs long life. Same.

KARL: I agree with you. When I was in Japan, I passed a restaurant that had a turtle in a box outside that was there to be eaten. It bothered

me seeing it trapped in a box and scratching to get out, so I bought it and set it free.

RINPOCHE: Oh, good! Yes, release the animals and you feel happy.

KARL: Yeah, really happy.

I'll never forget saving that turtle. It turned out to be quite a palaver as I had no idea what species it was, what it liked to eat, or where it should be put. I felt like that Elliott kid in *E.T.* who ended up with an alien in his bedroom. Most of the information online was about how it should be cooked rather than how to take care of it! I finally figured out that it needed to be put in fresh water so we ended up driving for a good few hours to a spot where it could be released. Once it was set free I had a really good feeling, so this is why I was looking forward to my day ahead with the monk.

Rinpoche found a safe secluded spot by a bush and handed me a plastic tub full of crickets. He said a little prayer and chant then finished by ringing a small bell. As I lifted off the lid all the crickets legged it. It

was like a school class hearing a bell for home time as they all scarpered in different directions unaware of how close to death they had come.

We moved on to another location. Rinpoche had found a patch of soil where we added some water to soften the ground before releasing a tub of slimy wriggly worms. Thinking about it, maybe the reason I like to save insects is because not many people care for them because of their slimy, wriggly crawlyness. I'm pretty sure if the panda was bald and slimy and had six legs it would have died out years ago. It's the cuteness that makes people want to save the panda. I see adverts on the telly every day asking for money to help save the beautiful snow leopard and the cuddly panda and yet I've never seen one asking for money to set up a sanctuary for the Daddy no-legs appeal. The only part of the world that doesn't seem to be put off by the look of insects is China. They like the look of them so much that they eat them. No creature is safe in that country. Noah's job of saving every animal two by two could have been sorted quite easily if he had just wandered around a Chinese food market as they'd have the lot on display. You know that nursery rhyme about the old woman who swallows the cat to catch the bird to catch the spider to catch the fly that wriggled inside her? At the end it goes 'I don't know why she swallowed the fly'. Well, I reckon I know why. It's because she was Chinese. All those creatures were part of her five-a-day plan. If I gave a copy of my dad's newspaper to someone in China they'd class it as a selection box. They're even trying to push their ways onto us in Britain now. You can't go into a Chinese takeaway these days without them asking 'Do you want flies with that?'

I thought our saving of insects for the day was over, but then Rinpoche said he wanted to free some other creatures back into the sea from a fishing boat, but wanted to stop for lunch first. As I suffer pretty badly with seasickness I decided to skip lunch and just have a walk while Rinpoche went to eat. After an hour I met him back at the harbour where he was holding a big polystyrene box that contained around fifteen crabs he had bought from a local fishmonger. These weren't like the small crabs I used to see crawling about between the rocks on holiday in Cornwall, these were bloody massive. They weren't moving at this point so I thought they were all dead until Rinpoche explained that they had been sat in ice, which puts them into a sleepy state. It's weird, as ice seems to have the same effect on my auntie Nora. She's forever nodding off when she has a large glass of ice in her hand. I suppose that could be to do with all the whisky that's also in the glass. Either that or my auntie is a crab.

ALL FOR A GOOD CLAWS.

We boarded a boat and set off. We weren't planning on going too far out, but the problem was there were loads of seals around the harbour so Rinpoche suggested we keep going otherwise we'd just end up feeding them with drowsy crabs. But the further out the boat went, the choppier the waters became. The captain finally threw out an anchor. The boat was now rocking all over the place and it made the task rather difficult as the once sleeping crabs were now wide-awake. We couldn't just tip the box into the sea as we could have ended up breaking their shells or legs, and then the whole exercise would have been pointless. So we took it in turns to grab a crab (sounds like some Saturday TV show presented by Ant and Dec). He told me to make sure to pick them up from the back so they didn't nip me. That wasn't as easy as it sounds, as they were all lying on top of each other like some sort of crab orgy. We had to concentrate.

We had managed to set free about three crabs each when Rinpoche turned to me with his hand on his chest while looking down. At first I thought he was about to do a little prayer, but then he belched. He was suffering with seasickness! Now I've been seasick many times, and it's not nice, so I suggested that he be sick as he would feel a lot better. It's at times like this that I realise I have quite an odd job. There I was, out at

TRIED TO GIVE A HELPING HAND . . .
THE CRAB WANTED TO KEEP IT!

sea, releasing crabs while holding on to a monk's robes so he didn't fall into the ocean as he spewed up his lunch, which by the look of things was seafood chowder. He's such a kind Buddhist that he even wanted to free the fish that he'd eaten for lunch back into the sea! It was never-ending. He seemed to be sicking up the whole cast of *Finding Nemo*.

We were down to about three crabs each and I was eager to get back to shore, but this was when a crab managed to get me. God knows how, as I had hold of him at the back, so the thing must have been bloody double-jointed for it to get its claw into me. It had one of its pincers on the end of one of my fingers. It was painful. Really painful. To the point that I actually thought I was going to lose the tip of a finger. It was like someone had hold of me with a pair of pliers. I leaned over the edge screaming my head off, hoping that once it saw the water it would let go, but for some reason it seemed to grab me even harder. Maybe it didn't like the idea of swimming in the lumps of sick that were bobbing around in the sea.

'Fuckin' hell!' I shouted. I'd been trying not to swear all day, seeing as I was in the presence of a Buddhist, but I had to help relieve the pain. 'FUCK!' I swung my arm about hoping it would let go but it held on tight. I don't know what its problem was. It was like the end scene in *Titanic* when Kate Winslet isn't letting go of Leonardo DiCaprio.

It eventually let go. I was shaking from shock, as I had no idea that crabs had that sort of power. To think that we went far out into the sea so they wouldn't get attacked by seals was a joke, as that one could easily have put a seal in a headlock.

My finger was bleeding quite badly as its claw had managed to cut quite deep and had also put a hole in my nail! If Mr Xtreme is ever short on members to help him patrol the streets of San Diego he should sign up some crabs.

BEING CHARITABLE

I was up early, as I had to wait for a man with a van to turn up. This time it wasn't for a delivery. It was for a pick-up. Suzanne was donating her old dressing table to an organisation that auctions off what you give them with the proceeds going to charity. I had already dragged the dresser down from the bedroom as the person Suzanne had spoken to on the phone said that the man who collects the furniture didn't do stairs. So as I waited for the Dalek to arrive I tightened the nuts and bolts, as me shifting it seemed to loosen everything. It's never been a very sturdy piece of furniture so I was glad to be seeing the back of it if I'm honest. It's what they now call 'shabby chic', where they take something old and battered and pop some fancy paint on it. I call it shabby shit.

There was a loud knock at the door – so loud I was worried the dressing table was going to collapse. It was the Dalek. Before he had set both feet into the house he said, 'Sorry, I can't accept that.'

'Why not?' I asked, as I stopped it rocking back and forth.

'Well, erm, the thing is . . . we can't take anything that is painted.'

'What! Why not?' I didn't understand this, as I'd say the paint was the best thing about it.

'Something to do with health and safety. It's considered dangerous. Those are the rules.'

'I guess with so many people dying from painted dressing tables it's understandable,' I said. I don't think he picked up on my sarcasm.

'Is there anything else you would like to donate, you know, now that I'm here?'

'Well, I've got a Monet and a Warhol that I'm sick of looking at, but you don't accept painted goods so . . . no.'

'Haha . . . yes. Sorry about that. Seriously though, are you sure you don't have anything else? I waste so much of my time turning up to addresses to find their donations can't be accepted and it costs the charity money, you know, with fuel for the van an' all.'

It was like he had some kind of Jedi power as suddenly the guilt kicked in. I looked in the front room and the first thing I set my eyes on was Suzanne's Nintendo Wii with the *Michael Jackson Experience* keep-fit dancing game. I bought it for her a few Christmases ago but as far as I was aware she hadn't used it in ages. I think the legs on the dressing table have had more movement than Suzanne's. Moments later, the man from the charity was walking down the path with said item in a carrier bag as he left me to carry the bloody flimsy dressing table back upstairs. He was right about the dresser being dangerous. Lugging it back to the bedroom nearly bloody killed me.

After some time had passed I felt really annoyed with what had happened. I should have just said that there was nothing else and sent the man on his way, but because it was for charity I let him take the piss. Or in this case, let him take the Wii.

Charity is a lot more in your face these days and it's difficult to go a day without having someone asking you for money at some point. I used to live in a flat in the centre of London on a fairly busy high street. Every fifty yards there was someone holding a bucket asking for spare change. Within a few hours it would be full to the brim. Shoppers didn't even question what the charities were raising money for; they would just throw their handful of coins at anyone holding a bucket. I think the local window cleaner probably ended up making a few extra quid on that street.

Charity collecting is different now. Spare change is no longer enough to solve the world's problems, and the people with buckets have been swapped for people with clipboards who ask for your bank details so you can donate on a regular basis. I found myself with about five or six monthly direct debits set up because I struggled to say no. It was impossible to leave that flat without having one of those charity collectors accost me, which in turn ended up accosting me a fortune. Before nipping out for some milk I'd look out of the window to check if the coast was clear and see a cluster of Hi-Viz vests dotted about the street. It was like there was a game of five-a-side going on there were so many of the buggers. The supermarket was only a five-minute walk away but I'd have them all confronting me: 'I'm collecting for the Salvation Army', 'Excuse me, I'm collecting for the British Heart Foundation', 'Have you got a minute? I'm collecting for Help for Heroes'. Whatever happened to just collecting stamps?! People talk about London being an expensive place to live, but it's not because of the price of rent, it's due to the amount of charity collectors on the street taking your money off you.

Next on my trip I was going to test my generosity some more by joining a man named Jason Buzi. He's a millionaire who has made his money from selling property and regularly gives away some of his personal fortune using Twitter. I met up with him early one morning on the beach in Santa Cruz where he was going to bury some of his wealth for his followers to find.

KARL: Why do you do this then, Jason?

JASON: Well, it's fun. People like finding money and I like giving it away. You can write a cheque to charity – there's nothing wrong with that – but you don't get to see people's reactions. They get so excited about it. I have over 600,000 followers on Twitter so I say I'm gonna be in Santa Cruz today or we're gonna be in LA or London. I give them some clues, then they run out to wherever it is and start looking for the money. You know it's going directly to somebody, and if they don't need it they tell us they gave it to another person that needed it and we try to spread that message. Sometimes they buy people ice cream if it's at the beach or they buy food for the homeless or they give the money to charity. It's inspired a lot of other giving.

KARL: Would you say this gives you more joy than buying something for yourself?

JASON: Yes, definitely. There are three things you can spend your money on, right? One, you buy something tangible – a sports car or something – two, you buy an experience – go travelling, for example – or three, you give it to someone. They've done studies, and the third option makes people the happiest, second is having experiences, and what makes people the least happy is buying something like a new sports car. This kind of thing only brings happiness for a short spell. Once your basic needs have been met nothing brings more joy than giving to others.

Jason was carrying $1,500 in a carrier bag along with some little plastic toys that broke into two pieces – similar to the plastic balls you get inside a Kinder Egg. He placed different amounts of cash in these before burying them on the beach. The minimum was $40 but others had been stuffed with $60, $80, $100 and $120. As we walked and talked Jason was dropping the toys containing the money onto the sand and pushing them under with his foot. The way he kept shoving his hand in his bag and throwing out the cash-filled toys was like he was feeding ducks. At this point he didn't seem to look like he was enjoying the process very much but he told me that the joy comes later.

It was odd to see cash being thrown away like this. Normally, if I drop any money I bend down so fast to pick it up it hits me on the back of the head. I guess I was brought up to respect money as you never know when it's going to run out. My dad always said it was important to be able to pay your way in life. This has stuck with me.

By doing the TV programmes and books I've earned more money than I ever thought I would have but I never waste it. Since I've had a bit more dosh I still buy the same stuff I always have, it's just that now I'll go for a better-quality version of that thing. So I like to have jam on my toast, but rather than a bog-standard jam I'm treating myself to Tiptree. It's a bit more expensive but it's worth it for the taste.

KARL'S FACTS

A burger chain introduced a burger that was bigger and less expensive than a McDonald's Quarter Pounder, but it failed because customers assumed a third was less than a quarter.

You have to be careful though, as just because something is more expensive doesn't always mean it's worth the extra cost. Suzanne bought some toilet paper that was 37p more than the stuff we used to use, and the only reason it was dearer was because it had a nice pattern on it. This wound me right up. It's not bloody wallpaper, it's for wiping my arse with! There's no need for it. I read recently that some woman had stolen three bikinis from Harrods valued at over £2,000. £2,000 for a few bikinis! How can they be worth that much? I'm struggling to work out who the robber is in this scenario.

There was another occasion when I wanted some paint to decorate a room so nipped to a shop that was close to home known as 'the upmarket supplier of paint'. I have never felt so out of place when buying a tin of paint in my life. I was the only customer in the shop, and the fella who worked there dressed and spoke like he was in *Downton Abbey*. I only popped in to pick up a tin of white paint, but almost thirty minutes later he still had me looking through colour charts. There were some really ridiculous names for some of the colours like Calluna, Cromarty and Babouche. This paint shop must be where Gwyneth Paltrow goes to get the names for her kids. The fella was so excited talking me through all the different grades. I think he was the only person who may have been disappointed by *Fifty Shades of Grey* as it wasn't actually about paint. He asked loads of questions like 'Which way does the room face as the colour changes in west-facing rooms?' I had no idea! 'It faces a Tesco Local,' I said. Honestly, it would take this fella a month to decide on what paints to use to design a chess board, so I left him and headed to Homebase. I might have a tad more money these days but I feel more at home in these big warehouses where you're not being watched and judged on what you buy. They also take on a lot of OAPs and disabled staff, which is nice. Though I did wonder if using the old bloke who had the shakes to hold the paint when the mixing equipment was broken was a bit wrong.

KARL: How much would you say you've given away in total then?

JASON: Close to seventy thousand dollars now.

KARL: And any idea when you're going to stop? Is there a figure where you'll think that's enough now?

JASON: No, I have no figure. I have no plan to stop. But I had to slow it down a bit. It was just taking up a lot of my time for a few months.

KARL: Seventy grand, though! I wonder if you'll ever regret it.

JASON: I won't ever regret it, as it's been an experience and it has brought joy to many people.

KARL: So how many people will turn up today?

JASON: You never know how many. One time we had three thousand.

KARL: What?! Where was that?

JASON: That was actually in Riverside, which is not a big city, near Los Angeles. But I think sometimes with the smaller cities there's less going on so people are really excited.

KARL: That's scary though when it's three thousand people, then you've got to get out. If they know you've got a bag of money.

JASON: Yeah, you do, but that's why you want to make sure it's in a big open space because when we started off we were just putting the money on parking meters and street corners and street lamps. But when you have hundreds of people coming you can't just put it on the street corner, it could be really dangerous.

Jason gave me some of his cash to hide, as he wanted to get rid of it fast before the sunbathers arrived. I put $120 in a plastic egg and hid it in a pile of seaweed (I checked for crabs first). It felt so wrong disposing of it this way. I used to go to Stretford Arndale Centre as a kid. There was a huge fountain in the middle of the centre, and if you were meeting someone you'd meet there. People stood around it and threw coins in before making a wish. It seemed like an odd thing to do and such a waste of money to me. Especially when I was on only 50p a day for my paper round. I used to make a wish but say I'd pay on delivery.

Jason had hidden just under $2,000 on the beach. For me to try and understand the joy he got from this I was to bury some more, but this time with money of my own. I got $200 out of a cashpoint, which also cost me an extra $5 to access. I wasn't happy at the thought of throwing all this away. You might be thinking, Jesus, Karl, it's only £140, but I can't help but think back to a time when this was the monthly mortgage payment on our first flat in Salford and it used to be a struggle to pay. Even though I treat myself to Tiptree jam it doesn't mean I can afford to go chucking away almost £150. Especially with Suzanne's expensive taste in toilet paper.

I STRUGGLE WITH GOODBYES.

It's odd how people mistake being careful with money as being tight. As I've said, I just don't like wasting money. It was Mother's Day recently and I sent my mam a card. But rather than also sending her some over-priced flowers, I sent her a packet of seeds inside the card. My dad ripped the piss out of me for it. I know some of you will think that's a bit shit but I'm not happy paying over the odds for flowers just because you feel under pressure to. The seeds are a much better gift as the plant will last a lot longer than the cut flowers ever will. I did something similar to this that I might have written about before, but it's another example of how life's rules confuse me. I left a job after ten years, and the boss asked me what I wanted. I told him I'd like a camera. Once I received it I wrapped it up and gave it to Suzanne for Christmas (or birthday, I can't remember). Everyone I've told that story to says it's a really cheap thing to do but I don't see why. I could have asked for something for me but I didn't – I got something I knew she wanted, and it saved me having to buy it.

I got to work hiding my cash. Rather than just burying it in random places I decided to make sandcastles, and hide the money within the castle. I suppose you could call them 'sandcashles'. My thinking was that if nobody found them at least I knew where my money was so I could go back and collect it. This was something that I don't think Jason could do as he kept no record of where he was dropping his cash.

So there I was, a forty-three-year-old bloke making sandcastles as the beach started to get rather crowded. I didn't bury the whole $200 in one go. I put $40 in one castle and $60 in another. I then set up a little area where I could sit and keep an eye on my money. The best that could happen is that nobody finds it and I get to pop it back in my pocket, which would

PEOPLE SEEMED TO
REALLY DIG IT.

give me some pleasure. I've had that a few times in the past when I've put on a coat I haven't worn for a while and found £5 or £10 in the pocket. I love that. Even though it's my money it's still like I've won a prize. I feel like a squirrel that has found some nuts it had hidden away.

Jason put a message out on Twitter that there was hidden money on Santa Cruz beach. Within minutes there were around a hundred people digging the place up. Some were using just their hands and feet, others had spades. It was the sort of chaos you see at a Black Friday sale. It was madness. I saw two young girls kick one of my castles. They had found the $40! But that wasn't enough for them. They kicked the other and found that too. I was gutted. They didn't even look like they were short of money. They ran off looking for more, no doubt reducing kids to tears as they kicked over every sandcastle on the beach.

Jason came to the spot where I was sat.

JASON: How many eggs did you put out?

KARL: I did two, one with $60 and one with $40.

JASON: I thought you took out $200. You're having a hard time letting go of your money? I guess I've just got used to it. I'm gonna throw out some more. I think this is addictive. I always feel bad for the ones that try so hard but don't find it.

KARL: Well, that's like life. There are a lot of people who work hard and never get a chance to get anywhere.

I didn't bother burying the other $100 as I'd had enough. Giving my money to these well-off Californians didn't do much for me.

I was about to leave the beach when I remembered the golden egg that I'd planted that contained $120 of Jason's money. If I found that, I could experience the other side of the joy. I was just about to set off on my hunt for the pile of seaweed when I heard a girl scream with excitement. Jason was with the thrilled winner.

KARL: How much did you find?

GIRL: I found a hundred and twenty bucks!

KARL: It wasn't in a golden egg, was it? In the seaweed?

GIRL: Yes.

KARL: Shit, that's the one I had my eye on!

JASON: Listen to this. She's minus forty-six dollars in her account and she's gonna use it to buy groceries. Doesn't that feel good?

KARL: Yeah, a little bit.

GIRL: And my birthday is in two days.

Once the sun went down, the beach emptied and Jason left. I spent another hour searching the areas we had covered earlier that day as I was convinced that there would be one or two toys left unfound. But I had no joy. The good news is, when I started writing about this experience it made me wonder what happened to the other $100 that I got out of the cashpoint. I checked my rucksack and found $80 in the shorts I was wearing that day. What a result. I might treat Suzanne to some fancy toilet roll.

'People talk about LONDON being an expensive place to live. It's not because of the price of RENT, it's due to the amount of CHARITY COLLECTORS on the street taking your money off you.'

LEARNING TO SHARE

At infant school I would be quite happy playing by myself in the sandpit until the teacher would come along and say, 'Karl, why don't you share that toy with Ryan?' 'No, I'd rather not, to be honest, love. Gary over there was playing with this toy for thirty minutes and I had to patiently wait until he got bored and put it down, so why is Ryan so bloody important that he gets fast-tracked to any toy of his choice?! He can bloody wait in line like I had to. Now piss off!'

I never actually uttered any of those words as I was only five. In reality I said nothing and just handed the toy over to Ryan before wandering off to find something else to play with. To be honest, I don't know why sharing was pushed so much at school when really 'waiting your turn' is a much more useful lesson to learn. The school introduced 'Bring a Toy Day,' which I think was another idea to get kids to share. It would often end in tears though. I remember a girl crying her eyes out after a lad who was dressed as Batman had shoved a lightsaber from a miniature *Star Wars* figure up the arse of her My Little Pony and stood there shouting, 'Feel the force.' I only ever took a pack of playing cards in as my toy, as anything that was half decent just filled kids with jealousy, which then often led to the item getting broken.

Since then, I've never been one for sharing as I think for it to work there has to be trust, and on the whole I don't trust people to look after things that don't belong to them. The amount of flights I've been on where I've finished filling out my customs form to be asked by another passenger a few seats away if they can borrow my pen, to then find out that they had then passed it on to someone else who had in turn passed it on to someone else. Honestly, I've had more pens stolen than Argos. I wish airlines had pens on chains like banks do, then none of this would happen.

Next I was meeting a bunch of people who have taken sharing to a whole new level. Five women who all share the one husband. His name is Brady Williams.

BRADY: When I was seventeen I joined the polygamous group for religion. And then got married at twenty-one, twenty-two, twenty-four, twenty-seven and twenty-nine.

KARL: I don't know much about the religion. Is it the more you marry the closer to heaven you get? If so, how many do you need to marry to guarantee a place up there then?

BRADY: Depends on who you talk to, but minimum of two. Some people think three. But I only chased one, and then after that the ladies came to me. They liked me. I left the religion and now we're just married because of love.

KARL: What are the advantages of having five wives then?

BRADY: Okay, well, you get five different types of people, and all of their strengths. I mean, you get their weaknesses too!

KARL: Did you go out of your way to make sure they were different before you decided to add someone to the collection?

BRADY: I didn't, no. But I'm just lucky. They all have different strengths and weaknesses but they all make me a better person. I mean, I'm a way better person because of what they've been able to bring out in me.

KARL: So they're all different to you. Would you say you're a different person to each of them?

BRADY: Well, I'm the same person, but because they're individual, yeah, I kind of take one head off and put another head on. Take the Rosie head off and I put the Rhonda head on.

KARL: And how is time shared out between all five wives?

BRADY: So I just honour rotations every five nights. So tonight I'm with Paulie, who's my first wife, and then Robyn tomorrow night, who's my second, and then I'll be with Rosemary, and then Nonnie and then Rhonda and then start over again.

KARL: That's five days, so do you have two days off for yourself?

BRADY: No, it just keeps going. I don't care what day of the week it is, it's every fifth night I'm with the first wife.

KARL: And you never change the timetable?

BRADY: Well, they swap nights. Say Rosemary has a concert, you know, she's a musician. And she wants me to come and watch but it's not her night, she'll just go to Robyn whose night it is and they kind of trade me around like a commodity. People think that it's me who's in charge of everything, but no way. You learn quickly the women are all in charge.

Brady went through what he considered to be the good points for each of his wives.

WIFE 1:
'Paulie is a great decorator.'

WIFE 2:
'Robyn, she's really good at artwork.'

WIFE 3:
'Rosemary, she's a masseuse.'

WIFE 4:
'Nonnie can figure out anything in technology. If we get a new TV or computer Nonnie will set it up.'

WIFE 5:
'Rhonda will get the sales, day-after-Christmas sales for the next year, she's real good with money.'

KARL: So has there ever been a time when you've got, let's say, wife number one and wife number two, and then you think you've found wife number three, but the others aren't keen?

BRADY: Yeah, that exactly happened. I had three, and then I was courting a girl, I thought I'd love her and that she was meant to be but the three wives just said no. They said they just didn't feel right about it.

KARL: Okay, what if it's the other way round, and you feel it's not working. Are you allowed to just get rid of one? (*Brady laughs*) Or would the others be like 'No, no, no! I like her, she's part of this family!'

BRADY: Oh yeah, I'm not like kingpin. It's not like I can say 'Just get rid of one.' They'd revolt, they'd say, 'Well, you're out of here, we'll just keep going without you.'

It seemed like an odd way to live, but just because it's not way that the majority of people do it, that doesn't make it wrong. I mean, I thought having salt in caramel was an odd idea until I tried it. Most of us have been brought up on Romeo and Juliet, not Romeo and Juliet, Sandra, Denise, Barbara and Norma.

Brady found it just as strange that I hadn't got married or had any kids. He asked why I wasn't fussed about carrying on the family name, which to him was obviously important. People never get my name right anyway so the sooner it dies out the better. Most of my post is addressed to Mr Dilkington or Tillington or Pillockingtun. One of the reasons I don't want to be buried when I die is that I worry what name would end up on the gravestone.

KARL'S FACTS

A farmer from Michigan had the dates of his life carved on his gravestone before he died. He carved the dates 1856–1950, but he died in 1948.

I wonder if having five wives makes each relationship last longer, as if Brady is only seeing each wife for twenty-four hours once a week, they're not going to spend it arguing. Suzanne is always saying that I wear her out with my moaning, but maybe if I had more women around the house to spread my annoyance it wouldn't get to her as much. I doubt Snow White would have put up with having just Grumpy knocking around all the time on his own. Having the other six dwarfs would have made his moods easier to handle.

I went to meet Paulie, wife number one, who Brady married twenty-three years ago.

KARL: What's in it for you then, Paulie? What are the good sides of it?

PAULIE: Well, we're really good friends. We eat together every night and everybody takes a turn in cooking. So my kids always have a really good dinner ready for them.

KARL: So how many kids have you got with Brady?

PAULIE: I have six.

KARL: How many in total, Brady?

BRADY: Twenty-five.

KARL: Twenty-five kids!

BRADY: I've got a three-week-old. Just barely born. In fact my youngest child is younger than my grandson. So my grandson's older than my youngest daughter.

KARL: And what about if it was the other way around, Paulie? If you could have had five fellas?

PAULIE: I wouldn't want five.

KARL: You wouldn't want five men?

PAULIE: I wouldn't.

KARL: Cos that's how I've been thinking about it. If Suzanne said to me, 'You can stay but I want five fellas', I wouldn't be happy. What about you, Brady?

BRADY: Yeah, that's a complex question because I don't think I'm as good as them. I'd be too jealous. I really would be. And I'd probably beat the other man up, I just wouldn't be able to handle it. Which says a lot for them. How good they do. I wouldn't be able to. But they should have that right. You know, I mean, it's fair. If they wanted it, that is.

PAULIE: I have no desire for that.

KARL: But you knew what you were marrying into? You knew there was gonna be more wives?

PAULIE: Yes, I knew.

KARL: How many did you think he was gonna go for? Is that even a chat that you have, or are you just waiting every day thinking, is he gonna come back with someone new today?

PAULIE: (*laughs*) It didn't work like that. But I didn't put a number on it. I just took it as it came.

BRADY: After two I thought I was done.

KARL: Who is wife number two?

PAULIE: Robyn.

KARL: So you were just with Paulie for how long?

BRADY: Eight months. And then I married Robyn.

KARL: And then, what are the rules? Obviously, you two are together, you're solid at the beginning. Just the two of you. Then do you just say, 'I want another one'?

BRADY: Oh no, Robyn showed interest in me. I wasn't out chasing girls.

KARL: Did you see Robyn hanging around, Paulie?

PAULIE: Robyn showed an interest, yeah. Her and her sister got really friendly with me.

BRADY: It's never behind the wife's back. Never. I'd be like, hey, it looks like Robyn likes me. And Paulie would say, 'Hmm, yeah, maybe.' So I went to talk to her dad, and said, 'Hey, I'm interested in Robyn.'

KARL: And you tell the dad that you have got a wife already?

BRADY: Yeah, they're all polygamists.

PAULIE: Then one day a week Brady set aside to go out and spend time with Robyn.

KARL: And what do you do while he's out? You're just staying in watching TV on your own?

PAULIE: Yeah, I just stayed at home while he went out and took her out on a date and whatever they did, and on weekends all three of us would go out together.

KARL: How long were you dating Robyn before she became wife number two?

BRADY: Two months.

PAULIE: I felt good about it. I was okay with it. So they got married.

KARL: Did you go to the wedding?

PAULIE: Yes.

KARL: Oh, that's weird. The honeymoon. Did you go on that?

PAULIE: No. (laughs)

BRADY: No. On the honeymoon you just take the new wife. It's a little more private.

Wife 2: Robyn, five children

ROBYN: Well, we all talk about big issues, different moral standards that we like to expect with our kids, but definitely every mother is different. Every mother has her own rules in her own home and that her kids will follow and that's just her right as a mother of her own children to do that.

Wife 3: Rosemary, four children

ROSEMARY: When Rhonda got married to Brady and they went off on their honeymoon, all the rest of us went and got ice cream and had a party.

Wife 4: Nonnie, six children

NONNIE: Brady's very determined. He's very responsible, he's driven. He's just got a lot of really good qualities. I was also able to watch how he treated his kids and other wives before I married him. I was impressed that he treated them so good. So I felt like if he treated them good, he'd treat me good.

Wife 5: Rhonda, four children

RHONDA: I think Brady has become a better husband each time he has married.

KARL: Say if it's one of their birthdays, can you keep track of what gifts they might like?

BRADY: Oh, I gave up trying to buy gifts for birthdays. I'm bad that way, I just take them on a date to a movie and dinner or something. But for Christmas I usually try and buy a nice little something.

KARL: Would you buy different things, or do you just get them all the same thing to stop any arguments?

BRADY: (laughs) Oh no, no. I tried that once, then they just think, well, I'm just the same, and so, no, I don't do that. What I do is I'll try and spend the same amount on each but on a different gift. So that they feel unique and loved.

Buying gifts for one is tough enough, buying for five would be a nightmare. I imagine it's also difficult for the wives not to look at what each other receives and compare. I normally make a card for Suzanne and do a little drawing and poem. She likes that as I've taken time to make it personal, but if I did that for all my wives it probably wouldn't feel as special. Here's a poem I did for her birthday card last week.

I know it hasn't been the greatest year, as the weather's not been the best,
Especially when the gale force winds have been coming in from the West.
Due to me having the book to write, I've mainly left you on your own,
Trapped inside – as the house got hit – by many a cyclone.
Cloudy days with no sun, you have the skin tone of an albino,
The Met Office says it's due to climatic change – what they call El Nino.
You've not had many cuddles or hugs, or any type of lust,
You've only felt the earth move due to a ninety-mile-an-hour gust.
But I'm hoping we can have a nice day today, and make it a celebration,
The weather man says it's going to be dry with zero precipitation.
The good news is, all this explains why you wake with hot flushes in the morning.
It's not your age or the menopause, it's probably just global warming.

I can also see how having a polygamous relationship could work for the better. If I was to do it (and I could as we do have two spare bedrooms) I'd like to have a wife who knows about plumbing and maybe another one who is good with electrics. I spend quite a few quid at the dentist too, so one of them wouldn't go amiss either. If you think about it, some people go through life being single and lonely cos they put too much pressure on looking for 'the one'. This seems barmy to me, as what are the chances of ever finding them?

Brady has taken away that difficult search for perfection – his family is like a bag of Revels. I've never got sick of eating Revels due to the mix of flavours that they offer all in the one bag. I still have a favourite though – the orange ones. But I think if I only had orange ones I could end up taking them for granted. In a way, the variety keeps my love for the orange ones fresh. Maybe if I had more than one partner I would appreciate Suzanne more?

KARL: Do you have a favourite?

BRADY: I would never go, 'Oh, Rosie's better than Paulie.' I'm not stupid. I know if I said that it would be hell for a month. You have to be smart if you're gonna be a polygamist, otherwise you won't be a polygamist for very long.

KARL: But surely a relationship is about being able to be honest?

BRADY: Man, you just don't compare.

KARL: You don't have to say who, but in your head you must have a favourite. You've got to have, haven't you?

BRADY: No. A lot of polygamous men do, but I don't. I think that's why we're happy.

What he said about them all making him a better person was an interesting thought. I'm pretty sure that Suzanne has changed me over the years in the way I think and act, so God knows what I'd be like if I had another four women changing my view on things. I really doubt there would be any of 'me' left. A few months ago I tried to sign into an old email account but couldn't remember the password. After a few attempts I gave up and decided to create a new account. Before I could do this I had to answer the security question, which was 'What is your favourite colour?'. Oh, nice easy one, I thought as I typed in 'red'. 'Sorry, incorrect answer' came the reply. I typed it in again just in case I had spelled it wrong, and then again with a capital R. It wasn't having any of it. But red is my favourite colour! Why would I have given another colour as my answer? After a few attempts I was locked out proper and had to get in touch with the email company. I explained to them that I'd typed in 'red' as my favourite colour and it didn't let me in. The guy on the end said that red isn't my favourite colour. So now this stranger on the end of the phone knows more about me than me! I felt like a right tit. In the end he asked me what my mother's maiden name was, which luckily isn't a question that can have different answers. All this goes to show that I don't really know myself at all. If I was to go on *Mastermind* and have 'me' as my specialist subject I would probably fail.

After being with Brady and his wives all day I was struggling to see why I couldn't get used to his way of life. But it's just dawned on me – I never met his five mother-in-laws . . .

LIVING EVERY DAY AS IF IT'S YOUR LAST

I was on yet another flight. I still get quite anxious as flying isn't a natural thing to do, is it? There I am in a metal tube flying at ridiculous heights at high speed and I'm just sat there, eating nuts and waiting to get back the pen that has been borrowed by every passenger on board. Every stage of flying makes me nervous. Even boarding the plane puts me on edge, as this is the part where you find out who you'll be spending the journey sat next to. It's a bit like going on a blind date hoping it will be someone who you will at least be able to get through the evening with. The difference being is that when you're on a plane you hope you'll be stood up so you can have the two seats to yourself.

On this particular flight I had an exit seat and was sat next to a small, grey-haired, ninety-one-year-old lady called Martha. I didn't get much of a chance to talk to her during the flight, because around five minutes after taking off, Martha jumped out of the exit when we reached 11,000 feet above sea level. I was on a skydiving plane. It was such an odd thing to see. One second she was there and the next she just stepped out like she was hopping off the back of a Routemaster. Just thinking about it is enough to make me feel ill. You see, I don't like that feeling you get from falling. Now and again I get that falling sensation just as I'm about to go off to sleep and I quickly grab the bedpost as my heart rate rockets. I certainly don't do the 'ROCK ON' hand signal and shout 'YEAH, DUDE' when it happens, so this is why I know skydiving isn't for me.

As Martha was hurtling through the sky at 120mph I was left with Mike the instructor. He was there for me to strap myself to if I got the urge to take on my first skydive. It shouldn't really be called skydive, it should be called a skyfall, cos that's what it is. I declined. Mike tried his best to get me to leap out of the plane by telling me that if the first chute didn't open there was always a back-up. This didn't help. One back-up wasn't enough to persuade me to jump. Just one! I carry four pairs of underpants when I'm in India as back-up. I'd want at least five parachutes before I would even contemplate hurling myself out. And a jet pack.

Mike went on to tell me how he'd done 12,000 jumps but that didn't help either. I'd say the fact that he's done 12,000 jumps means he's due a bit of bad luck. West Brom hadn't beaten Manchester United at Old Trafford since 1978, yet they got beat recently. Their luck ran out, and the same could easily happen to Mike. He then said that he had packed the chutes himself, which still didn't make any difference. I pack my own bag for all the trips I've done, and now and again I forget to pack a deodorant or my toothbrush. Human errors happen. Mike backed off. Now Richard the director got involved and said that he believes that 'if it's your time to go, it's your time to go', which is all very well, but what if it isn't my time to go but it is Mike's time? How does that work when I'm bloody strapped to him?! Then a few of the other jumpers started to join in: 'Jump now! You'll regret it tomorrow if you don't.' 'Show us what you're made of!' said Richard. Thing is, I know what I'm made of. I'm made of stuff that tends to splat when making contact with earth at 120 miles per hour.

There was nothing anyone could say that would make me change my mind. This is because I'm quite strong-minded. I was never one for following what others did. At school when some of my best mates were smoking drugs and sniffing glue, as much as they tried to get me to take part I always stood my ground and said no. I don't like the idea of doing something that takes me away from being in control. Plus I might get addicted. The mate who sniffed glue couldn't stop. Not because it was addictive, just cos the pot got stuck to his nose.

Soon my feet were back on the ground. I ran over to see Martha, who had just completed her second ever skydive. She was still on cloud nine even though she'd passed through that over twenty minutes ago.

MARTHA: It was wonderful! The view was unbelievable. I couldn't have picked a better day in the whole year. I'm just sorry you didn't do it because it was awesome.

KARL: Maybe when I'm ninety-one.

MARTHA: I wish I was around to see that, but I won't be. I can't tell you any more except that it's the most wonderful experience I've ever had in my life.

KARL: But were you into things like this when you were younger? Were you a bit of a maniac?

MARTHA: No, no, I've never been a maniac. And I didn't do a lot of things when I was younger. I didn't have time, I didn't have the money.

KARL: Would you say it's because you're older now and you're more willing to take the risk cos you've been here for ninety-one years anyway? If the parachute doesn't open . . . you know . . .

MARTHA: *(laughs)* Thanks!

KARL: No, but you know what I mean. I've got a long way to go. If your chute doesn't open you'll probably say 'Aw well, I've had a good innings.' I'm only forty-three.

Who knows, when I'm older I might have a go at it. I'm never in a rush to do things. I'd mentioned to Martha that I was in a supermarket with Suzanne a while back and heard a kid say to his mum that he wanted some lychees. The kid must only have been about ten years old. I am thirty-three years older than this kid and I didn't even know what a lychee was. The funny thing was, Martha didn't know what they were either.

Martha lives her life by the popular mantra 'Live every day as if it's your last', which I think, without wanting to be rude, for Martha it could well be. I mean, she's ninety bloody one. It makes sense to live by that rule when you're that age. Suzanne often tries to get me to do things by saying 'Life is short'. I don't know what she means by this, as life is the longest thing you'll ever do, and if I live to be as old as Martha I still have another fifty years to go. Like Martha, Suzanne has also told me to live as if every day is my last, but then she had a go at me when I ate an Easter egg that she had bought me a month too early. I told her that this was me living my day as if it was my last. It's hard to please some people.

Richard the director was a bit pissed off that they had paid for me to do the skydive and I hadn't done it. I could tell he was annoyed as he's normally quite an easygoing bloke, but he said he wouldn't let it go and said that I'd chickened out. I don't even understand what that saying means. Why do people say you're a chicken when you don't do something? What is it that a chicken never did for them to be slagged off in that way? To be honest, if I was a chicken I probably would have done the skydive as at least they've got wings. They're not the best at flying but at least they offer some sort of back-up if the chute doesn't open.

If at first you don't succeed skydiving's not for you.

I wanted to prove to Richard that I wasn't a chicken and that I could take on an exciting 'living every day as if it's your last'-type challenge. It's just that I wanted one where I could be a bit more in control. So for this last part of my trip I was going to meet a fella called Mike who got his buzz in life from something that seemed interesting. It was called E.I. We had arranged to hook up in Moab in the Utah desert. There were quite a few people trekking and climbing around the incredible sandstone landscapes, but it was easy to spot Mike in the crowd. And it was easy for Mike to spot me as we were both carrying ironing boards. This is the vital piece of equipment needed when taking part in E.I., which stands for Extreme Ironing.

Extreme ironing is an adrenaline sport, which can take place anywhere and borrows disciplines from other extreme sports, such as rock climbing, scuba diving and running. What I like about the idea of this is that it involves taking an everyday job that needs doing while giving it a bit of an edge. It winds me up when Suzanne has been to the gym and then gets back and can't be arsed doing any housework because she's knackered. Mike has managed to blend the two activities together.

We lugged our ironing boards through the bizarrely-shaped dark orange boulders of the Moab desert for about forty minutes until we reached an odd-looking rock that Mike suggested was an ideal spot for some extreme ironing. It was mental. A big boulder balanced on top of a 300-foot-high mound. There are many of these weird formations in Moab. They're created over years and years of erosion from the strong wind and rain. At this point I felt pretty nervous, as there were professional climbers involved with hard hats and ropes to help us get to the summit. As much as these rocks were an unfamiliar sight to me, so was the ironing board I was carrying as we've not owned one for years. When we lived in our small flat the place was really tiny, with no storage cupboards, so we stored the ironing board behind the bedroom door. The problem was, when you closed the door it would end up falling on us. One day I just got so sick of being attacked by the ironing board that I took it to the charity shop. So I'd say 2002 was the last time we

ever used an ironing board or iron. We find that the creases in our clothes tend to sort themselves out once you've been wearing them for a few hours.

Mike could sense I was shocked at how difficult the climb looked.

> MIKE: There's a reason why they call it extreme ironing. The point of extreme ironing is you put an extreme sport in there. Who would wanna climb that and then not do anything up there? It's anti-climactic. It's about a three-hundred-foot drop on the back side of that. So you just gotta make sure that you keep a tight hold to the ironing board.

Mike climbed it first. He does this sort of thing a lot so made it look fairly easy. He set up his ironing board and ironed his shirt, which he changed into before descending. Now it was my turn. Just as I started, the wind picked up. I was now really bricking it. The professional rock climbers were creasing themselves at my fear, but I was determined to iron out those creases by making sure I made it to the top. I wanted to prove to Richard that I was no chicken. I started my climb up the rock. A 300-foot drop with no parachute. I think this was more dangerous than the skydive. The thing is, I'm happy to take on dangerous stuff as long as I'm in charge. My life is full of danger all the time. I'd say going to bed is one of the most treacherous things you can do. That might sound odd, but think about it: how many times do you hear about people dying in their sleep? It happens all the time. Sleeping is perilous. I reckon it's that falling sensation that does it.

What I didn't like about the skydive was that once you step off that plane you are no longer in control, but with the climbing I was running the show. It was a crazy thing to be doing but not the most insane thing I've ever done. I think that title goes to the wing walk I did during the filming of *An Idiot Abroad 2*. A wing walk is when you climb up from an open cockpit while the plane is in the air and then stand on the wing. A lot of people have told me that they were surprised to see me do this, but as I've said, when it's me who is in control of deciding when to climb up and what to hold on to and so on, I can do it. Once I stood up on the wing and buckled myself into a frame I actually enjoyed the view. Being stood up there, thousands of feet in the air, looking at the curvature of the earth was pretty stunning. The part I didn't like was when the pilot took the plane into a dive, a side roll and a bloody loop da loop! I didn't know he was going to do any of those things, so that was when it became the most dangerous, ridiculous and idiotic thing I've ever done. I no longer had control. People say when you die your life flashes before your eyes. If that's true it means I have to relive that sodding wing walk again. When I've spoken about how much I hated that incident a few people have said to me, 'Well, at least it's a moment you'll never forget.' The thing is, I wish I could forget it. I've done loads of better things than that and yet my memory doesn't seem to remember them.

I don't have any say over what my brain wants to remember. Normally, when you ask someone what their earliest memory is, they have a fond recollection of a time they were playing in a park or on holiday. My earliest memory is when I accidentally farted loudly in public for the first time. It was in my first year of school. The memory is as clear as crystal (the air wasn't). The teacher (Mrs Robinson) was reading the story of Rumpelstiltskin to the whole class, who were sat cross-legged on the floor engrossed in the tale, when my arse let one go. It wasn't a quick burst either. It sounded like a lost whale. The whole class turned and looked at me. Even kids who were sat rows away stretched up like meerkats to give me the stare. I felt so embarrassed that I had a slightly dizzy feeling. Mrs Robinson knew it was me, as I was the only one who had a look of surprise on my face while all the other pupils were over-reacting and showing their disgust by crunching up their faces and holding their noses. Mrs Robinson asked me if I needed to go to the toilet. I declined as I didn't like using the toilets at school. She carried on reading.

Now, you'll notice that I said I can't get rid of the memory of me farting for the 'first' time in public. It happened again! About six years after my first public expulsion, I nodded off in my religious education lesson and a trump of mine woke me up. Twenty of my classmates were roaring with laughter as Mr Davies yelled at me: 'GET OUTSIDE, YOU DISGUSTNG BOY!' I was given 200 lines of 'I will not disturb the class with my dirty habit again'. Now, I want to make it clear that I don't make a habit of breaking wind. Both of those incidents were accidents and took place years apart. But I do think his reaction was a bit over the top. Like I said, I hadn't done it on purpose.

I've never understood why if you sneeze people accept it and say, 'Bless you', and yet if you fart all hell breaks loose. Why doesn't an unexpected trump get the same blessing as a sneeze? They don't spread as many germs and yet the shit hits the fan when one slips out. Not literally, obviously. If that was the case I should have been given more than 200 lines. But who makes these rules?! This is what's peculiar with my memory. Why on earth does it bother keeping those instances stored up? I've heard people say they will never forget the birth of their first born or the day they got married; they never talk about never forgetting their first public trump. Maybe it's worth me getting married and having a kid to replace my flashbacks of flatulence.

KARL'S FACTS

A woman farted on a plane and tried to cover up the smell by lighting matches, causing an emergency landing.

I was slowly making my way up the rock face. I'd taken my time connecting myself with the various metal spring-loaded connectors on the ropes. There were two of these carabiner clips that I had to move along and undo to get past certain knots in the rope, but I had to make sure that I was focused and always had one connected. I found this quite therapeutic. It took my mind off everything else. The most difficult part was pulling my own body weight up round the big boulder. I was so close I didn't want to give up. The wind was picking up again (not mine) and was blowing grit from the ancient red rock into my eyes. I was

THOUGHT I'D END THIS CHAPTER WITH A CLIFF HANGER.

adamant that I was going to make it to the top. I used all my might and gave one final push. I was up. I was knackered and out of breath, but there was no time for me to worry about that, as there was ironing to do. I got a couple of T-shirts and boxer shorts out of my rucksack, fired up the battery-charged iron, and got to work. In all honesty I felt a great sense of achievement. The idea makes sense to me. It was the ultimate in multi-tasking. Taking part in an extreme challenge and getting the ironing done at the same time. I remember really enjoying it, or as they say in America 'I was having a gas'. I hope I remember having a gas as much as I recall expelling it.

A lot of time has passed since that trip, and I still don't regret not jumping out of that plane.

CHAPTER 4

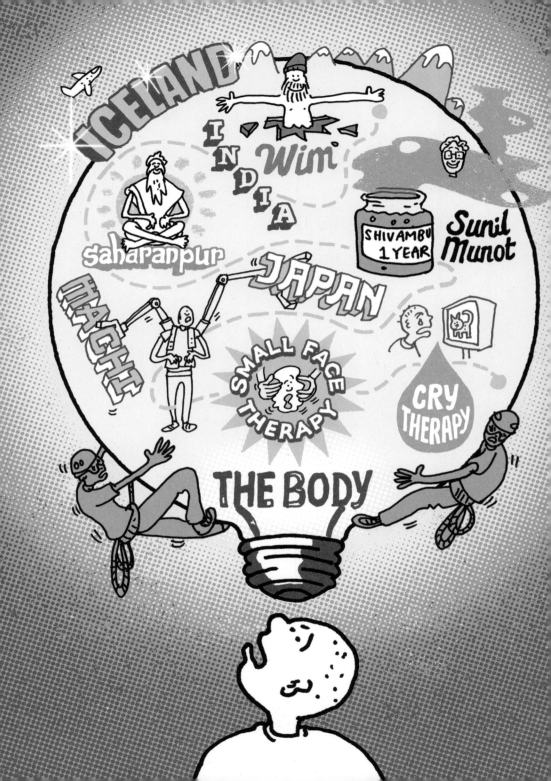

I CURRENTLY GO to the gym (or 'germ' as I call it) four times a week. I don't go for me, though. I give Suzanne a lift in the car to her yoga class, that's about as close as I get.

I call it 'the germ' as since Suzanne's been going, I've had more coughs and illnesses than ever before. She may as well go and do the lotus pose in the doctor's waiting room as she'd pick up the germs without having to cough up £65 per month for the pleasure. To be honest, I don't mind the germs, as getting ill is just part of life and it's helpful to be a little bit off colour now and again to appreciate how good it is not to be ill.

The problem I have with the idea of working out in a gym is it just seems like such a waste of energy. I prefer to work up a sweat by cleaning my windows or raking or cutting the lawn; that way I've used up my nutriments in a useful way. This kind of workout might not make my abs poke out of my stomach, but I don't understand why you'd want that look anyway, as it looks weird. It's your insides poking through! Why is that attractive?! You may as well swagger about showing off your haemorrhoids.

How fit do we really need to be these days anyway? I understand that back in the hunter-gatherer days it was essential to be in good shape so you could chase food, but that's not the case any more. The last time I chased food was when the ice-cream man pulled away in his van and I had to peg it after him to the next street. It's funny really, cos apart from other kids legging it for the ice-cream man, the only other people I used to see sprinting when I was growing up were criminals. Someone running back then was a sign they'd been up to no good, but now everyone is running and the criminals no longer stand out in a crowd. We're at the stage now that if a gang of masked robbers were running down the street, everyone would just presume it was some kind of fun run.

As for pumping iron, what do we need huge muscles for? The only time I need a bit more power in my arms is when it comes to separating shopping trolleys at Asda. Apart from that, I don't think they're required as everything is smaller and lighter these days. I've found that people who have enormous muscles are almost always fans of tattoos, so maybe that's the only reason to be buffed up these days – when the muscles stretch the skin they give you more surface area to ink up.

FINDING YOUR INNER POWER

The point of this trip was to look at how different people around the world take care of their bodies and the lengths they go to with diets and medicines. The plan was also for me to experience how I'd fare when I face my biggest fear and have the most complex organ in my body taken away from me. You'll find out which one it is later. (Or you could just whizz a few pages on and find out now if you can't be arsed waiting.)

I knew the next nine days were going to be gruelling as my trip involved visiting India, which has always had a bad effect on my guts, and then Japan, where based on past experience I knew I'd be facing some serious jet lag. So what better way to get warmed up for such a journey than spending time with a man who is known for putting his body through extreme challenges to prove just how much our 'inner power' is capable of. His name is Wim Hof. As I write this, he has twenty-six records in the *Guinness Book of Records*. One of those was for running a marathon in the Namibian desert without drinking water, another was for hanging from one finger at an altitude of two thousand metres, and he was also immersed in blocks of ice for one hour, fifty-two minutes and forty-two seconds to claim the record for taking the longest ice bath, which then got him the nickname 'The Iceman'. He did all these activities not with the use of magic or drugs, but by channelling his 'inner power'. As impressive as that list is, I think I still hold the record for most time spent sat on a toilet – two hours twenty-six minutes (Agra, India, 2010). After that incident I'd say any 'inner power' I had beforehand was well and truly flushed away.

I was meeting Wim in the snow-covered area of Langjökull in Iceland. I made my way there wearing a thermal vest, a jumper, a thick insulated coat, thick trousers, gloves and boots, even though I'd have to remove all of it soon. Wim believes the layers of clothing we wear and the way we control the temperature at home and work means we have changed the stimulation on our body and weakened it, and we are therefore no longer in touch with our 'inner power'. I could relate to what he was saying as Suzanne wears way too many layers. It's a good job I'm not a passionate man, cos if I wanted to whip her clothes off in a moment of lust, it would be more like playing pass the bloody parcel. She's always saying she's cold. She's the only person I know who has to put her coat and gloves on to get the milk out of the fridge. I'm looking forward to her getting hot flushes with the menopause as at least the gas bill will go down.

Wim was a bearded man in his fifties from the Netherlands, who sounded like Schwarzenegger, had the face of a villain from *The Bourne Identity*, and the look of a man who could take on the world, survive the apocalypse, and win all the Bushtucker trials on *I'm a Celebrity . . . Get Me Out of Here!*

We entered a small wooden building and Wim got me to strip down to my shorts before we went outside. It was below freezing. The strangest thing about cold places like this is the silence. There are no trees rustling as no trees survive in this temperature, and there are no tweeting birds out in this bitter cold either. The only sound was my teeth chattering. This was my body's alarm letting me know that I was bloody freezing. Apparently the chattering happens when your muscles contract and relax to try and warm up your body. This could explain why a lot of old people die from hypothermia – they have no teeth left in their head to chatter so they don't realise how cold they are.

KARL'S FACTS

Yakutsk in Russia is the coldest inhabited city in the world with an average January temperature of −40°C.

As well as my teeth letting me know how chilly I was, I was also aware that my testicles were not happy. In a way my testicles are like an elderly person – they're wrinkly, they need to be treated gently, and you see them less when it's cold. Mine were like heat-seeking missiles looking for warmth inside my body. They had raised themselves so high to escape the arctic conditions that I almost choked on them. It annoys me how the testicles seem to escape the ball bag in the cold and go up inside, as if there's room for them to be higher up and out of the way. Why don't they stay up there all the time and be safe from harm?

WIM GAVE ME THE COLD SHOULDER . . . IN FACT HE GAVE ME TWO OF THEM.

I'd say Wim must have balls to do this regularly but in some ways I'd imagine it would be a lot easier if he didn't have any. This is another health issue for us blokes: checking our balls for lumps. I've never really done it. I'm all for doing DIY, but I think when it comes to plumbing, the electrics or checking balls for lumps, you should get the experts in. I had an idea recently while going through security at the airport. They should get a doctor to sit at the X-ray machine and check for lumps in testicles and breasts while security look for weapons. At least then passengers would get something out of the trouble of having to wait in line to be scanned.

Anyway, after feeling the cold wrap itself around my bare body, I ran back inside the hut to try and psych myself up. If it was as cold as this at home it would be a day of staying in, popping on a *Columbo* box set and working my way through a packet of biscuits with a pot of tea.

WIM: Come on!

KARL: It's fucking freezing out there!

WIM: It's not cold.

KARL: Aye, it is!

WIM: It's because you ain't got your inner power. Do not fear, man. You just need to cope with the cold.

KARL: Yeah, but I've not been in Iceland that long.

WIM: COME ON! Now, let's breathe shallow. That's why the body gets acidic, that's why you do not feel good. If you breathe better and you let a little bit of the cold in to stimulate the vascular condition, then you feel good!

If it was anyone else I'd have probably thought 'this is a load of bollocks' and left, but Wim has been involved in many scientific tests that prove his method is a natural way to combat illness. Wim explained it was vital for me to relax and untighten as much as possible, as only then could my body process the signals and start thermogenesis, which means it produces its own heat. I ran outside again and joined Wim for some breathing exercises. I didn't mind getting involved as I was planning on breathing anyway. I'm also pretty good at it as I've done it every day for the past forty-three years. I don't want to brag, but I'm such a dab hand at it that I can even do it in my sleep.

Wim got me to take in big breaths until my body was saturated with oxygen. I very rarely fill my lungs to full capacity. I treat my lungs like filling my car up with fuel – they never get a full tank. The air is far too polluted, and I can't imagine getting much good out of it. On the plus side, the dirty air has probably put an end to people receiving calls from heavy breathers. There's a positive with every negative.

All this inhaling and exhaling really did wake me up. Honestly, just stop reading for thirty seconds, take in ten deep breaths and you'll feel loads happier for it. These idiots who sniff cocaine and think it's the drug that makes them feel good, it's not, it's just cos they've taken in air! We then went for a run. I'd say we must have covered a good five or six miles, breathing heavily as we went. At this point I was feeling warm. It was like someone had turned up a thermostat inside my body. Though it might have been due to the amount of carbon monoxide we'd both been exhaling – we'd probably melted a few icebergs and that's why it didn't feel so nippy.

I'd enjoyed my run and it really did make me feel more alive and alert, but Wim didn't want to just leave it there. He had this idea for us both to get into a frozen lake. My mood changed at this point, and I'm pretty sure the thought of it must have brought me out in a cold sweat, though it was impossible to tell in those conditions.

A bloke from Health and Safety turned up.

HEALTH AND SAFETY MAN: Okay, guys, you know the water is freezing, well below zero. There is a danger of hypothermia. It's at your own risk you go in there. This is a lagoon, and we don't know how deep it is so just go a few metres in and play it safe. And we have the ropes on you here so we can pull you out if need be.

WIM: I've been in more dangerous places than this. Karl, I will do a dry run, and then we do it together.

I took a moment to go and have a pee. Thinking back, I should have peed in the lake to warm it up a bit. Surely this could be classed as using my 'inner power'? As amazing as the lake looked, there was nothing that made me want to have a dip in it. I was proud of how well my body had coped with running around half naked, but getting into the frozen lake seemed a step too far. I used to have to face cold showers every day in our old flat due to a knackered boiler and I have no fond memories of that. As the urine left my body I started to feel the cold again. It was like draining a radiator of hot water.

I made my way back over to Wim. He was now hacking away at the thick layer of ice that separated him from the dangerously cold lake.

Not only was it absolutely freezing, the ice was so sharp that Wim had already cut his feet on the shards. Not that he had noticed. I imagine he wouldn't have had much feeling in his feet at this point. He created a bath-sized hole and calmly climbed into it and lay in the water. He didn't make a sound and he looked relaxed. Or maybe 'chilled out' is a more suitable expression. The only other person I know who loves ice as much as this man is my auntie Nora. She can't drink her daily intake of whisky without it. Anyone who holds her cold hands could be mistaken for thinking she has bad circulation, but it's cos she's always got hold of a freezing glass of ice and whisky.

Once Wim was in the water he tried to tempt me in by saying it would be a great end to the day if I joined him. I stood there speechless, the only noise coming from my chattering teeth. It was as if they were sending a message for help in Morse code. I sat on the edge of the lake and put one foot in. It was so cold that it felt like it was burning. That was enough for me. I'd literally got cold feet.

I was impressed with Wim, but he proved to me that the problem with exercise is that people always want to push themselves further. Just running in the cold air wasn't enough for Wim, he had to take it a step further and enter the lake. It really wouldn't surprise me if one day he's found dead at home, surrounded by frozen potato waffles after deciding to take a kip in his freezer.

I had enjoyed my time with him, but like visiting the gym I didn't have much to show for the energy I had burned. Maybe the next time I rake and cut the lawn, I'll do it half nude with some Freezepops shoved down my undies.

JUST CHILL IN.

CHANNELLING
THE SUN'S ENERGY

When I was growing up I had constant problems with my teeth. The tooth fairies could have set up their head office in the corner of my bedroom. To be fair, I wasn't on my own – everyone's were rotten. My mate has one of those class photos of us and we often look at it and laugh while playing spot the tooth. Once at school they tried to get us to stop drinking Coca-Cola by showing us how bad it was for our teeth. The teacher dropped an old dirty penny into a glass of Coke and left it for a few minutes before emptying the glass to reveal a shiny clean coin. I didn't see the point he was making – if it could clean up a grubby penny, then it should bring my teeth up a treat.

I think the reason I never had great teeth is because they had to share space in my mouth with my tongue. For me, this is an example of where nature got it wrong – sticking something that enjoys sugar in the same vicinity as teeth was never going to work. I lose count of the amount of times a week my teeth take a bite of the side of my tongue. Suzanne says it's because I eat too quickly, but I'm convinced it's because my tongue keeps picking food that my teeth don't want near them. And it's daft how if you're a fan of sweet food you're described as having a 'sweet tooth', when really it should be a 'sweet tongue'.

KARL'S FACTS

Sticking your tongue out is a greeting in Tibet.

These days, bad food is blamed for more than just tooth decay. It's the main cause of an increase in heart disease, obesity, diabetes and high blood pressure. The way they harp on about it, having no teeth might not be a problem as it seems there's not much that's safe to munch on anyway. Jamie Oliver is obsessed with telling us what we can and can't eat. He probably wouldn't let a prisoner on death row have a bowl of greasy chips, even if it was his last meal.

I just tend to eat what I fancy. My weaknesses aren't so much sex and drugs and rock 'n' roll as biscuits, cake and chocolate roll. Food is what makes living worthwhile. Even when I'm not eating, I'm thinking about what to eat next. So what I was about to get involved in was going to be tough. I was in Saharanpur in northern India where I was going to meet Uma Sankar Sunyogi. Rather than getting energy from eating food, he gets it from the sun, and I was going to join him for breakfast to see how long I could go without eating actual food.

In preparation for this mammoth task I decided to eat as much as I could the night before. The problem was, Saharanpur didn't have much to offer in terms of fine dining, so I had to fill my face with roti, spicy dips and chilli chips. Waking up at the crack of dawn turned out not to be a problem as I was up and down all night using the loo. Every time I go to India I get a dodgy stomach, but this was the quickest it's ever hit me. I thought I'd been careful with my food selection but obviously not careful enough. That car sticker that says 'Shit Happens!' should be used by the Indian tourism board as when you're here, it generally does.

I find it hard to believe that India is now the third most obese country in the world. How can you get obese when the food doesn't stay in your body long enough?! I've had meals in India that have gone through my body before the bill has arrived. You know how you see men of a certain age out and about in the evening wearing a jumper tied around their shoulders, just in case it gets a bit nippy? Well, I was thinking about doing the same when in India, but instead of a jumper I'd do it with a pair of trousers as there's always a chance you'll be calling for an extra pair at some point.

Anyhow, Uma Sankar Sunyogi was a very small thin man, which I suppose wasn't that much of a surprise. I helped him lay out a few mats on his roof terrace where other people would be joining us.

KARL: So how does this work then, how do you get energy?

SUNYOGI: Through the sun you receive cosmic energy. And that cosmic energy goes to the brain and pineal gland. The charge that we normally get from the food, we are getting directly from the cosmic energy of the sun.

KARL: How long have you gone without food, then?

SUNYOGI: Four months.

KARL: Four months without anything?!

SUNYOGI: Without food, without water and without sleep.

Even if it is possible to live only off the sun, I really wouldn't want to do it. For me, eating is the best perk of being alive, if not the *only* reason to be alive. Evidence of this is that if you don't eat, you tend to die.

Whenever we move house I like to make sure there's an off-licence or garage close by so I know I can treat myself to a late-night chocolate bar if need be. I call it the Twix test. Some people pick houses that are close to good schools or have good transport links. All I need to know is how long it would take to get a Twix.

As odd as living off the sun alone may seem, the way things are going with food allergies, the sun might be the only option for energy in the future. I've been in restaurants where I hear customers asking what they can have off the menu that doesn't contain eggs, wheat, milk or shellfish. For them it's basically an 'all you can't eat' buffet. Anteaters probably have a more varied diet than these people. Having a nut allergy is the really serious one. People die *every* year from this. I can't remember having my first nut, but by rights it should be the most nerve-wracking experience of your life. You should be surrounded by family and friends and someone to read you the last rites when taking in your first nut.

I sat down cross-legged with Uma Sankar Sunyogi. He asked me to gaze just a few inches above the sun while also looking up at my eyebrows so the rays could enter through my eyes without my having to stare directly into it. You could say he was a solar-powered human, but if he had been born in Manchester like me, he'd have starved to death a long time ago. There are more sightings of the woolly mammoth than the sun in Manchester.

Seeing as my guts were in a bad way, I was willing to give this sun gazing a go to get a break from food. The chilli cheese chips I'd eaten for tea the night before were probably only slightly milder than the sun, so I was prepared.

KARL: What about damage to the eyes?

SUNYOGI: No!

KARL: You sure?

SUNYOGI: Yes, I am! Three million people are practising all over the world. You will get better eyes.

There weren't millions with us this morning but we were joined by around thirty or so people. It was the most stress-free dinner party ever. Thirty guests to cater for and the host is sat getting a sun tan. I'd love to see him pull this stunt off on an episode of *Come Dine with Me*. Still, no washing up would be a bonus.

HAVING A BLINDING TIME.

The sun started to rise, and we all sat and stared at it. It wasn't long before I was struggling cos my eyes are really sensitive to light. I have to put a pair of shades on if I have my eggs sunny side up, so this was a big ask. As the sun got brighter I began to get more and more fidgety and couldn't help but rock from side to side. Maybe it was charging me up. I was twitching and getting irritated like I sometimes do after eating a full bag of Haribo to myself.

SUNYOGI: Give thanks to the sun! To have given us beautiful life. Very nice experience. Pray to the sun. For peace. Prosperity. Wisdom. Good health. And love. Enlightenment for all of us. For all the humanity, better man and good woman. Pray to the sun to burn all the darkness from our life.

All I wanted to pray for was a box of Nurofen to get rid of the headache I knew I'd be getting later. I couldn't relax at all, so after twenty-five minutes I had to get up and walk about a bit and rest my eyes. Like I said, it might have given me some energy but I don't eat just for energy, I eat for taste. Also, the sign of a good meal is the burp. It gives you an extra little taste of what you've just eaten and it's a nice bonus. It's like the food is doing an encore. The sun didn't give me that.

Overall I didn't enjoy the experience and left with a red eye, which was funny as I was suffering from red eye at the other end of my body at two o'clock that morning after eating those chilli chips.

The first thing I did after saying my goodbyes was eat a banana.

URINE THERAPY

I'm at the age now where drying myself after a shower, I will regularly find some new itchy patch of skin and wonder if it's eczema, psoriasis, razor bumps or ringworm. You could say I'm always having to make 'rash decisions'. It's usually followed by a visit to the chemist to buy yet another tube of something or other. It's no longer a quick undertaking now that the chemist is a huge multi-floored megastore and finding a cure for athlete's foot is harder than finding a cure for the Ebola virus. Endless aisles of creams and potions that never seem to work. I'd probably be better off rubbing the rash with the five-pound note it cost to buy the same white watery substance that seems to fill most of these tubes.

Suzanne is forever buying creams to get rid of her wrinkles, and I swear they all contain the same stuff. It rattles me the way they sell 'night cream' and 'day cream'. What a con that is, as if the skin on her face knows what time of day it is!

As a kid, any illness could be cured with the one unlabelled bottle of bright pink fluid in the bathroom cabinet. If you had a rash you'd rub it into your skin. If you had a cough you'd drink it. And if dabbed into the carpet it could get rid of a stubborn gravy stain. It was a multi-purpose medicine and cleaner. And if that pink concoction didn't do the job, there was my auntie Nora who always had a good supply of medication to cope with anything. She has so many chemicals in her system to keep her going that if she cuts herself she has to call hazardous waste disposal to clean up the blood. Honestly, I'm not exaggerating, the amount of pills in her house, she could gravel her driveway with them.

Next I was on my way to meet Sunil Munot, a man who doesn't waste money on narcotics and stimulants. He thinks we all have the answer within us in the form of Shivambu, or to use the more familiar word – urine.

SUNIL: It saves loads of money. I don't need to pay for the medicine. This is the medicine. This is my soap, this is my shaving cream, this is my aftershave lotion. Everything is this.

KARL: Toothpaste . . . you don't use that to clean teeth, do you?

SUNIL: Yeah, I do.

KARL: What!

SUNIL: I don't brush. What I do, I take some urine in my mouth and swill.

I'd arrived just in time for his morning ablutions. He grabbed a big jug he had filled earlier that morning and washed his hair in it. He washed his body in it. He cleaned out his nostrils with it. He shaved with it and then used two small cups of pee to clean his eyes. You could say he was proper pissed up.

During the process, his urine was sloshing about everywhere. I only have to leave a little bit on the toilet seat at home and Suzanne goes apeshit, but I guess his wife wouldn't have to worry about that as he'd never pee in the toilet. To him, flushing urine away was literally money down the drain. The amount of uses he had for his urine, I wouldn't be surprised that if his doctor ever asked for a sample, he'd ask for it back once it had been tested.

A NEW MEANING TO THE EXPRESSION 'PISS POUR'.

Sunil informed me that the name 'Shivambu' comes from the Hindu god Shiva, and 'ambu' meaning the purest water. It would be a good name for a shampoo. Shivambu could easily sit next to Elvive, Pantene or Fructis in the chemist without anyone batting an eyelid.

One of the major benefits here was how much easier it would make travelling as I'd be able to carry a lot less in my suitcase. And I'm always leaving my soap and toothpaste in hotel rooms and having to replace them. This would never happen to Sunil as he's basically carrying his toilet bag around with him at all times. And to be fair, he did look pretty good on it. He had no blemishes on his body like I do, and his hair was soft and shiny, and the thing that surprised me the most was he didn't stink of piss.

All this needs is some celeb to back it, like a Victoria Beckham or a Jodie Marsh, and everyone would be at it. In fact, if one of these celebs had nice radiant skin from using their own urine they'd probably end up bottling their own and selling it. Stick it in a fancy bottle and call it 'Pee-Pee' (said with a French accent to make it seem classy).

After Sunil had finished cleansing, he took a glass of his urine . . . and drank it.

SUNIL: It tastes very good. I had all raw fruits and vegetables so I had a very good taste here. No smell, no cloudy and no problem in this urine, it is totally energetic urine.

KARL: But why do it?

SUNIL: Because I'm getting health benefits and no side-effects with this medicine. When you are in your mum's womb you started drinking your own Shivambu. We call it embryonic fluid but it is Shivambu. Already by nature we started drinking the Shivambu. I've never been to any doctors. If I have any problems, I go with this.

I suppose the fact that he eats lots of fruit means he doesn't stink of urine. He's eating that much fruit and veg his pee tastes of Lilt. A totally tropeecal taste. He finished off the glass without gagging. He never called it pee, piss or urine, he always called it Shivambu, which probably helps him deal with drinking it. It's like honey. I'm happy popping a bit of honey in my porridge, but if on the jar it said 'bee sick', which is basically what it is, it might not be so appealing. In fact maybe that's it, and for all we know our urine is already used in various ointments and we're just not told as we'd never use it otherwise. Think about it: every time I go to the doctor's he asks me to pee in a bottle. Where does it go? Maybe it goes down a special drain where it's all collected and rebottled and made into antibiotics.

KARL'S FACTS

Urine can be used to make gunpowder and was used to whiten teeth in ancient Rome.

Sunil took me through to his bedroom where he had a cabinet stocked up with old jam jars and bottles of all sizes full of different shades of Shivambu.

SUNIL: These old Shivambu we cannot drink, is for external use of the body. Like skin problem or any wound.

KARL: How old are these?

SUNIL: Three days, seven days, one month, four month . . . I have a Shivambu one year old.

KARL: No!

SUNIL: That is the very medicated Shivambu. If someone is having chronic disease of the skin I can use that for their massage and it heals them. I do fasting. When I do fasting I get the purest form of the Shivambu. If I keep it for two years, three years, four years, it will be like a wine. The older it is, the better it is.

KARL: So you get excited by looking at this?

SUNIL: Yeah, they are the most precious thing I have. You can see these bits in the bottom, these are the minerals. We call it the Shivambu cream. Ladies are using this as a face lotion and their skin will be very silky.

KARL: What, ladies are rubbing that in their face?!

SUNIL: My wife also use this.

There was a jar with some old pee that looked as thick as treacle with some thicker fermented gloop in the bottom. He took the lid off and the smell was horrendous. A mix of rotten fish and off milk. It burned my eyes more than the sun worshipping ever did. If the gases from it had been visible it would have looked like the spirits that escaped from the tomb at the end of *Indiana Jones and the Temple of Doom*, where Harrison Ford is telling his girlfriend to keep her eyes closed.

KARL: Oh God! I am not convinced by that one. Honestly, I believed everything you said up to this point but that is rank! That is proper rank! Oh Christ . . . I can't get away from it! Let me out of the room!

At this point I must confess that I have stored old piss of my own before, but only by accident. I have a hot water bottle under the passenger seat of my car. I find it comes in handy on long journeys when I need to have a pee. It holds a decent quantity of liquid and the neck on it is nice and large so it's easy to pee into, with a surround that can deal with spillages. Now and again I have used it and then forgotten to empty it so it's been left for close to a month. If Sunil found that under my seat he'd say my car had a mini bar.

I was handed a couple of glasses and I filled them both with my own pee for him to inspect. His eyes lit up with the excitement of getting to see and smell another blend.

SUNIL: There's no smell. It's good!

KARL: Would you know yours? If I had different glasses of piss lined up, would you go 'that's me'?

SUNIL: Errr, no. It's not possible.

KARL: Right. I just wondered whether that's a unique sort of blend.

SUNIL: There is no smell. And colour is sort of yellowish. Your body needs a little bit more water.

Sunil said he was presenting a seminar where he was spreading the power of Shivambu and invited me to go along. There was a good turnout of maybe thirty or forty people. Sunil was preaching to the crowd.

SUNIL: Pharmaceutical companies, they are not curing the diseases. They are creating the customers. Once you are affected by disease you are a permanent customer for the doctor. Doctor will support you so you can live, but they won't want to heal you permanently. Those who are taking medicines have to heal themselves twice: once from the disease, and again from the medicines and their side-effects. So what is the greatest medicine?

He spoke for a good forty minutes about the benefits of Shivambu and how it is being used to cure all sorts all over the world. But still, when he had finished his speech and asked for one of the audience members to come and drink their own Shivambu, no one was keen. So I put my hand up to volunteer. God knows why, as my guts were still not fully recovered from the chilli chips. I went and had a pee into a plastic cup and then faced the crowd with it. I took a big sip. It was surprisingly warm and made me gag. I tried again but my fussy taste buds were rejecting it so I couldn't help but spit it out. Sunil stepped in and suggested I start off

BOTTOM'S UP . . .

with a small amount until I got used to it. He used a pipette to put four or five drops into my mouth. It wasn't the worst-tasting thing I've ever had. It tasted quite woody, like the flavour you get when chewing the end of a pencil. It was also a little salty and left a thin slime on my tongue like cheap orange juice. The crowd clapped.

Thinking back on the whole Shivambu experience, it's hard to know if it does Sunil any real good. But I doubt it's doing him any harm as the extra fruit and veg he's eating to make his urine more palatable is probably doing something. And while it's a mad thing to be doing I can see what he means when he says it saves him money, especially now water isn't as cheap as it used to be. It can be costly if you have a big family all having baths every week, but if you take Sunil's advice you're in the money. Or should I say 'urine the money'.

THE BODY OF THE FUTURE

The human race is a bit like the *Police Academy* films. The longer we exist, the weaker we get. We aren't strong bulky animals like our prehistoric ancestors. Let's face it, there's no way a caveman would fit into a pair of those skinny jeans that young blokes are wearing today. I'm sure there are more crossdressers nowadays because it's easier for fellas to fit into women's clothes.

I often wonder if the biggest error we made in our evolution was leaving the sea. The planet is seventy per cent water. I mean, it's known as the Blue Planet for God's sake, so why on earth did we decide we'd prefer the measly thirty per cent of land?! It's clear that most of us miss being in the water too, as why else would we work hard all year to be able to afford a two-week holiday by the sea, the very place we left all those years ago!

I've tried to pinpoint the time when it all went wrong for us and I've decided it was 800 million years ago, as that's when we had our last common ancestor with the octopus. I wish we were more like the octopus. Experts say the common octopus has about 130 million neurons in its brain, which makes it about as intelligent as a dog. Humans have 100 *billion* neurons, but I really don't think we're all that. We're probably the only species who can lock ourselves out of our own homes. How stupid is that?! An octopus would never get locked out of its home, and even if it did its boneless body means it would be able to just climb through the keyhole. Having no bones would be a good thing. When I've backed out of doing a bungee jump or skydive, people have said I have no backbone. Honestly, I wish I didn't have one. I've had nothing but problems with my back since being in my teens. Octopuses also have more arms than us, which would be really handy. It would mean we could carry things in our arms instead of carrier bags and we wouldn't clog up the seas with plastic.

Its penis can also be used as an arm, which for me would at least give it a use.

And, if it loses an arm, it can just grow one back, so there would be less pressure on our health service. There are so many other astonishing things they can do that make them so much more impressive than us humans.

The thing is, it's too late now. We moved on and left the sea so here we are, years later, stuck on land as humans. Which begs the question: what is next for the human body? Our organs are lasting longer and longer, but how long can our bodies carry on? I've been waking up with aches and pains for a few years, but now I'm finding I'm getting more and more of them, and it does start to get you down after a while. Aches and pains are like clouds – one or two don't get you down but a skyful makes you feel miserable. I wonder if it's going to get worse too, with all the exercise people are doing these days. We haven't witnessed the repercussions of what people are putting their bodies through at Zumba and Bokwa classes.

KARL'S FACTS

Artist Neil Harbisson has an antenna implanted in his skull and is the first officially recognised cyborg.

The thing that might help us keep up in our old age when we're living to be 120 is a robot that assists your body. This was exactly the idea Machi had, a Japanese inventor I was meeting at his workshop just outside Tokyo.

Machi is a quiet lad who prefers to let his invention do the talking. Or should that be the lifting. As I entered his garage, there it was – a metal structure hanging from the ceiling like a praying mantis. It had two long arms made out of metal rods, similar to the sort that are used to make those rotary dryers you hang your washing on, and apart from the lightweight frame there really wasn't much to it. Just a few small boards of computer chips. A lot less complicated than the endless bits and bobs constantly working away in our bodies. It's like a woman's handbag inside the human form with every space taken up with something – some of which are surplus to requirements. Nature is a bit of a hoarder in a way, keeping stuff like the appendix that we no longer need and a thing called the Darwin's tubercle which is a small bump on the rim of the outer ear. Apparently it's a hangover from years gone by that allowed the top part of the ear to swivel or flop down over the opening to the ear. You could say our bodies are like a Poundland store – we have a few really good items but also a lot of other useless stuff.

Anyway, Machi buckled the contraption to my back and inserted four AAA batteries to give it power. The motors for the arms were under covers on top of my shoulders that gave me an '80s shoulder-pad look, a bit like Joan Collins in *Dynasty*. But where she would have been spraying herself with expensive Chanel No 5, I'd be spraying WD40 under my armpits. The odd thing is, I'd probably look after this bit of kit more than I look after my own body. I tend to take care of things that I might have to sell on at some point, like a house or a car, so it keeps its value, whereas my body isn't going anywhere so I'm fine with a few scratches and bumps here and there.

KARL: Is this what he hopes everyone will be using in the future?

MACHI: Not for everyone.

KARL: Give me an example of someone who would use this.

MACHI: Construction workers. Enable them to bring heavy stuff, and holding things.

KARL: How long will the batteries last?

MACHI: About twenty minutes.

Twenty minutes isn't a long time. The last thing I want is yet another item that needs charging all the time. It sometimes feels like the reason for my existence is to walk around the house charging things up. Suzanne never remembers either, which means if we did have to rely on these robot bodysuits I'd end up doing all the lifting as she wouldn't have any power in her suit. Charging batteries really is a bugbear of mine. I only watched *Star Wars* fairly recently and couldn't help but wonder how long Darth Vader would get out of that lightsaber of his before it needed plugging in and recharging.

Machi flicked a switch to bring the arms to life. I then had to use my own arms to operate the levers that would give me extra power and an extra reach of around five feet. It seems to me that rather than making us stronger, these suits would make us even lazier than we are now. Some of the little exercise I get is reaching over to pick up the TV remote off the coffee table.

My question is: would wearing these suits stop us evolving longer arms in the future? Giraffes developed longer necks in order to get food from the trees. A lot of supermarket shelves are getting higher and harder for us to reach, and maybe in time nature would have taken care of this, but now we're interfering. This is what makes me wonder if we've taken over from nature. I believe it got sick of us thinking we know what's best, and now rather than looking after us I think it spends its time coming up with diseases to try and get shot of us. Think about it: we've been around in this form for 200,000 years and nothing has really changed. I mean, I don't expect the body to get as many updates as an iPhone but it would be good if we saw a few changes to iron out some faults. I find it odd that we have to put food down part of the same pipe that we need to keep clear so that we can breathe. It would have made sense for nature to do some plumbing so we could breathe through our ears and not choke to death on food. This would also mean I could sleep face down on my pillow instead of having to twist my neck. It's a good idea, isn't it? It could well happen in years to come. Maybe not in my lifetime, but possibly before they finish the roadworks on the M3.

IRON MAN'S DISABLED
BROTHER.

The idea was for me to have a day out wearing the battery-powered long-armed suit to see how much it helped me. First, I took it for a test just outside the workshop. It wasn't too heavy, to be fair; it was like carrying an aluminium sun lounger around. I got used to the distance it could reach and the speed that it moved by grabbing a few leaves from trees. This was difficult, as normally I can reach and grab things with very little thought, but now I'd replaced my flexible fingers and thumbs with three claws, and picking things up was like playing one of those games in an arcade where you have to try to grab a teddy in a glass box. Has anyone ever managed it? Just like the arcade machine, the robot hands had the grip of a ninety-year-old with arthritis. I wasn't sure how this would aid construction workers, when I doubt it could manage handling a pick 'n' mix counter. I didn't feel like it was going to make my life a lot easier, and it certainly didn't make me feel stronger. In all honesty, I felt and looked like Iron Man's disabled brother.

As I was heading back to Machi to get a supply of batteries to get me through the day, there was a loud crackle and I saw some sparks and flames in the corner of my eye followed by a puff of smoke. The arms no longer moved.

KARL: Is it broke now? Did I do that? Did I do something wrong?

MACHI: It's not your fault. My product is not perfect. I'm not sure I can fix this today.

KARL: Oh. That's that then, innit.

And that was that. It was out of action. Even though my body suffers with aches and pains and is slower than it used to be, it has never let me down as much as this suit had. Even when I've not been well it has taken care of me. I remember when I had kidney stones and the walk-in clinic was too busy to see me, my body walked back home, even though I have no memory of it. It went on autopilot, and the next thing I knew I was waking up in my own bed without knowing how I got there. As much as I moan, me and my body are a good team. The only thing it does now and again that I don't like is give me arse cramp. I always forget to ask my doctor what causes it. It doesn't happen often, but when it does it really stops me in my tracks for a few seconds. It feels like something has crawled up my arse and is strangling my anus.

Anyway, Machi is a clever lad, and there's no way I could make something like the suit he had built, but after the short time I'd had with it, I wasn't sure making us stronger was such a good idea anyway. The problem is, I reckon this extra body power would just end up in the wrong hands and be used to commit crime. Spider-Man and Superman had special powers, so their arch-rivals came up with other special powers to try and defeat them, which then ended up in a full-on battle causing loads of damage. I wouldn't want to live anywhere near Spider-Man as he seems to cause more damage than good. He can't have a fight without taking out buildings and bridges. I imagine if Spider-Man moved into your neighbourhood, your home insurance would shoot up. The monthly council tax bill would shoot right up too, as someone would have to pay for all the damage he caused. I'd prefer to stay well away from all that and stick with Neighbourhood Watch.

In my opinion we should just work with what nature gave us. Unless someone can figure out how to turn us into octopuses.

CHANGING FACE

The thing that gets my heart pumping isn't exercise, it's getting wound up. My heart can pound like I've just completed 200 star jumps if someone has annoyed me. I once bought a birthday card for Suzanne that had a £3 price tag on it. A bit pricey just for a card, but I thought she'd like it so decided to take the hit. I'd come to terms with the price by the time it was my turn to pay, but then was told it would cost me a further 60p for the envelope. How bloody cheeky is that?! It made my blood boil. Surely the envelope is part of the card? They'll be selling shoes individually next. If I'd been rigged up to a heart monitor as the cashier told me this, my beats per minute would have matched that of a Fatboy Slim track.

The problem is that research says that my heart beating fast due to stress isn't good for it or for the rest of my body as it can cause deterioration and make you more susceptible to illnesses, from the common cold to cancer. But I find it difficult to control what my brain chooses to get stressed about. I could have pretended that I wasn't that fussed about the extra charge, but inside, my heart would still have been pounding.

I've always said there's a little part of the brain that is there especially to hold stress and worries. If I wasn't getting uptight over the cost of an envelope, I'd find something else to get in a tizz about. I call it the 'worry hole' – a small area that is there to fill with annoying crap. It's like a landfill for the mind where the worries rot away more slowly than a plastic bottle.

What I was having a go at next proves that people will always find things to worry about. I was going for a session of small face therapy. This is a non-invasive method of bone remodelling for people who stress out about the size of their face. Many Japanese women want to have a smaller face as they feel it makes them appear more feminine and attractive. Now, I'm aware my face isn't perfect – the main problem being that the bottom half is big but the top half is small. I have more of a twohead than a forehead. Although my odd-sized head isn't taking up any 'worry space' in the 'worry hole' I was up for seeing if the procedure works, if nothing else.

I lay on the bed in a quiet room in the clinic as a man named Tsutomu Muramatsu in traditional Japanese dress got to work on my head. For me, the problem I have with alterations like this is that styles change. Small faces might be the trend now but what happens when people suddenly prefer the larger face? Then you'd have to book yourself into big face therapy. I'm telling you, it will happen. It's like mobile phones. When they first came on the scene they were about the size of a house brick, and then as time went on they got smaller and smaller until suddenly in the last two years or so they've got massive again. The other possible issue is with a smaller face my eyes and teeth might look bigger and I'll end up looking like Gollum.

Isn't it best just to accept what size face you've been dealt? This whole trip was about looking at the body and health, and for me this is one of the most unhealthy things about today's world – the amount of money people spend on changing their looks. Suzanne used to have quite a bit of fat on her head so I told her it was bubble wrap for her beautiful face. She accepted that, and then moved on and started worrying about her body shape! I told her that her figure is 'pear-shaped, which is pretty normal'. What I didn't say was that with the size of her fat head she was more an upside-down pear shape.

Tsutomu Muramatsu started by gently pushing either side of my face with his palms and massaging the flabby skin on my jawbone, which was all very nice and relaxing, but that was just the warm-up. Suddenly he switched and it was like he was kneading dough. Pulling and pushing at my face and sticking his thumbs in my eyes and tugging at them as if he was peeling an orange. He then rubbed my twohead really hard with his knuckles, like he was doing a brass rubbing, laughing maniacally as he went. I'd had enough. He said he needed to do the other side of my face but I told him I didn't want any more.

After twenty minutes of having my head used as a stress ball I made my way over to the mirror to see the results. I was gobsmacked. I could genuinely see the difference to the side of my face he had worked on. My skin seemed a lot firmer and looked like it fitted my head better. Normally I look like I have no jawline and carry the look of a jelly baby, but he'd manage to give me one. The only problem was that I looked like one of those before and after adverts as

LOOKING AS GOUGE-OUS AS EVER.

he'd only done one side of my face. It didn't matter too much though, as by the time I got back to the hotel and looked in the mirror again, I was back to my normal fat-headed self. Everything he had squashed had returned to normal, like when you scrunch up a crisp packet and it slowly unfolds. I was told the procedure I'd had normally cost £500! Clearly, people have bigger empty spaces in their head than my little worry hole if they're happy lashing out £500 for that.

CRYING AWAY THE STRESS

I haven't had a good cry in years. It's just not something that my eyes do. I find that blurting out expletives helps me release my frustrations. We haven't got kids, but if we did I think I'd teach them a few swear words at a young age that I'd allow them to blurt out if they fell over or stood barefoot on an upside-down plug. I'd much prefer to hear a quick 'FUCK!' 'WANKER!' or 'TWAT!' than put up with five minutes of whimpering.

Suzanne on the other hand gets teary-eyed far too easily. I sometimes get home to find her sat there with red puffy eyes and snot running down her face and immediately presume that someone in the family has died. I'll ask what's wrong, only to find that no one has passed away, she's just been watching the new John Lewis Christmas advert! If she was ever properly upset I'd have no idea. She's like a sensitive car alarm – after a while you just ignore it when it goes off.

Then there are crocodile tears that people use as a way of getting what they want. The saying used to be 'If at first you don't succeed, try, try, try again'; now it's 'Cry, cry, cry again', especially on TV talent shows. They're the worst for it. Contestants hoping that they'll win votes from the public if they sob their hearts out. It's got so bad on *X Factor* they should put out flood warnings before that show is broadcast. I struggle to understand who's lost and who's won as they all cry. I'm sure this is why they suggest that we should drink two litres of water a day; it's not to hydrate the body, it's so the blubbers don't run out of tears. Talent programmes, dance programmes, cooking programmes, even hard-headed wannabe businessmen and women on *The Apprentice* break down and start scriking like a mard arse if Sir Alan Sugar points the finger.

Suzanne tells me to stop being cold-hearted and that 'it's natural' and 'it's better to let it out', but I say it's also natural to shit yourself when nervous and I doubt I'd get the job if I 'let that out' during a job interview. It's true though, there's a relationship between fear and bowel control.

Veteran soldiers have admitted that in combat during the Second World War many soiled their pants, but they never show that in war films. Sobbing and tears look cuter on film than other bodily functions. Prime example is Naomi Watts in the *King Kong* remake. When King Kong picks her up she just screams and cries a bit, but in reality she would have well and truly shit her pants. That would be a real 'motion' picture.

KARL'S FACTS

The melody of a newborn baby's cry matches the intonation of the language they heard in the womb.

Anyway, research says a proper cry is a really good way to help fight against the 'silent killer', otherwise known as stress, which is also one of the worst enemies for your body and mind to deal with. In Japan, to help battle against modern-day stresses there is a new social activity called 'rui-katsu' (tear-seeking) where people gather to watch sad movies and cry in public as a way of releasing their burdens.

The crying therapy session event I attended had around twelve people. Men, women, young lads and girls. From what I could gather they all seemed fairly happy and relaxed and the atmosphere was quite upbeat. That was until a traditional Japanese storyteller narrated a sad tale about the relationship he had with his granddad.

STORYTELLER: When I was nine years old I went to the amusement park with my grandfather. In that park there was a rollercoaster. At the time I was very terrified getting on the rollercoaster. We waited in line and we watched the ride. Wow, everybody was screaming. I was very scared, very, very scared. At the time I grab his hand. We got on the rollercoaster. I closed my eyes. After the ride my grandfather said to me how brave I was. 'I'm proud of you. I'm very happy.' I then saw his arm. I was surprised because his arm was bleeding.

At this point the storyteller started crying, and I mean crying! His body was shaking and his voice was breaking. I was nowhere near ready yet, I was still getting myself comfy. Had I nodded off and missed something?! I was now more concerned that my body would react another way to deal with the surprise of him being upset. Laughter. It happens quite a lot. I don't do it to be mean. I suppose it's a genuine nervous reaction to a situation, it just isn't the right one to use. When I was younger, about eight or nine years old, my mam and dad bought me a computer called a ZX81 for Christmas. It only had 1k of memory so to play any games on it you had to insert a RAM pack into the back of it to make it 16k. Problem was, they didn't realise this, so on Christmas Day I couldn't play with it. Most kids at this point would cry with frustration, but because I wasn't a crier, my body chose a different method to release the stress. I was sick in the kitchen sink! All over the vegetables that my mam was preparing for Christmas dinner. It really surprised me and hasn't happened since.

Anyway, the man continued with his story. I could hear a few others bawling behind me now. I dealt with it like a newsreader reading some breaking news, looking sincere, thoughtful and solemn and trying not to laugh.

STORYTELLER: My nails had scratched his arm when I was holding so tight. But he never said, he never said it's painful. He never said, let hand go. I had great strong grandfather. In 2010 that rollercoaster closed, and last year in June my grandfather passed away. Please look at this picture! This is my grandfather in hospital. I visited him sometimes. Look at this picture! This is his hand. Do you think it's weak?! I didn't think so. This hand for me is very strong. I can't meet him again but I will remember his warm hand.

By the end he was making a noise like a lost whale. I was shocked, not just by how upset he was, but also by how odd he looked when he was crying. It was freaky in the same way that when a friend you've known for years takes their glasses off. It throws you a little bit and you need a few moments to get used to how different they look. I peered around at everyone else and a good majority of them had tears in their eyes. I, however, still had nothing. Don't get me wrong. I was happy that he loved his granddad, but I think for me to get upset I would have needed a bit of back story.

As he was talking he was looking through his tears to see who was sharing his sorrow. Believe me, I was trying. I tried opening my eyes really wide and not blinking, to force a tear, as I thought maybe if one came, others might follow. Then I thought my body was going to do something as bad as a laugh – I could feel it producing a yawn. I held my lips tight and kept it trapped in the back of my throat, and as luck would have it this caused my eyes to water a little bit, and I think he noticed. What a result.

Next, the pressure was off a little bit as they played a few short films. There was one about a girl getting bullied at school, which is an unpleasant situation, but I thought it was badly acted. And I found that I wasn't concentrating fully on the film as I was too busy looking round at the others who were crying again, while I was sat trying to find a pulse just to make sure I actually had a heart.

The next tale was about a young lad who had always wanted to cycle the whole of Canada but couldn't due to the fact that he had no legs. So his dad ended up cycling the distance while his son sat in a basket on the front of the bike. Again, everyone around me was watching through tears and blowing their nose, but the story was ruined for me as the music kept fading in and out. It was some ridiculous sickly sweet music that just wasn't needed. It cheapened the whole thing. The dad and son seemed quite happy with their achievement. They were having quality time together, the son was getting his wish, so why the sloppy sad music?! I would have preferred them to use 'Agadoo' by Black Lace as they cycled over the finish line as it would have been less corny. It was just trying too hard, like they felt the viewer needed telling what emotions they should be feeling at certain parts. They'll be sticking sad music under reports on *News at Ten* soon, just to try and make the sad stories that little bit more sad. Or how about doctors having a CD player in their surgery so they can slap on a soppy song by Celine Dion while they tell me they've found a lump on one of my bollocks? This evening was meant to reduce my stress levels but I felt like it was increasing them.

At this point I thought it was never going to happen. I wondered if there was just too much pressure on my eyes to produce real tears. It's like when someone says they've got a really good joke they want to tell you and you're suddenly too busy worrying about getting it to listen properly.

Just when I thought I was wasting my time, a video came on featuring a kitten. If anything was going to work, it would be this. I love watching animal and nature programmes but always have to leave the room if any sad bits happen. Recently, there was a David Attenborough series called

The Hunt that I couldn't watch. It was all about how different species hunt their prey. Muggings and attacks, blood and guts everywhere. It was like a version of *Crimewatch* for the animal kingdom. Honestly, no wonder a lot of stuff in the wild is nocturnal. I don't think I'd sleep at night if I had as many enemies as most animals do. It's strange, as Suzanne can quite happily watch this without getting upset. She likes animals as much as me but watching them getting mauled to death doesn't bother her. Mind you, she's the only person I know who when passing lambs in a country field says, 'Do you fancy lamb chops for Sunday dinner?'

The footage was of a child playing with a kitten, and it was rolling around and hiding in boxes and diving in and out of paper and chasing a ball. Various photographs of the cat dressed up in daft outfits were mixed into the footage. It made me smile. Then more video of the same cat with the same kid, who was now a bit older and was still having fun playing with their pet in the garden. Then it faded to black and faded up again. Now the cat was not being so playful as it had a big bandage around its waist. At this point I got a bit of a lump in my throat. I could hear sniffles around me. More than I'd heard all night. The kid stroked the cat but she appeared to be sad. Then the video cut to a photo of the cat, still in its bandage, with text underneath the photo – 'R.I.P.'. It had died of a tumour.

This caused my bottom lip to quiver and my heart rate altered, and at last my eyes glazed over a little with real tears. I looked around the room and the others noticed my shiny eyes. They smiled at me like they had accepted me into their gang. They seemed happy to see that I had got upset. I felt like Andy Murray. He didn't show any emotion for years, and even though he won a few competitions he wasn't very popular with the public. Then, in 2012 he lost in a final at Wimbledon and burst into tears and the country loved him for it. He didn't win the final that year but he won over a lot of fans by spilling some tears.

Will the director ripped into me afterwards, taking the piss that I'd cried at a cat video. I told him that I wasn't crying. I'd just yawned.

COPING WITH A DISABILITY

After making my eyes upset at the crying therapy, I thought they deserved some time off. Which was what they were going to get, as the plan was for me to face my biggest fear. I was going to experience what it is like to be blind. Whenever I see a blind person out and about on their own it always stops me in my tracks, and I take a moment to watch them for a while as they make their way down crowded streets and cross busy junctions. As much as I'd pushed my body quite a bit during this trip, running in temperatures way below freezing, drinking my own urine, and having my face pummelled, I knew confronting blindness for a day was going to be the toughest thing I've done on all my travels. I knew it would probably be one of the most intriguing things I've ever done too. I had other senses to help me, like touch, taste, smell and hearing, but without the use of sight I'd be lacking the lead, like Queen without Freddie Mercury.

To give my other senses confidence I considered what was bad about the eyes. As amazing as they are, they often make decisions for me that aren't always for the best. They can pick clothes that please them but are uncomfortable for the rest of my body. My eyes don't always give certain things a chance. When I'm buying a sofa, if my eyes don't like the look of what they see, my arse doesn't get a say on the comfort levels. Eyes are probably responsible for many break-ups in relationships. And it's the eyes that make people worry about the way they look and force them to have daft procedures like small face therapy. I also wonder if I didn't do well at school because of them. These days loads of kids seem to suffer with Attention Deficit Disorder. Back then, I don't think I had ADD, but my eyes might have had it. I did try hard in lessons to learn things from reading books, but regularly

BONO HAS LET HIMSELF GO A BIT.

the eyes would just turn and look out of the window at something they found more interesting.

I was going to be blind for a day by wearing some blacked-out goggles and I decided to put these on before meeting Kobayashi, my blind guide for the day, as I wanted us both to be in the same situation. I felt that if I got to see him first I wouldn't be experiencing what he was as he wouldn't get the chance to see me. The goggles blocked everything out. I was one hundred per cent in the dark.

Will the director led me to Kobayashi's front door and placed my hand on the button of the intercom. From then on I was on my own. Kobayashi's voice came on the speaker moments later and I could hear him release the lock on the door. After a few moments of feeling my way around, I found the handle and pushed. I was faced with a problem instantly, as in Japan you are always expected to remove your shoes when entering a person's home. Kobayashi shouted hello and said he was upstairs, so I shuffled tentatively towards the direction his voice was coming from until my feet hit a step. I then felt with my hands to see if there were any other shoes on the step. There weren't, so I placed my trainers on the right-hand side of step number one so I would know where to collect them later. I slowly made my way up the stairs, one hand holding tightly to the banister and the other outstretched. I was already sighing to myself with frustration. I realised it was going to be an extremely long day when something as basic as entering a building took so much effort. Once I got to the top of the stairs I explained to Kobayashi what my trip had been like so far and what I wanted from today.

KARL: I just want to experience what it's like being blind. I don't think I'm gonna enjoy myself today at all. So I don't want you to do anything that you don't normally do, just have a normal day.

KOBAYASHI: I think that my daily life is boring, just make a coffee, make a breakfast, and start the job using the voice-controlled PC and mobile. It's similar to your daily life, just little bit different to use sight.

KARL: Have you been blind from birth?

KOBAYASHI: No, my eye sickness appeared when I was twenty-eight years old.

KARL: How long ago was that then, how old are you now?

KOBAYASHI: Now I am forty-six. I was born in 1968.

KARL: Would you say that you're a different person to who you were when you had sight?

KOBAYASHI: Umm, I think my personality has not changed but I need more patience. I have to take a long time more than before. So I feel frustrations.

He gave me a quick tour of his place by feel. At this stage I didn't ask many questions about what it was like living with blindness. I was too busy asking what I was touching so I could build an image in my mind of the layout of the place while stumbling my way around the edge of the room. Usually when I enter a property I always head for the window to see what the view has to offer, but on this occasion it didn't even enter my head.

Kobayashi made coffee and some toast while taking my hands so I could feel where the appliances were.

KARL: Is there anything on this appliance for blind people? Any sort of Braille? Do you read Braille?

KOBAYASHI: No, I don't. I use only the kind of voice supporter, in a PC, in a mobile phone that can talk everything. I cannot understand Braille well. Most of the people who do understand used Braille from young age.

I reckon both Braille and sign language would be pretty useful to have, not only to communicate to the deaf and blind but to use in everyday life. When I'm on a train or bus talking with whoever I'm with, I don't like the way people can listen in, and sign language would get rid of this annoyance. Braille would be useful too. It does me head in when Suzanne reads when we go to bed as she has to have a light on. And then she tends to fall asleep with a book in her hand and I have to get up and turn the light off! If she could read Braille she could read in the dark and stop that happening.

The fingertips contain more touch and temperature receptors than any other part of the body, except for the genitals, apparently. I don't know why they have to be that bloody sensitive. I don't know if anyone can read Braille using their genitals, but if they can, that means every book would literally be keeping them on the edge of their seat from start to finish.

As I was talking to Kobayashi I could smell the toast was done. I couldn't tell you how often my nose normally gets involved when making food. I had a bite of it and it was done to perfection. Who knows, maybe there's a chance my nose is a better cook than my eyes. This gave me a bit of hope for the day ahead.

Once I'd eaten I volunteered to do the washing up. This is one of my jobs at home, and it made me wonder if I would be as keen to do it if I didn't have sight. Part of the reason I enjoy it is to see the kitchen nice and tidy afterwards but if I had no sight would I be so keen? While I'd been away I had moaned at Suzanne on Skype as she'd been wrecking the house in the short time I'd not been there. She mentioned that she'd knocked over a cup of tea in the bedroom and stained the carpet. If I didn't have sight she wouldn't even have had to tell me and that little argument wouldn't have taken place.

KARL'S FACTS

Miniature horses are used
as guides for blind people who
are allergic to dogs.

Kobayashi suggested that we should go and have a walk outside, so I used his toilet first, as the prospect of touching my way around a public toilet to find a urinal didn't seem like a good idea. By the time I'd found my way back I'd totally forgotten where I'd left my cup of coffee, so I made my way downstairs to move my shoes off the step before Kobayashi came down and tripped over them.

He gave me a stick and then led the way. He walked pretty fast for a blind man, so fast that if he ever got a blind dog, it would have to be a greyhound. I was worried about tripping off the edge of the pavement into the road but he said there were no pavements, only white lines dividing the road for cars and pedestrians. He used his stick to feel for the white line. He knew when he got to a junction as there were concrete slabs with bumps on them. Once I'd stood on them I recognised the feeling, as we have these slabs at home, but I had no idea they were for the blind. I'd always thought they were to offer more grip on an icy day so people wouldn't slide into the road.

The white lines and dimpled slabs were a good idea, but the use of the sound of chirping birds at a pedestrian crossing to let the visually impaired know it was safe to cross seemed like an odd choice. Especially for me, as I was new to it all. If a noisy flock flew overhead at the wrong moment I could get knocked down. A noise from an animal that doesn't exist any more like a tyrannosaurus would have been a safer bet.

My eyes had now adjusted to the darkness and found a tiny pinprick of light at the top left of my blacked-out goggles. That little dot was what let me know if my eyes were open or shut. I actually thought my eyes

would have just closed by now, as they couldn't help me in any way, but I've since read that it takes more muscles to close your eyes than it does to have them open. I suppose that makes sense, as when I close my eyes at night, it wears me out that much I often go to sleep.

KARL: I'm just wondering whether your eyes get as tired as mine. For me, my eyes are the thing that let me know if I'm tired. What time do you go to bed?

KOBAYASHI: It depends, but normally twelve o'clock.

KARL: And what is it that happens, do your eyes still feel tired? Is that the sign you get of being tired?

KOBAYASHI: No. Eyes not tired. It's my mind. So my brain tired from making images. So eyes is okay but brain is tired.

He nipped into the local barber for a haircut and then took me for lunch. He navigated his way there by the light from the sun. He knew how many blocks he had passed by the slight light change as he passed tall buildings. This was impressive. I mean, I can make my way to and from the toilet at night in the dark, but he had been walking for almost a mile. He then stopped and asked me to sniff. I could smell food. We were at his favourite noodle bar.

I was saying how much I enjoy eating food earlier in this chapter, but it was weird having to decide what I wanted to eat without vision. Rather than reading the menu, I'll often look around at what people are eating at other tables to see what takes my eye, but today that wasn't possible so I went with the safe bet of chicken. When the meal arrived it was yet another strange experience. Eating without seeing takes a lot of the enjoyment away. I couldn't tell Kobayashi this, as he has to deal with it every day, but what I did find surprising was the way I stopped eating once I was full. My eyes are definitely bigger than my belly, and I eat all of whatever is put in front of me, but this wasn't the case when I couldn't see what was there. I've got no research to back this up but I reckon because of this you don't see many fat blind people. Sometimes I'm not even hungry, but if I've seen a KitKat in the fridge I'll want it and won't stop thinking about it until it's gone. I have little to-dos with Suzanne about jam donuts, as we'll buy a bag of five, which is always going to end in tears when there are only two of us. You might be thinking, why not just cut the last one in half and share? But you can't cut a jam donut in half as you never know where the jam is, so one of us is always going to be losing out. If either of us were blind, this argument wouldn't take place.

I thought this was going to be the end of my experience, but everyone had kept me well and truly in the dark about Kobayashi's hobby. When he was younger he had completed several major climbs, but as his sight deteriorated from an inherited, degenerative eye disease called retinitis pigmentosa, he climbed less and less. That was until he realised he wanted to focus on the things he could do rather than the things he couldn't. He set up a non-profit organisation that promotes free climbing for those with visual impairment and in 2011 won a world championship event. The idea was for me to have a go.

We met a friend of his called Suku, who was a climber with sight and was going to help me. We had to travel across Tokyo using various underground trains. It sounded extremely busy. Normally when using public transport at peak times at home, I'll pop on some headphones to block out the chaos, but that's not possible when your ears are taking on the role of your sight.

My grip on Kobayashi got tighter and tighter as the journey went on. My back and neck were now hurting too. I was holding myself differently to the way I normally would, shuffling along slowly while tilting my head so one of my ears was facing the way I was walking. I was exhausted.

Finally we made it to a park. I knew it was a park as the ground was softer and more dusty under my feet. I could hear kids playing and dogs barking. I don't think my senses were working any harder than normal, but when touch and hearing are all you've got, you tend to take more notice of them.

I've done a few climbs in my life, but normally the incentive was the view when you got to the top. Today that motivation wasn't there. I didn't ask how high the climb was as I didn't want to be put off giving it a go. That's the other thing with eyes: if I could see what Suku was asking me to climb it would be easy for my eyes to make a judgement as to whether I was capable or not. But even though I couldn't see it, I was aware it was a tough climb as both helmets and ropes were involved. I climbed first as Suku gave me instructions about where I should put my hands and feet by using a clock face, shouting out commands like 'Put right hand at two o'clock'.

SUKU: Okay, use your right hand. It's eleven o'clock.

KARL: Eleven o'clock?!

SUKU: Yes, eleven o'clock. That's one o'clock, remember.

KARL: (feeling around) That's not one o'clock!

SUKU: That's one o'clock.

KARL: No. One o'clock is over here, isn't it?

SUKU: No. Come on, I said eleven o'clock. That means to the left up, see?

KARL: Hang on. Okay, got that! Where now?

SUKU: Go! Come on, Karl.

KARL: What you on about, 'come on'?! I'm taking control from you! Where's the clock? What time is it?!

SUKU: Left foot higher, bring higher! Eight o'clock!

KARL: Higher than this?

SUKU: Yes, higher, higher!

KARL: Fucking hell, that's more a nine o'clocker.

> SUKU: Yeah, it's now from your left hand, it's twelve o'clock. One metre, twelve o'clock. That's actually one o'clock. You have to go to the left and about another half a metre, so you have to push yourself. Come on, little higher, you got it.

I don't know how long this went on for. I didn't want to ask Suku the time as it would just have confused matters, but it felt like a good forty-five minutes to an hour, and I didn't feel I got much higher than five feet off the ground. I'd had enough, so Kobayashi took to the ropes. Suku shouted the clock commands to him and within four or five minutes he had made it to the top. I could hear a few cheers from spectators who I wasn't even aware had been there. I probably wouldn't have tried to climb for so long if I had known people were watching and seeing how rubbish I was. I put two and two together and worked out that this is why he doesn't have a guide dog. It would be pretty tricky climbing up with a Labrador on a lead!

Kobayashi's voice sounded a lot happier once he'd reached the top. Not dissimilar to my own sense of achievement when I used the loo on my own with no sight. I thanked Kobayashi for spending so much time with me. He asked me if I was impressed with his climbing skills and I told him I hadn't seen it as I was still wearing my goggles. I said I was keeping them on as I didn't think it would be fair to take them off when he couldn't do the same. He said I was a gentlemen and appreciated that.

I only got to see Kobayashi and the cliff edge that I tried to climb once the TV programme had been edited. It was around forty feet high, with very small cracks to grip. It's hard to say, but I'm pretty sure I would have given up a lot earlier if I had seen the distance I was expected to climb.

I think my fear of being blind was justified and hopefully won't be something I'll have to face again. After facing my number one fear, I decided that once I was back at home it would be worth facing my second. I had my testicles checked for lumps. Like my vision, they were all clear.

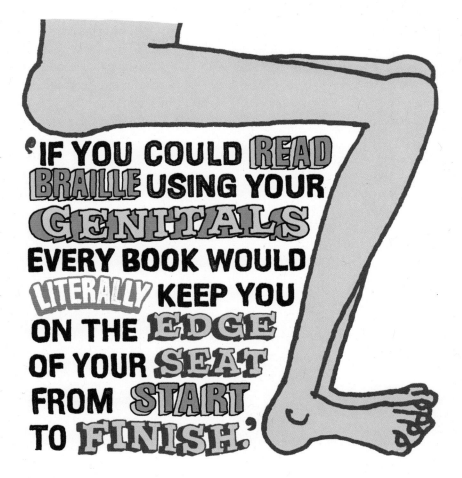

'IF YOU COULD READ BRAILLE USING YOUR GENITALS EVERY BOOK WOULD LITERALLY KEEP YOU ON THE EDGE OF YOUR SEAT FROM START TO FINISH.'

WHEN I WAS younger I couldn't give a shit. I'm not talking about my attitude towards life; I'm talking about my bowel movements. I really couldn't shit. I think it was down to my diet of nothing but potatoes and bread. I read somewhere recently that ninety-two days of our life are spent sat on the loo. I reckon when I was a kid I probably did that amount of time in one sitting – without anything leaving my guts. I could never understand why the toilet was named 'the restroom' as there wasn't much rest going on in there for me. I'd often have to remove clothing after getting a right sweat on due to me pushing so hard.

These days, even though I'm very rarely bunged up, my trousers still spend more time round my ankles than they do around my waist. But it's not due to me being bunged up, I just like sitting on the toilet. I'm not going to lie: I enjoy it. It's what I class as 'me time'.

Sometimes I've been sat there so long I've actually gone twice without having to wipe in between. Some people have pastimes like fishing, and I guess this is my fishing. I have the same disappointments as fishermen now and again where I was expecting to land something a lot bigger. Every so often it feels like nothing is going to occur but I don't give up. If I haven't got red patches on my legs from where I've been resting my elbows I feel I haven't really invested enough time.

I can be seated for yonks, and usually the only thing that stops me staying longer is when I start to lose the feeling in my legs, or my phone battery dies. The invention of the smartphone has definitely increased the time I can sit on the lav, though. I'm surprised Apple haven't pounced on the market and released the iThrone especially for this purpose. Some might say it's a disgusting habit but I believe it to be time well spent. Reading the news or educating myself with YouTube videos while emptying MyTube has to be a good thing, surely? Before the smartphone I'd just sit there reading the ingredients on the back of shampoo bottles. I don't think I'm the only one using my phone when I download a brownload, as a trend I've noticed recently is men queuing for the toilet at service stations. That never used to happen. It was just the ladies' facilities that had queues longer than those for rides at Thorpe Park, but now it seems blokes are opting for the cubicle over the urinal so they can do their business while sorting out their business on email.

DIVING FOR TREASURE

Anyway, there is a reason for all this toilet talk. Next on my travels I was going to look at the waste that the planet has to deal with, and I was starting with body waste. So what better place to begin than Mexico City, one of the most densely populated and polluted cities in the world.

The smell is probably the first thing that hits you on arrival in Mexico City. And it's not a pleasant one. It's a constant reminder of the pollution problems, along with the signs in a big red font reminding you not to drink the infected tap water. An estimated nineteen million people live in Mexico City, but with the constant internal migration the numbers could easily be closer to thirty million. With each of those citizens in possession of an arse, that's a hell of a lot of crap to keep moving through the city's pump stations.

I was to meet the man whose job it is to do just that. His name is Julio, job title: sewage diver. I met up with him at a pumping plant where his colleagues were helping him into his wetsuit and helmet, ready to be lowered down in an open cage by crane into the raw sewage.

At this stage I could only smell the human sewage as the top layer was covered in plastic bottles that acted like a scab, protecting us from the lethal excrement that lay beneath. This is the major problem with this city: much of the sewer system runs in open canals and flows through the surrounding villages, and residents dump in all sorts of places which causes blockages. If they're not cleared they could lead to the city and subways being flooded with toxic waste.

But it's what causes the blockages that's even more disturbing. Julio and his team have had to remove dead animals and people that have either fallen into the open sewers by accident or have been dumped. How mental is that! To think I shout at Suzanne for blocking the washing machine with coins seems a bit harsh after hearing this news. It does annoy me, though. She always picks coins up off the pavement that folk have dropped while saying 'See a penny, pick it up, and all day long you'll have good luck', but then she forgets it's in her pocket, and her trousers go in the washing machine and the coin ends up blocking the filter. Now, whenever she sees a coin on the street I jump in with 'See a penny, pick it up, the very next day, the washing machine's fucked!'

As Julio's cage hit the bottles the top layer cracked as if he was breaking the caramel on a crème brûlée, which then revealed the bubbling murky greasy sludge underneath. Once he was under the deadly crème poo-lée I could hear him talking to his colleagues via a microphone in his helmet. A few minutes passed and then he was on his way back up. The good news was that he was empty-handed. No dead dogs or people to speak of. Knowing it was all clear, he asked if I'd like to join him for a dive. I can't say I was jumping with joy at the idea, as it wasn't exactly the Great Barrier Reef, but I felt it would be rude to turn his offer down as it's something he has to do regularly, keeping over 400 miles of drainage pipes clear, and something he has been doing for over thirty years. He was basically keeping the city safe for my visit, so it was the least I could do to thank him.

His mob went and got me a drysuit and helmet. When they returned I got a bit worried as the suit looked a tad worn out, and seeing as Julio was being dunked in shit more than a toilet brush, I imagine he doesn't have much time to thoroughly inspect his back-up suit. If there was a tiny rip in it I'd only find out once I was submerged in the filth. Like when you make a cup of tea with a ripped teabag and it's not until the water is added that you find your mug full of loose tea.

KARL'S FACTS

About once a year, a house in the United States is hit by sewage falling from a plane.

We were now in the crane together, being lowered slowly into the toxic slush, and I could see the top layer a lot clearer now. Plastic was the main culprit. Plastic bottles, plastic footballs, a washing-basket lid, polystyrene cups and hundreds of those friendly-bacteria Yakult drink bottles. I was sure that any friendly bacteria that may have been left in those bottles must have felt well out of place mixing with this dodgy crowd of microbes. Cardboard plates floated on the top, a few lightbulbs, some rubber tubing and even a ladies' brassiere drifted by, which just goes to show where there's muck there's bras.

As we entered I could feel the thick muck wrap around my legs. Soon I was up to my neck in shit and, more worryingly, I could smell it stronger than ever. Even though the suit was supposed to be airtight the poo particles had somehow made their way to my nostrils. Once my head was under the coating of plastic I got to see what was causing the stench. Human turds floated by. Loads of them. It was a shoal of shit, which dispersed as I entered it. I was like a headmaster breaking up a school fight, as most of the turds scampered

WELL AND TRULY IN THE SHIT.

off and I was left with just two pieces fighting it out around my helmet. As one piece was just going out of my vision, the other would pass by. The sight would have made a unique screensaver.

Seeing this evoked memories of my local swimming baths. They were known for being full of little shits, and I'm not talking about toddlers. A weekend didn't go by without the pool having to be closed for a short space of time due to 'logging'. It happened so often I'm surprised they didn't produce a card like they do on aeroplanes – 'in the very likely event of turdulence'.

I only experienced it once. The lifeguard announced on his megaphone that there was a 'stool in the pool' and this led to a full-on panic with around fifty people trying to make their way out using just one of the four ladders in the pool. It was chaos. Like a scene from *Jaws*. The lifeguard then used a fishing net to scoop the offending piece out, which once caught was greeted with a big cheer, and the pool was announced open again. I didn't bother going back in. He may have captured the loose body boulder, but it was like being offered the same bowl of soup after a fly had been scooped out.

But here I was, thirty years on, in sediment that had more stools than IKEA. This must have been the most dangerous thing I'd ever done. I was a bit fearful when I did a shark dive during *An Idiot Abroad* but at least I was fairly safe in the cage. These waters were much more dangerous. One little malfunction with this suit or helmet, and a mouthful of the crappoccino liquid that surrounded me, and I would have been in the shit. Literally.

I couldn't understand why Julio had to do this for a living. Surely this is what robots were invented for? It seems to me that androids are getting the more cushy jobs these days. I saw a TV programme not so long ago about a cruise ship that has robots working behind the bar serving drinks! What is the world coming to if robots are having fun making bloody cocktails while Julio, a human, is wading about in thirty foot of shite?!

Unlike the liquid I was in, it soon became clear why robots can't do this job. Once you get to the bottom you're in total darkness. It's so dark that if Nemo got lost in these waters, there would be no finding him. No light is strong enough to cut through this thick contaminated goo, so all of Julio's work from this point is just done by feel alone, which I doubt any robot would be capable of.

Julio can spend anything from thirty minutes to six hours in these lethal lakes trying to sort a blockage, but lucky for me, I was up and out after just five minutes. Once back on land, the lads hosed down our suits and then they were off, as Julio had a call to get over to another 'jobbie'. It must be a never-ending job in Mexico City, so I can't imagine he gets much chance to have time off from work. Maybe he gets time off in lieu, or should that be in loo.

LIVING ON TRASH

The things we buy these days are only stored in our homes for a short time until they are thrown away and replaced with newer 'improved' versions. And because we live in this wasteful way, nothing is made to last any more. I'm pretty sure if *Antiques Roadshow* is still on the TV in 200 years' time, they'll still be looking at the well-made furniture of Victorian and Edwardian times, as I doubt the stuff that is manufactured today will stand the test of time.

I bought a dressing table online for Suzanne as a Christmas gift, and it was broken before she even had a chance to use it. It had been packed in three boxes, bundled up in bubble wrap and then wrapped in Ethafoam, but it still arrived in pieces. I'm not sure having all this packaging is a good idea as I'm certain the delivery people would be a lot more careful and less inclined to throw it all over the place if they could actually see what it was they were handling. The Ocado man delivers a box of eggs to us every week and they aren't individually bubble wrapped, yet they always arrive in one piece. The bloke is just careful with them as he can see he's handling eggs.

I called the company I bought the dressing table off and the conversation went something like this:

ME: Oh, hello. I ordered a dressing table. I didn't realise it was a self-assembly.

SHOP: We don't sell any self-assembly furniture, sir.

ME: Well, the one you've sent me has just turned up and it's in bits!

SHOP: Oh, you mean it's damaged. I see. Is it possible to put it together, sir?

ME: What do you mean 'put it together'?! I bought a dressing table, not a bloody jigsaw. It's buggered!

SHOP: Yes, it happens quite often. What if I knock a bit off?

ME: I think the delivery man has done enough damage without you joining in.

SHOP: I'm terribly sorry. I can take seventeen per cent off the price or we can arrange to pick it back up if you wish.

Seeing as it was a few days before Christmas I had to accept the offer of seventeen per cent off, otherwise Suzanne wouldn't have had much to open on Christmas Day, and then she'd be the one in pieces. Thinking about it, I should have individually wrapped all the broken parts to make her feel like she had more gifts, but I didn't. I sorted it all out with a few blobs of wood glue and she was none the wiser. But I'm telling you this as it's an example of how it seems to be the norm for things not to last. No doubt the firm would have collected the dresser, chucked it in the company skip, and claimed the costs back through insurance, which in the long run is paid for by the customer as the price of their goods goes up to cover their insurance premium. But fixing the dresser gave me a sense of achievement and made me feel good. I had saved it (and saved a few quid). Yes, they may have broken it down and recycled it to make more furniture but all of that still takes a lot of energy. Stuff doesn't get recycled magically.

This brings me to what I was looking at next on my travels. I was going to spend some time with an eco architect who had made his home from recycling products he had found, mainly plastic bottles. His name is Richie Sowa, and I met him at his home on Joyxee Island in Cancun where he's been living since 2008. Richie's plastic bottle island is thirty yards from the shore, so we got over to it by using his plastic bottle boat.

RICHIE: This, I believe, is truly a solution to what we're doing to the planet. We have so much trash and that trash can actually make sustainable land. The bottles that are supporting this whole island are well preserved away from the sunlight. Corals actually grow on them. It's only the UV rays that break plastic down, so they are doing no harm down there.

It would be easy to think this bloke in his sixties was a bit mad with this idea, but it really was impressive. He had used around 160,000 bottles to create a metre-thick, eighty-foot-diameter island, which keeps his two-bedroom, two-storey house afloat, complete with roof terrace and plunge pool. He even recycles his own body waste as fertiliser to help grow the vast amount of mangroves and palms that populate his island. The plants help to bind the island together as the roots twine around the bottles, and they offer a little shade from the midday sun.

RICHIE: The compost toilet is just like a little compost heap. A little bit here and a little bit there is just fine, and when it's covered it goes back into nature and feeds the trees. It's just perfect.

KARL: You've taken something that is bad and made it good, haven't you?

RICHIE: Yeah. A nice little statement I came up with is 'from trash to treasure', as nature is the greatest treasure we have, right? We think of treasure as money but the real treasure is the nature that supports us all and gives beauty to the planet.

Richie tries to use anything he finds that would otherwise be left to rot to add something to his home. He has fashioned ornaments out of Coke cans and his plunge pool is decorated with broken glass and tiles to give a mosaic effect. He has a use for everything. I didn't look in his kitchen drawer but I wouldn't have been surprised to find a crab's claw can opener in there. Even the bioluminescent jellyfish in the waters surrounding his island offer free outside lighting at night-time. Actually, talking of jellyfish, I was thinking recently that they're probably one of the few species that are quite happy with all the polluting of the oceans that we do with our plastic carrier bags, as they can probably use the bags as decoys to escape from hungry turtle predators. This is one of the reasons there is now a 5p charge on carrier bags; it's to stop them ending up in the seas and choking turtles who munch on them thinking they are jellyfish. I think it's a daft rule, though, as the powers that be are basically saying you can carry on choking a turtle if you're prepared to pay 5p to do so. If plastic bags are so bad for the planet we should just stop making the bloody things. I think I have a solution for this issue. I propose we look at somehow using the washed-up dead jellyfish that you see on beaches to create carrier bags, then the problem would be sorted. If the jellyfish bags ended up back in the seas, turtles would be able to eat them without choking while also keeping the oceans clear of our mess. Sorted. Everyone's a winner.

KARL'S FACTS

A certain species of jellyfish has been deemed 'immortal' for its ability to revert its cells to their earliest form and grow anew when in crisis.

Richie was going to show me how easy it was to make a small island for myself, which I could then spend the night on. We headed off on bikes with eight or so fruit sacks the size of a standard bin bag that we would fill with plastic bottles from the bottle banks that were dotted around the local village. For me, this is proper recycling. The thing I hear most about plastic bottles is the way they are bad for the environment because they are difficult to break down. Well, how about not breaking them down and just reusing them as they are? When I was around twelve or thirteen I used to gather the small plastic Panda Pop bottles from the bins and fill them up with fizzy drinks that I made using a SodaStream machine. Then I'd sell them to kids at school for 20p a go. I made an absolute fortune in the summer months from the little thirst quenchers. There weren't enough bottles in the bins to keep up with the demand as they were so popular. All I used to do was give them a quick soak in hot water and they were good to go for the next day's earnings. Why can't we do this now? Some might say it's not very hygienic but surely they could at least give it a trial run with bleach as that stuff is supposed to kill any germs stone dead.

Me and Richie were out on the bikes for a good couple of hours. We collected 200 or so plastic bottles to make my island. Each one had to be checked to make sure it still had its lid and was not split anywhere.

KARL: So have you got a favourite bottle?

RICHIE: Well, the thing is, the Coca-Cola bottle is quite strong. It is better for island building because it's got a really good top. Gatorade are usually good. The tops have good grip and you can tighten it very well.

I'm pretty sure if we tried this in the UK we'd be done for stealing rubbish. I may have mentioned this story in my last book but seeing as this chapter is about recycling I think it's a fair place to recycle a story about me trying to recycle. It was a few years ago now. I broke a glass shelf in the fridge when I was scrubbing off a few milk bottle rings. Then, on one of my weekly trips to the recycling centre I passed a row of broken fridges, one of which was like the one we had at home. So once I'd got rid of the stuff out of the back of the car I walked over to the fridge to see if it still had the shelves. Luckily it did. What a result, I thought to myself. As I was walking back to

AFTER A LONG DAY
ME AND RICHIE
WERE FLAGGING.

the car with the glass shelf under my arm the bloke who worked at the recycling centre came limping over (people with these jobs always seem to have a limp) and asked me what I was doing. I told him my story, thinking common sense would prevail, but that wasn't the case. He said I couldn't go helping myself to rubbish, to which I said, 'It's not rubbish to me. Surely the whole point of this place is for stuff to get recycled. Well, I'm recycling it.' But he wouldn't have any of it. You could say he was being proper shelf-ish, and he sent me on my way empty-handed. How stupid is that?!

Once me and Richie had checked all the bottles, we got to work on making my island. He used to be a carpenter by trade so it didn't take long to make a base using two pallets he'd picked up from a construction site (the sort that bricks are delivered on). He attached those together using rope and then tied each bag of bottles to the pallets with string until they were fastened tight. Once the bottles were in place, we flipped it. We then made a soft base for me to lie on with grass he had hacked down from a local field, and then nailed material over it so it wouldn't be too itchy. Finally he made a pyramid shape by nailing four pieces of 2 x 6 from each corner of the base and tied string around the other ends to join them together. Once he was happy with that, he draped some waste material around the frame for privacy and protection. We then launched it. It floated perfectly.

RICHIE: I used to think the trash was awful, and then this idea came. It's a godsend. With the trash of the world we could save the planet. There's enough ocean area to build another Australia or lots of small islands.

After all the cycling around gathering the 200 bottles I slept well on the island that night. And I've since looked Richie up online and noticed he still has it in use. I often wonder how he's getting on when I see storms hitting that part of the world. As much as I enjoyed my night on the floating island, I'm not sure I'd have the nerve to stay on it in bad weather. But I guess if there's one thing I know about Richie, it's that he's got a lot of bottle.

HOUSES STUFFED WITH STUFF

'The best gifts are sometimes the ones that you wouldn't necessarily buy for yourself,' said Suzanne as I looked in bewilderment at the fondue set I'd received from our 'friends'.

'What does a fondue do?! There's no way they bought that for me,' I said.

It was definitely an unwanted gift of theirs that they had palmed off, I'd put money on it. That old trick of passing on unwanted presents has gone on since the year dot. The first record of this happening was probably when the three wise men gave baby Jesus the frankincense and myrrh. They had to be unwanted gifts that the wise men had received from a neighbour, hadn't they? I mean, they're pretty odd gifts for a baby. Frankincense and myrrh is the equivalent of giving a toddler a can of Glade air freshener for its birthday.

It's pretty bizarre to give a baby gold too, to be honest, but that sort of thing still goes on today. I was dragged along to a christening a few years ago and virtually everyone had turned up with a silver spoon for the baby. What the hell for?! It was like some kind of Uri Geller convention. The baby had only been in the world for a short while and already had a bigger collection of spoons than a Little Chef.

It's as if the only reason for our existence is to accumulate stuff, whether we want it or not. Our species started off being hunter-gatherers; now we're just gatherers of stuff, with some people gathering more than others. And it was this problem I was looking into next: hoarding.

I was on the outskirts of Las Vegas to help someone who had accumulated so much stuff over time that their home had become unsafe. They had items blocking exits and heating vents, which could cause mould and infestations that could lead to respiratory and other health problems.

I met up with a team from a specialist cleaning company who were happy for me to tag along and give them a hand clearing out the property. It was a decent-sized, two-bedroom prefabricated home. It looked fine from outside, but I knew I was going to be faced with something bad when Glen, the lead cleaner, handed me some white overalls, rubber gloves and a face mask.

Once I'd put all the protective clobber on, I made my way inside. It was unbelievable. There wasn't a clear space in sight. In all my years of travelling this was probably the first time I had entered someone's home without asking if I needed to remove my shoes. Every surface was piled high with stuff. Plastic bags and empty wrappers, but also clothes, batteries, shoes, packets of food, sprays, newspapers, magazines, leaflets, cuddly toys, tubs of face cream, a coconut Twix (I didn't even know they existed), ornaments and more. It was strange, as a lot of this wasn't trash, but we were making it so by putting it in bin bags.

It was the stuff that hadn't been opened that puzzled me the most as it shows that it hadn't been bought through need. When I buy something it's because I need it and it comes out of the box as soon as I'm home. I don't go shopping unless I need something, and when I do go shopping I only tend to buy the item I went for. My mam, however, is the sort who says 'I'm going shopping' and if you ask 'What for?' she says 'I don't know yet.' The problem with this is that she buys things like this mug.

HALF A CUP FOR PEOPLE WHO HAVE A BRAIN TO MATCH.

I'm pretty sure when she left the house she didn't even know these things existed, and to be honest they shouldn't. But it's like she has to buy something to justify going to the shops. On top of that, sometimes she brings other useless things home from the street. I remember my mam and dad coming to visit me in London, and we were walking back home after having an Indian, and I heard my dad say 'What you doing with that shit?! Put it in the bin.'

'No. I want it,' said my mam.

I turned round to see a two-foot-tall plastic model of Jesus she had found on the roadside. Almost eight years on and she still has it. It's of

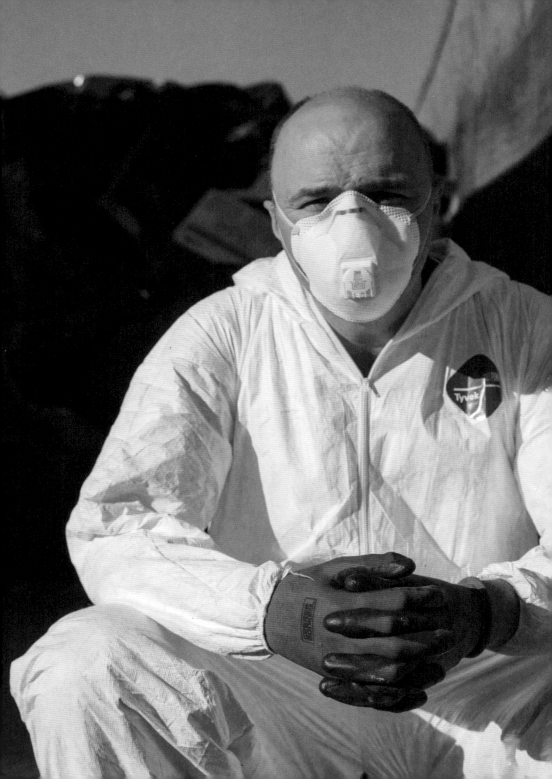

no use whatsoever but that doesn't stop my mam from keeping it. If it wasn't for my dad sneakily shoving the odd thing in the bin, I could see my mam being quite a hoarder.

KARL: Do you think the world is to blame in any way here, Glen? You know, with the amount of stuff you can end up with that you don't really need? Cos what would the owner have been like back in the day if they were a caveman or woman when there wouldn't have been stuff to buy and hoard?

GLEN: They would have collected a lot of rocks.

KARL: Is that what you think?

GLEN: I do. That's just my personal opinion. I think it's part of their DNA. For some reason, they don't have the ability to dispose of items, regardless of whether or not they have any true value.

The funny thing is, you can get away with collecting rocks nowadays as people do it for scientific reasons – they're called petrologists. People don't tend to think you have a problem if you only gather one thing, as you can say you're an enthusiast, but if you're a collector of many things, suddenly you're a hoarder and you need help.

I grabbed another bin bag to fill. There was no order to the bagging as we had far too much to shift to worry about separating and recycling any of it. There was no sign of the

WE THREW AWAY EVERYTHING BUT THE KITCHEN SINK.

chaos spilling outside the home though. Maybe this is the difference between a scruffy, inconsiderate neighbour and a hoarder. I've lived next door to people who had no shame in tipping half their belongings out the front door without a care in the world. About ten years ago I had a right scruffy bastard for a neighbour.

On one occasion there was so much furniture stacked up outside their gaff I asked them where they were moving to. They just laughed and said they weren't moving, a relation had been off their head and pissed on the sofa. Rather than using the en suite, they had taken a leak on-suite. Everything stank so they put it all outside to air. The day I moved away from that area the furniture was still outside.

Make-up, packets of sweets, empty milk bottles and ant killer filled another bag. I'm not sure why the person would want to kill any ants. They'd have helped to tidy up a little bit by eating some of the sweets that were left lying around.

Against the walls, protected by the piles of stuff, were display cabinets filled with porcelain dolls. It was weird how the blokes clearing the house didn't touch them, probably as they were part of a display, which I guess made them more acceptable to keep. Yet to me they seemed more like rubbish than some of the useful stuff we were actually throwing away.

I've never really been one for collecting anything. Apart from money. I don't mean foreign coins and notes, I mean money that I can use. As a kid, while mates were sniffing glue and collecting football stickers, I'd be out making cash by doing a paper round or washing neighbours' cars and selling fizzy drinks, and I'd look forward to getting enough coins to change it into a £10 note to add to my growing collection of other £10 notes that I'd hide in a drawer under my bed in a white plastic tub. I wasn't saving for anything, I just enjoyed watching it grow. To this day I'm still a hoarder of money, though the trouble is the taxman keeps ruining my collection.

The one item I do have – and have had for years and can't really explain why – is a small toy of the alien from the film *E.T.* It's all worn out and its skin is so flaky that the slightest movement of him makes more mess than eating a McVitie's Boaster. But for some reason, each time we've moved flat or house I've always made sure to pack him personally.

KARL'S FACTS

Statistically speaking, being a trash collector is more dangerous than being a police officer.

The cleaning went on and on, and I was sweating in my overalls and mask. It was a warm day, and the accoutrements the hoarder had gathered acted like insulation so the place was boiling hot. More and more products passed my eyes. A brand new omelette maker, unused slippers, an opened box of jelly, more old magazines, a broken DVD player and a copy of the book *Fifty Shades Darker*, the follow-up to the filthy *Fifty Shades of Grey*. I say filthy, but it couldn't have been any dirtier than this house was.

It surprised me that the person had bought a book, as I can't ever imagine being relaxed enough in this place to want to read. I think this is where I have something in common with E.T., my little flaky alien friend. I'm a big fan of space. I think in this overpopulated world, space is becoming a rare luxury. Think about it: people with money pay to have more of it, whether it's a big roomy house, a first-class seat on a plane, a stretch limousine or a holiday to a remote location – it's all to do with having space. The places that are making a load of dough at the minute are these storage units. I know a few people who pay monthly fees for one of those lock-up units to hide away loads of crap they don't actually need but don't want to throw away. In some ways they're hoarders, but, like a lot of things, if you have the money to deal with it, it's not so much of a problem.

I shifted some bags and found yet another omelette maker. Who has two omelette makers?! Actually, who has one?! After six hours the place had got back to looking more like a home rather than an Argos warehouse, and the unit outside was full and ready to be taken to a landfill site before the homeowner came back and had a chance to start taking bits 'n' bobs back inside.

KARL: So do you expect to be back at this address emptying it all again sometime soon?

GLEN: You know, we have a psychologist that is on staff and she comes out to speak to these people and will say 'You didn't know that you had it' or 'If you haven't used it within a year there is no reason to keep on to it and you don't need it in your life.'

KARL: Apart from maybe a fake Christmas tree. You don't use that for a year.

GLEN: (*laughs*) Apart from a Christmas tree! That is true, that is very true!

Before I left I half thought about keeping one of the omelette makers to give to Suzanne as a gift. After all, the best gifts are sometimes the ones that you wouldn't necessarily buy for yourself.

'The first record of an unwanted gift being palmed off was when the THREE WISE MEN gave BABY JESUS the FRANKINCENSE and MYRRH.'

COMBATTING FOOD WASTE

I used to find Christmas one of the most stressful times of the year. It wasn't the financial pressures or family arguments, it was the rubbish. Just as I'd managed to break one box down, another batch would be escalating. Dealing with this sudden mess did my head in. I'd find it difficult to get excited about receiving big presents, as rather than wonder what the gift was inside the giant package, I just ended up worrying about how I was going to get rid of the bloody box and all the protective packaging inside it. The mass of wrapping paper, boxes, bubble wrap, cellophane and polystyrene took over the house. Suzanne used to think I woke up early on Christmas Day from excitement, but it wasn't that. I'd just want to get my stuff in the bin before our upstairs neighbours filled it with their shit before me.

And it doesn't end with the gifts. Just as I'd cleared all that up, out would come the Christmas crackers! If I had my way I'd put them straight in the bin. That's where they were going to end up anyway as they're one hundred per cent shite. They start off as one piece of rubbish and just reveal more crap with the 'gift'. Every part of a Christmas cracker is rubbish. Even the jokes are shit.

Nowadays, this stress over boxes doesn't only happen at Christmas, it's something I have to deal with on a daily basis. It seems to me that the use of packaging has increased tenfold in the last decade – especially when it comes to food. Meat and fruit that once came in a paper bag now comes in clear plastic containers. I'm convinced whoever invented the game Tetris must have known this was coming. They were training us to cope with stacking oversized two-for-one offers in our fridges. As well as the hassle of getting rid of said containers, the really annoying thing is you're paying for the pleasure. It's reported that packaging adds twenty per cent to the cost of a product, which when looking at some of the contraptions that food turns up in, doesn't really surprise me. We ordered a chicken recently, and rather than it being in the usual shrink-wrapping, it arrived in a plastic dome-like structure. I think it had more room in that packet than it probably ever did when it was alive. It looked like it was having a day out at the Eden Project!

I was now in North Carolina where I was to spend time with a man called Alan Muskat, who doesn't have to deal with all that food packaging. He is a forager. He hunts and gathers some of his food like our ancestors would have done many years ago. Alan was a bearded, softly spoken fella, like a Mary Berry of the foraging world.

The day started off pretty relaxed, walking around the land near his home as he talked me through some of the local plant life that can be picked and eaten.

ALAN: The way I see it, wild food is really good for you and anything else is not. This is natural food. It's more sustainable and it's ultra local. It doesn't have to get transported here or raised with pesticides. You get to know where it's coming from and it's more meaningful and rewarding.

I tried something called beautyberry, and I ate some pine tree that Alan said was used by Indians to stop scurvy as it is full of vitamin C. I also nibbled on some onion grass while he collected some more to go with our meal later. It was nice to be able to sample some of the goods as we walked around. Before all this packaging was wrapped around our food it used to be possible to do this while shopping in most supermarkets. No one batted an eyelid if you took a few grapes or cherries and ate them as you walked around the shop pushing

your trolley. They didn't mind the odd bit of 'try before you buy'. It made sense. After all, why would you buy the produce if you didn't know what it tasted like? But now, just like everything else in the supermarket, fruit is sealed in plastic cartons to protect it.

As well as all the plastic adding an extra cost, according to a British study over 60,000 people receive hospital treatment each year due to injuries from opening food packaging. There's also a stat that says we throw away seven million tons of food every year in the UK alone. I reckon it's not always because we don't want to eat it, it's cos we can't get into the bloody packaging. The news is always telling us how more people are carrying knives these days. I don't think they carry them to threaten people with, it's so they can get to their food in these plastic sealed boxes. But seven million tons of food going to waste is disgusting. In some ways we shouldn't have a go at fat people, as if it wasn't for them filling their faces every minute of the day we'd be chucking even more food away.

KARL'S FACTS

The toy company Mattel sold Wonder Woman's 'invisible jet' as an April Fool's joke — the package was an empty plastic shell with nothing inside.

Alan's real love is mushroom picking. There are around 3,000 varieties growing around him. I've never been that much of a fan of the mushroom. I was put off them when a girl at school ate a few magic mushrooms from a field at lunchtime and ended up off her tits. She started screaming because she said a king-size Mars Bar was chasing her. To be fair, king-size Mars Bars were a lot bigger back then.

Alan pointed out the lobster mushroom, which he said tasted a little bit of fish, and the sulphur shelf that is nicknamed 'chicken of the woods' as it tastes just like chicken. But the plan wasn't to eat something that only tasted like meat. Alan had another method of hunting down real meat to go with our free veg. When I say hunt, no weapons were going to be used as there was no way I could kill something. I love eating meat but if I had to kill the animal myself I'd be eating acorn pie tonight. No, the food we were going hunting for was already dead. As well as Alan using food that has grown around him, he is also prone to eating a bit of food that has been killed by traffic on the local roads. You may have heard of the surf 'n' turf meal, meaning fish and meat, well, now another option is surf 'n' turf 'n' tarmac. Alan eats roadkill.

ALAN: I was looking at statistics as to how many are out there and depending on who you ask there are one hundred million to four hundred million roadkill in the US per year. Which is about two hundred and fifty thousand a day.

KARL: Two hundred and fifty thousand things a day are being hit by a car?

ALAN: It's shocking.

KARL: God, yeah. Really then, we should be eating it. It's a waste, innit, if you don't?

ALAN: Yeah, you could say that for sure.

I hate food being wasted. Putting edible food in the bin feels as wrong to me as throwing litter on the street. I was brought up not to waste food, so much so that the story of Goldilocks wound me up as a kid with her 'this porridge is too cold' and 'this porridge is too hot'. I never understood why the silly cow didn't just mix the lot together and sort the problem that way. I never bother checking use-by dates either, as I think they're responsible for a lot of food being chucked that is really quite safe to eat. I have my own methods of testing if food is edible or not. I use my eyes and nose, and if they're not sure I'll pop the food in front of the cat, as he normally eats anything. Not so long ago I caught him with his head in the neighbours' recycling bin licking away at a jar of Marmite. So if he can eat that but then turns his nose up at some slightly shiny ham, I know something is wrong.

But most of the time, even though stuff can look a little bit off, it can be sorted quite easily. I suppose this is where I do my risk-taking in life. I might not be one for doing adrenaline-fuelled activities like sky diving and bungee jumping but I will risk eating slightly rotten food, which could give me more of a stomach-churning experience than any bungee jump. A trick I use for saving a few dodgy-looking beef slices is wiping them with vinegar. Normally I like to slice a couple of pickled onions to stick on a beef sandwich anyway, so I'll tip some of the vinegar from the jar onto the beef and wipe it down with some kitchen roll. I came up with it after watching those two cleaners Kim and Aggie on TV. They said vinegar shifts all sorts.

KARL: What could be on the menu for tonight then?

ALAN: Well, I found a turkey. And I've picked up snake, squirrel, skunk, possum. You just never know.

I'm not sure we have enough roadkill in the UK to make this a way of life for everyone. Alan lives in an area with quite a bit of woodland where the animals are not used to people and their fast cars, whereas in London foxes are so streetwise they look both ways before they cross the road. I swear there's a fox where I live that is so accustomed to modern life he always turns up in our area on the nights when the food bins full of scraps are put out. I can tell by its markings that it's the same one each time. That fox has a better grip on the waste collection timetable than I do. Many a time his appearance has reminded me to put the bin out.

Outside London, the roadkill I see the most is the badger. If it wasn't for the fact that they are useless at crossing the road I don't think I'd ever see one as they are very elusive. It's as if nature knew they were going to get run over often and gave them a white line on their back so dead squashed ones could act as road markings. Anyway, I'm not sure badgers would be safe to eat as they carry TB, and I don't think even vinegar from a jar of pickled onions could get rid of that.

We were not driving for long before Alan spotted something lying by the road. It was a dead raccoon. We got out of the car to go and inspect it. It had obviously been hit by a passing vehicle and used its last moments of life to crawl to the roadside. It was a beautiful creature with no visible damage to it, but it was letting off quite a smell.

KARL: Poor sod. How old's that, do you think?

ALAN: I guess just a day or two. The thing is, the weather is so cold this time of year that it gets preserved for quite a while. I've had raccoon before. It's pretty good for a stew. It can be too fatty for some people. But that was fresher than this.

KARL: So we'll leave that?

ALAN: Yeah, but we can give it a burial.

We moved the raccoon off the road and put it in some bushes thirty feet away from the passing traffic, where it could be eaten by other wild animals without the danger of them being hit by cars too.

Alan continued to drive while I kept my eyes peeled. Five more minutes down the road there was another raccoon, but it looked like it had been there a while and driven over quite a few times. I don't know much about raccoons but they're certainly not good at crossing the road. North Carolina could carpet the pavements with the crushed creatures. The 'why did the chicken cross the road?' jokes would never work with raccoons as the answer would always be 'to get run over'. Nowadays it's easy to guess why the chicken wanted to cross the road. It was probably to get away from the numerous fried chicken shops.

ALAN: I have friends with dogs who have really nice coats, and I've asked them if their dog dies could I make a rug out of it.

KARL: How did that go down?

ALAN: Well, they laughed . . . I don't know.

KARL: It is a funny one. If you had a cat or a dog and you looked after it properly, should you be allowed to eat it? You've spent money on it. If anything, it might stop animal cruelty, because if you know you're gonna have a good meal when it dies, you're not gonna want to give it rubbish food.

I think killing foxes and other animals just for their fur is disgusting, but if Alan was to find a dead animal, eat it, and then go on to make a pair of slippers out of it, surely that's a good thing. Does reincarnation always mean living on as another creature? What about living on through a garment of clothing? To me that makes a lot more sense than an animal just being left to rot or driven over until there's nothing left of it. Thinking about it, Alan mentioned that he'd picked up quite a few possums that had been hit by cars. Possums are marsupials, which means they have a pouch for raising their young in. This is an ideal animal for clothing as it comes with ready-made pockets.

KARL: I don't understand why eating roadkill is such a taboo.

ALAN: Well, there is a taboo on foraging in general. Picking up something from the ground instead of buying it is the image of scavenging.

KARL: But that's how it all started! Caveman wasn't nipping into a Tesco Local, was he? He was walking around finding food.

ALAN: Yeah, you're right, and we like to think we are past that and better than that. That's why it's looked down on now.

There are loads of taboos that are worse than this. You've got people who are going about sticking their knob in women's shoes (not while they're still wearing them – well, at least I don't think so). Necrophilia – people who have it away with dead bodies! I wouldn't even give a thing like that a name as by doing so it almost makes it seem like a 'thing'. Giving the act a name pretty much gives it a reason to exist. I'd say the word 'mental' should be used for people with these fetishes.

Apart from another couple of raccoons, there wasn't much else on offer in terms of roadkill (which I was kind of glad about), but Alan said he had one or two pieces in his freezer at home that we could eat. He wasn't lying. He lifted the lid of his freezer and it looked like he had the whole cast from a Beatrix Potter book sat in there. Between his ice cubes and choc ices were a rabbit, a fox and a wing from a turkey! Having just the wing seemed odd at first, and then I remembered I had a full bag of

THERE'S A RAT IN MY KITCHEN WHAT AM I GONNA DO? POP IT IN A 180° OVEN FOR 30 MINS.

chicken wings in the freezer, so what's the difference? He said he also had a squirrel in his fridge. In the end I opted to try squirrel. I thought if I didn't enjoy it at least there would be less waste.

I see squirrels almost daily at home but never get the chance to get as close up as I did with this one. It was a gorgeous-looking thing. Perfect, apart from a damaged head, which made me think it might have killed itself by falling from a tree. I wasn't worried about eating it in the slightest. I've been greeted many a morning by a crumpet that was in worse condition than this creature. Sometimes the crumpets are covered in so much mould they look like Kermit the Frog's brother, but after a bit of scratching with a knife it comes away quite easily. Compared to that, this roadkill squirrel was positively fine dining. Or should that be 'find dining'.

In some ways I've never been more confident that what I was about to eat was more environmentally friendly than most of what I've been eating for years. I didn't feel guilty about eating this squirrel as it hadn't been killed to eat; it had been running around freely and had an accident – whereas I remember not feeling so happy when I went out to a fancy place known for its steaks with Suzanne. Instead of having your bog-standard menu, some bloke comes out with a few different cuts of meat and starts telling you information about how the cow was treated to massages when it was alive and enjoyed drinking beer, which all helps to create a better flavour. I'm not joking.

The fella even said it liked to listen to rock music. The thing is, after being told all of this, it put me off eating it. I felt like I knew so much about the animal I was close to sending a condolence card to its family.

Alan got on with preparing the squirrel. I went and sat down as I didn't fancy watching the early stages of the dissection.

ALAN: I gotta tell you it's amazing inside. It's beautiful. It's life changing to actually do it. It teaches you something about your own body that nothing else can. It's just like us in there. I mean, it's virtually the same organs. It's a very sensual experience, the way it feels. All right, it's done. You can come over. It's no longer an individual, it's just a body. Is that easier?

KARL: Yeah. I'm stupid for acting like this. I eat meat all the time. Suppose it makes me a bit of a hypocrite . . . That's a standard-sized squirrel. How many people would that feed?

ALAN: Good question. It's probably for one. What's a meat serving? Three and a half ounces or something? After the skin comes off I think that's all you're gonna have.

KARL: But look, no packaging! No plastic packaging . . .

ALAN: That's right, and no truck had to go across the country to bring it to us using gas and polluting everywhere.

KARL: Yeah, it makes sense.

I helped remove the fur from what was left of the body and was surprised how easily it slipped off. I've had bananas that didn't leave their skin as easily as this creature did.

I didn't feel sorry for the squirrel any more. Well, at least not as much as I'd felt sad for the raccoon that had been bashed and left for cold, neglected and uncared for. Alan was treating the squirrel with respect, like a surgeon with a patient, as he carefully removed the bladder and intestines that were not to be eaten. He was careful not to waste the heart, kidneys and liver; they were some of his favourite parts to eat as they are full of goodness. He then fried it with some of the greens we had picked up earlier that day. While that was cooking he put the leftover parts of the squirrel in his garden for other peckish animals to find and feast on.

I'm not going to lie. It was pretty tasty. Similar to the sulphur shelf mushroom that Alan told me about, it tasted just like chicken. I've eaten a lot of odd foods on my travels around the world and most of it ends up tasting like chicken.

We ate the lot, so none of it ended up in the bin and neither did any plastic. I wouldn't say there was much chance of eating roadkill in London as there's so many speed bumps and cameras and 20mph speed limits in force that there's more chance of a badger overtaking me than actually hitting one. And anyhow, I wouldn't want that fox of mine to get hit and then eaten, as otherwise I wouldn't know what day to put out my bin of unwanted packaging.

MAKING RUBBISH MUSIC

In 2010 I felt like I had finally made it. After living in flats for over twenty years, me and Suzanne finally got our very own house. Family and mates said things like 'Oh, it'll be nice for you to have your own front door' and 'Finally you've got a bit of a garden.' But, as nice as those things were, the biggest change I was looking forward to was having our own bins.

If you've ever lived in a flat you'll know that it's virtually impossible to see eye to eye with your neighbour if you have to share a bin with them. One of the Ten Commandments states that you should 'Love thy neighbour'; well, I'm sure it was a lot easier back when that list of rules was put together as there was no bin-sharing to argue over. Sharing a bin is like trying to share a gobstopper. It can't be done. And you can't just go piling your rubbish around the bin, as there's now hard and fast rules that the bin men will only take what is in the bin, not what is left around it. And if the lid can't close due to the bin being overloaded, your bin men can refuse to take it altogether. Many a time I would have to throw my leg over and push down on the waste to get at least some of my crap in our bin and make sure the lid would close. I've noticed nowadays a lot of kids seem to have trampolines to jump up and down on, and I'm convinced this is parents preparing their kids for bin-sharing when they get older.

There have been times when I've wished I had the artistic skills of Banksy. Not for the money or admiration he receives for his art, but for the way that whatever he daubs his paint on becomes valuable. The walls he has painted on in the past have ended up being removed and sold, so I imagine if he needs to get rid of an old mattress or some empty cardboard boxes, he would only have to do a quick doodle on them and someone would go and steal his unwanted crap and sell it for thousands at auction. How handy would that be?

Back when I was a bin-sharer, I'd regularly have to take a few carrier bags of rubbish out with me if I was nipping to the shops and dispose of them in the various public bins. I felt like I was feeding ducks, walking around town like a mad bag lady, feeding the bins until they were full. I must have been the only shopper who left the house with more bags than I came back with. I soon had to stop doing this after an old fella said that he would report me for using public bins to get rid of home waste!

Thinking back to all the trouble I had getting rid of my rubbish, it's ridiculous. It would have been easier to get rid of a pork chop at a bar mitzvah. I got on to the council in the end and they dropped off another bin, but the problem didn't go away, as the neighbours filled that one too. That's the weird thing with bins. No matter how many of them are there, there will always be more rubbish to fill them. A bit like TV channels.

After a long twenty-year wait I am now the proud owner of two black wheelie bins for general waste, a blue recycling bin for bottles and paper and card, and two green ones for garden waste. And on the last day of this trip, I was given another wheelie bin – this one was to be used to make music.

I was going to be spending a few hours with a group of eight lads who had formed a band called the Groove Onkels in Osnabrück, North Germany. They use the wheelie bin as their main instrument during their trash percussion performances, by kicking, smashing and hitting it using drumsticks. They want to prove that you don't need to spend lots of money on fancy instruments to make music.

I've always loved music but I've never mastered an instrument, so I was looking forward to this. I went through a short spell of trying to teach myself the guitar but found that my fingers don't work well as individuals. They're great at grabbing things, but expecting them to pull strings at separate times was never going to happen. Especially my little fingers. I've had them all my life and I very rarely see them getting involved. Even as I'm typing this now, most of my fingers get involved hitting a key at some point but my little fingers just hang around being useless like an unwanted work experience kid. Even when I do dirty work, the little fingers remain spotless. The only time I think they get involved is when I make shadow puppets. So, for this reason, I've always thought that the drum would be my ideal musical instrument of choice.

One of the members called Joni gave me a quick introduction to the three different sounds I could get out of the wheelie bin. A kick to the bin gave the sound of a bass drum, opening and closing of the lid played the part of the snare drum, and finally the hi-hat sound was created by hitting the bin anywhere with a stick. I then spent around thirty minutes playing a basic sequence in time with everyone else: kick of bass drum, hi-hat, snare, hi-hat, bass drum, hi-hat, snare, hi-hat, bass drum, over and over. It might sound quite simple but I really had to stay focused to keep up and in time. But I did well enough for the lads to ask me to join them for a performance in the town square later that afternoon. I was keen to keep practising but was cut short when someone came out of an office block who was a bit irate and asked us to move away. Jan, one of the other Groove Onkels, suggested we go to the scrapyard where we could rehearse some more, and also get to pick up some items of waste that could be used to make more sounds.

JAN: Our philosophy is that everything might be an instrument, and there are tons of things that are thrown away by people that we can use to make music.

KARL: So it's not just wheelie bins? You pick all sorts, anything that you can make a sound with?

JAN: Anything! The wheelie bin is just a drum example, but . . . yeah, everything might be an instrument.

It was their passion for making music out of rubbish that got them on the German equivalent of *The X Factor, Das Supertalent*, in 2012. I'm sure there has been more useless shit onstage in that programme than the items that the Groove Onkels had taken from a scrapyard. Although they didn't win it, the experience gave them a platform that now means they're being booked to play around seventy gigs a year.

We got to the scrapyard where there was every sort of scrap metal you could think of, piled as high as a house. There were sections for

scrap cars, broken washing machines, car tyres, steel girders, radiators and piping. There wasn't one bit of metal they didn't have. I reckon they'd have taken the metal fillings from my teeth if I'd let them.

There was such a racket from the mashing machines and cranes throwing the waste around, the noise we were making while practising our drumming wasn't going to offend anyone. It made me wonder if scrapyards and refuse centres should be hired out for private events. You can make as much noise and mess as you like. Any boxes from gifts, party hats and empty bottles of booze could be disposed of instantly. I mentioned earlier how Christmas does my head in with the amount of mess it generates – well, most celebrations make a mess so why not hold them in places like this? I've never understood the point of confetti and party poppers and streamers. Why do we celebrate a special moment by chucking bits of paper all over the place?! If you were to throw shit around at any other time you'd get fined for littering. But at the refuse centre it wouldn't be a problem. Thinking about it, churches should try and do weddings on the same day as funerals so that all the crap thrown in the air at the wedding could then be swept into the hole in the ground or burned at the cremation. I'm always full of ideas.

We jammed using the objects around us before picking some pieces to take to our performance in the town square. I mentioned earlier how my mam doesn't throw much away as everything holds a memory for her – well, I could understand this a bit more as I went through the rubble in the yard. Some of the gear brought a few recollections of my early childhood. There was a broken DJ mixer that took me back to my mobile DJing days, a Black

& Decker Workmate like the one my dad used to have in his shed, and an exercise bike that reminded me of an old school mate called Neil. He wanted a bike for Christmas, but his mam was a bit overprotective and didn't like the idea of him cycling about on busy roads so she bought him a bloody exercise bike. He was well gutted. She mothered him that much she even bought him a helmet for him to wear when he used it. I'd forgotten all about that until I saw it in the scrapyard.

Me and the lads walked around picking things up and hitting them with a drumstick to see what noise the various bits of clobber offered. If the Groove Onkels ever made it really big I could imagine they might take to trashing hotel rooms and throwing TVs out of hotel windows, just like the Sex Pistols and The Who used to, though these lads would then go and pick up the smashed items and make a new album out of them.

After searching for a good forty minutes I left the yard with a dome lid off a barbecue (provided a sound like a triangle), an oven shelf rack (not unlike a harp when a drumstick was dragged up and down it), a petrol tank from a Ford Fiesta (a sound similar to a Jamaican steel drum) and an ironing board that would act as a bench for all my bits and pieces. But the bit of trash I was most happy with was a piece of plastic that I think may have been a lid off a flip-top bin (when rubbed with my drumstick it made a sound like scratching a record).

After putting all our findings into our wheelie bins I was given a pair of orange dungarees to wear that gave us an industrial boy-band look. They were an unnaturally bright shade of orange, much like the orange your fingers turn when you've had a bag of Wotsits (not the little finger though). Once dressed, we dragged our instruments to the town square. That was another good thing about the wheelie bin as an instrument. It has a handle, it's on wheels, and it's quite lightweight, so it's easy to shift. I've seen so many big instruments that, as much as they make some amazing sounds, I could not be arsed moving them about. There was a photo of Myleene Klass in the paper (out of the band Hear'Say) lugging her harp down the road. What a bloody daft design they are. On first glance I thought she was windsurfing. And I'll never forget seeing a bloke who had a double bass on his back,

caught his foot on the pavement and fell over. He struggled to get back up cos of the size and weight of the thing strapped to his back. The funny thing was, as he hit the floor the noise from the bass became the soundtrack to his fall, so it seemed more dramatic than it was.

We got to the town square. It was quite an upmarket place – I'd say comparable to towns in the Cotswolds. Quiet cobbled streets where posh-looking old people in brightly coloured chinos were hanging around outside cafés drinking coffee and chatting. God knows what they made of us as our debris clanged around in our wheelie bins on the cobbles. We must have looked like bin men on some kind of protest march.

We got to a spot and started with the basic sequence of kick of bass drum, hi-hat, snare, hi-hat, bass drum, hi-hat, snare, and then we all took it in turns to improvise. I guess you could call it 'trash jazz'. The crowds sat outside the cafés were now up on their feet, clapping along and taking photos. I found I could do anything as long as I kept in time with the beat. I gave a nod to Joni who counted me in to do a scratching solo using my drumstick on the plastic bin lid. I had the audience to myself. I felt like Bono must have done when singing the line 'Well, tonight thank God it's them instead of you' at Wembley for the 'Do They Know It's Christmas?' song. We played for a good forty minutes, with my petrol tank giving a bit of a calypso sound to each track, and I loved it. Only one spectator at the end said they thought it was a load of rubbish, but I'm still not sure if that was his review or if he was just stating a fact. It's the most fun I've ever had with rubbish, and the memory always comes back to me when I put my bin out for collection.

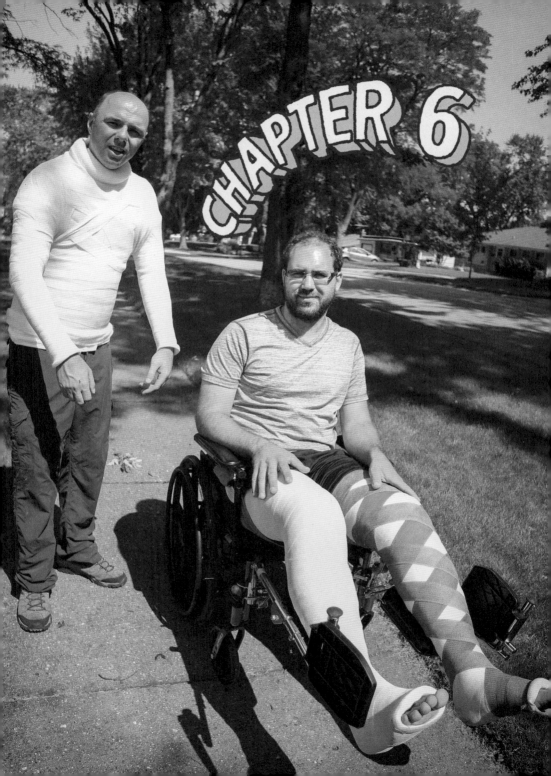

CHAPTER 6

I'VE NEVER BEEN one of those people who has a five- or ten-year plan. I've never really been one for wanting to know too much about what lies ahead either, to be honest. None of us can see what circumstances are on the horizon. We only know one thing for sure, and that is that we'll die in the end. To me it's the bit of mystery between now and then that makes getting up in the morning worthwhile. Well, that and the bacon.

Some people seem to want to plan everything in their lives and if we could invent something that meant we could see into our future I'm sure people would be lining up to have a peek at what's coming for them. I'd imagine seeing my future wouldn't make much sense, and could just end up worrying me. If ten years ago I'd had my future read and been told I was going to write seven books and do thirty TV episodes where I travel the world and spend time with all kinds of strange people, I would have been a nervous wreck. It would have absolutely terrified me as it wouldn't have been something I thought I could do or wanted to do back then. It would be like seeing a massive pile of food and someone telling you 'You're going to eat all that over the next ten years'; it would make you feel a bit ill. But because in reality it all happened fairly slowly over a long period where I've just taken each challenge a step at a time, it has been less daunting.

I also think that if I knew what was to come, life would be rather dull, like watching a recording of a football match when you already know the result. We're living in a world where we want everything NOW and on demand, and I don't think it's a good thing. It doesn't seem to make us any happier. If anything, it's making us more miserable as it's taking away 'the wait' and we're left with nothing to look forward to.

PREDICTING THE FUTURE

So anyway, here I was in Berlin, lying face down on the bed in my hotel room with my pants around my ankles while a blind man felt my bare arse with his fingers. This isn't me attempting to write an erotic Fifty Shades of Grey-style novel. This was actually happening. It was the beginning of my next trip where I was going to be looking at the topic of time. And I was starting with my future.

Now, if you think that being able to have your future read is a load of old arse, Ulf Buck would probably agree with you, as he was the visually impaired fella who was touching my buttocks. He uses this unique way to predict what is in front of you, by having a good feel of what is behind you. He believes that everything is predetermined and is recorded on your butt. This method is called rumpology.

I lay there in silence as he touched my backside very gently with soft strokes, like he was skimming through photographs on an iPad. He didn't utter a word for a good few minutes so I was lying there wondering what was going on. I mean, with my arse being so hairy and him being so blind, I was convinced he had forgotten about me and thought he was just stroking a cat. I asked what was going on back there and he said he was busy analysing (appropriate word) every lump, bump, crack and crevice, which according to Ulf held the story to the rest of my life. While I waited patiently and anxiously for the verdict, I wondered if being blind was the reason he got into predicting the future. It puts him on an even par with his clients in some ways as we're all blind when it comes to our future.

Although I'm not one for obsessing over my future, I was still intrigued to see what my arse had to say. Even though there was a possibility it could be a load of hot air (after all, that's what it usually gives out), I was interested to hear about its plans for me. To be fair to Ulf, I suppose we use other parts of our bodies to come to conclusions. We sometimes trust the 'gut feeling' we get at certain points in our lives, and we are always being advised to 'do what your heart desires', but maybe it's the arse that really has all the answers.

Ulf blurted out his first bit of future news.

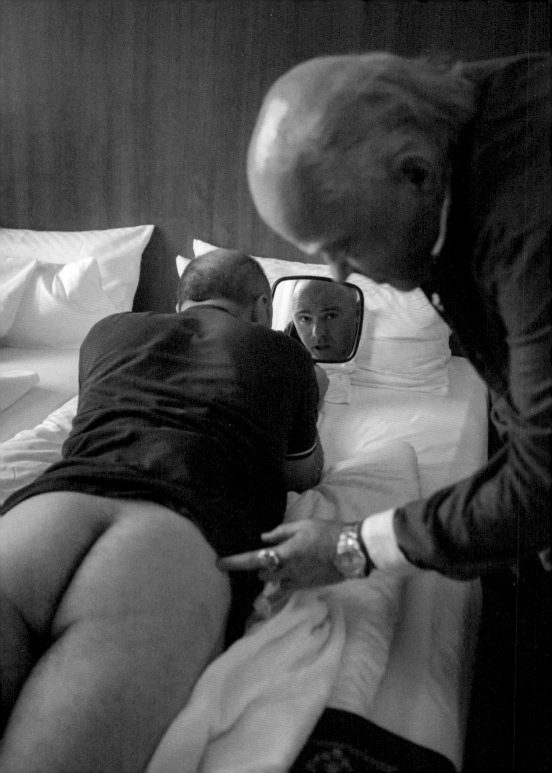

ULF: There is going to be a house abroad.

KARL: Whereabouts? Where are we looking here? Europe? America?

ULF: One moment . . . (*carries on feeling*) . . . It is south bound . . .

KARL: South bound?

ULF: I can say it is going to be Spain or Italy.

KARL: It is going to be Italy. My girlfriend likes Italy . . . In fact three days ago we were talking about buying a place in Italy. That is weird, that is weird . . . When are we looking at then, what year are we talking?

ULF: February or March next year.

KARL: Jesus, that is quick.

This was pretty spooky as we really had been talking about going there, and since getting back from this trip Suzanne has mentioned that she'd like to go away for her birthday, which is in March, to a place in Italy called Puglia, which believe it or not is pronounced 'Poolia'. Of course my arse would want to go to a place called Poolia.

I wanted to ask Ulf if he could do rumpology on animals as I imagine a chimp's arse would be a really interesting read – it would be like a pop-up book – but he seemed to be so engrossed I didn't want to disturb him. His fingers were now moving faster on my hairy arse cheeks. It was like he was foraging, as if he was looking for a lost earring in a shaggy rug. Maybe he was speed reading, trying to find something of interest to report back to me.

KARL: Anything else?

ULF: You need to watch out for your heart. There's just too much going on.

KARL: Too much what? What – too much stress? What do you mean?!

ULF: No, no, no. Wife. Girls.

KARL: What? Girlfriend?

ULF: Yes.

KARL: No, We're all right. We're quite happy together.

ULF: No. That's a problem.

KARL: What do you mean, there's a problem?!

ULF: Yes.

KARL: Hang on, what are you talking about? The woman I'm with now, or is this someone else?

ULF: Someone else.

KARL: Well . . . anything else you can tell me about her? What does she look like? What does she do as a job? Just so if she comes along, I know this is the woman that is going to ruin my life, and I can knock it on the head.

ULF: She works in justice. Judiciary system.

KARL: What, in courts and stuff, do you mean? I don't know anyone that does that.

ULF: It is going to happen in the future, and whether you like it or not there is going to be a child.

KARL: No.

ULF: Yes.

KARL: No chance! There is not going to be a kid.

ULF: There is going to be a child. It doesn't matter if you believe it or not, you have to think what you're going to call him. It doesn't mean you're going to become a father right away, but in your life there is going to be a child. You may not like it but it is going to happen inevitably.

I didn't know what to make of this information. It seemed to me that my arse was doing what it does best, and that is spouting shite, as there's no way that I'm going to break up with Suzanne. I couldn't envisage me saying the line 'Listen, we've got to split up. It's not you, it's my arse.' But when I got back home I took some time out to try and get to the bottom of what my arse was going on about, and after a while it came to me. I think the stuff Ulf had reported had hidden messages. They were

THE EXPRESSION 'RING FINGER' MEANS SOMETHING DIFFERENT TO A RUMPOLOGIST.

cryptic clues – or should that be craptic clues? – as to what lay ahead. I reckon when he hinted that there was a woman who works in the justice system who could come along causing problems, he may have been talking about my mother 'in law'. Maybe she's the one who's going to rock the boat at some time in the future. Now *that* I can believe.

The bit he touched on about me having a child – another word for a child is a little nipper, and me and Suzanne have been talking about getting a puppy, which to begin with are little nippers, aren't they? I don't know, I might be clutching at straws here but that's the best I could come up with. One thing is for sure, though, if Ulf actually meant I was going to have a real child then I'd go as far as to say that I think he was well and truly talking out of my arse.

LIVING ON AFTER DEATH

I'm not very sociable. The idea of entering a room full of people I don't know usually fills me with dread, and yet here I was mingling with a good forty-odd strangers. I spent a short time with each of them, and they were all fascinating in their own little way and all had something different to teach me. As I moved on from person to person I didn't have to worry about what their opinion was of me as I knew they wouldn't have one. The reason being they were all dead.

I was at the Plastinarium in Guben, Germany, a fully operational plastination laboratory, set up by physician and inventor Gunther von Hagens. If you're not aware of him, or aren't one of the forty million or so people worldwide who have attended one of his exhibitions, you might not be familiar with his Plastination process. I'll explain. In short, by using various chemicals and a few complicated techniques he is able to take a bunch of once living bodies and arrange them into a variety of stretching and leaping poses, while at the same time exposing the organs, muscles, nerves and tendons through sliced skin. The end result looks pretty mental. To give you a rough idea, imagine the cast of *Dawn of the Dead* doing a Zumba class. Gunther hopes by touring the bodies around the world it will educate the public about health and the anatomy.

I had been to one of these exhibitions years ago at the Science Museum in Manchester and had taken my auntie Nora along for a day out. I remember her walking round and pointing at the bodies stripped of skin, saying 'I've had that removed, and that replaced, and one of them taken out.' There's nothing left of her these days. In fact I think there are probably more contents in a bag of crisps. She's been so messed with over the years that I'm surprised the surgeons haven't considered using Velcro instead of stitching her up time after time. She's been opened up more times than a branch of Starbucks.

The odd thing was that I remember some of the exhibits looked in better shape than she did. She's had so many joints replaced with metal ones that if she donated her body to this show, once she'd been stripped of her skin it would look like they'd hired bloody RoboCop for security.

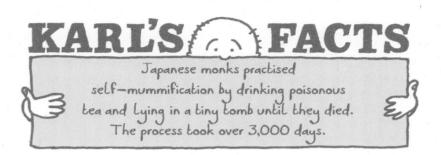

KARL'S FACTS

Japanese monks practised self-mummification by drinking poisonous tea and lying in a tiny tomb until they died. The process took over 3,000 days.

Anyway, that was back in 2008. Seven years on, there I was at the actual Plastinarium. And I wasn't just looking at the finished posed bodies, I was there to help prepare a specimen and think about whether this would be a good way to increase my time on earth once I was dead.

It's funny how people are always planning for the future. They plan a career path, they plan holidays and even organise a pension plan for the future, and yet not many seem to like the idea of planning what happens to their own remains after death. It's almost like they believe that if they don't plan anything then they won't die, but unfortunately it doesn't work that way. There's no escaping it. Death is a bit like jury duty, in the way that you don't know when you might be called up, but when you are there's no getting out of it. But if you were to be plastinated, it kind of gives you more time on earth. Yes, okay, if I was plastinated I wouldn't be aware of what was going on around me, but to be honest there's times when I feel like that now.

Let's face it, as weird as this option sounds, the other choices aren't that great, are they? You can be cremated and totally disappear off the face of the earth, or you can be buried and left to rot away. At least if you're plastinated you're still around to mix with the living at one of Gunther's exhibitions or in a medical school where students can look at and touch your undecaying plastinated parts. I quite like the idea of being useful and educating people after I die. There's a bit of pressure to say something profound with your final breath and to pass on some useful knowledge, but I just know that I'll have nothing important to say with mine. I reckon I may as well blow up a balloon for someone with my last breath. But if I was plastinated I would teach someone something. It is a bit annoying that I have to be dead before that happens, but better late than never.

I actually recognised one of the bodies in the Plastinarium from the exhibition I went to in Manchester. It was a man presented as a goalkeeper, diving in mid-air to save a ball. He hadn't aged since I'd last seen him, as plastination freezes you in time. It was odd to think that I never met this man when he was alive, and yet since he'd been dead I'd bumped into him twice in two different locations.

Some of the displays were pretty mental. There was one person who had been made to look like he had exploded. All the individual parts that make up the human body were being held by different lengths of fishing wire. It was hard to imagine that this person once walked and talked, worked and maybe had a family, and yet here they were dangling from the ceiling like a wind chime! Hundreds of separate pieces. It reminded me of the cured meats you see hanging behind the counter in Carluccio's, except there was no chance of this fella being cured.

There was another display of a body that had been cut into slices as thin as wafer-thin ham. I struggle to cut a neat slice of bread from a freshly baked loaf yet Gunther had managed to flawlessly carve this body from top to bottom, through bones and organs. It was like looking at a sliced pork and egg Gala pie, where you can see the layers of pastry, jelly, pork and egg.

It looked mad, and it really hit me how much stuff we're carrying around to make our bodies operate. I really don't understand how it can all be made from just a sperm and an egg. The more I looked at how complicated it all was, and thought about how all that gear runs twenty-four hours a day just to keep me alive, the more I started to feel guilty about feeding my body doughnuts as fuel.

While I was enjoying the company of the 'plastinites', which is the name given to the bodies, a real living person came along to say hello. Her name was Angelina. She has been working with Gunther since 1988 and ended up marrying him in 1992. She now runs the business side of the exhibitions.

BUMPING INTO STEVE MERCHANT WAS A NICE SURPRISE.

KARL: I am wondering whether this is for me, if this is the way that I would like to go – you know, a way of staying on the planet for a bit longer.

ANGELINA: You are welcome.

KARL: Yeah? Is it as easy as that?

ANGELINA: We have a body donation programme where people sign up during their lifetime. You sign a form, send it in – it is a sort of 'declaration of will'. If you change your mind over the years, of course you're welcome to withdraw. We initiate body donation meetings, where donors come together. We like to inform our donors about ongoing projects, our exhibitions, and they're entitled to see our laboratories. And interestingly when they come afterwards they say 'I am totally relieved because now I know what will happen once I am dead.'

KARL: So hang on then . . . This dead body stood here, do you remember meeting this man?!

ANGELINA: To be very honest, I don't know whether I have met this person in life.

KARL: Right . . . Well, at the moment I'm looking at it all and thinking, it's not a bad option, so why not?

ANGELINA: I mean, I am a body donor myself as well.

KARL: You're definitely going to do this?

ANGELINA: Yeah. I hope it is not coming too early, but it is just a body. It is not me any longer, it is not what I regard myself to be 'me'.

Even though time has now passed since being at the Plastinarium, I still don't think it's a bad option. I mentioned the idea to Suzanne and she said that if it was what I really wanted, then she would be fine with it, but she wasn't sure if she'd want to visit the finished thing. That made me look at it the other way and wonder if I'd be happy if Suzanne wanted to donate her body. I wasn't sure. It's probably an easier decision when it's your own body. Luckily I've never had to deal with the death of anyone who I'm really close to, so I have no idea how I'd feel about this being done to someone else.

Some car companies use dead bodies as crash test dummies. Sensors locate and measure the force upon impact and give more accurate data as to what happens to the internal organs during a crash than a plastic dummy could. I couldn't imagine being keen on Suzanne being used like that. The other place I wouldn't like her to end up is the body farm, which is a research facility for studying the decomposition of human bodies. The donated corpses are placed in private woodlands and then monitored to see how they decompose under various circumstances. If you watch TV programmes like *Midsomer Murders* or *CSI* you'll be familiar with the person who comes along to a scene where a dead body has been found and predicts how long they've been dead for. Well, it's thanks to this research they can work it out. It's daft that I wouldn't like Suzanne to donate her body to this important cause as I know that the same rotting process would take place if she was buried in a coffin six feet under, but I'd just find it a bit much to handle. The idea that she would be left abandoned in a field somewhere in all weathers would do my head in. At least with plastination she wouldn't be left out in the cold. In some ways the Plastinarium is like a spa – one that gets rid of fat and wrinkles and gives you the ultimate skin peel.

The only problem I can foresee is that I could get protective over her plastinated body and end up wanting to keep it. I wouldn't be surprised if someone has requested this to be done privately. I mean, if you think about it, it's not unusual to keep a loved one's lock of hair or their ashes in an urn. We're told that we shouldn't forget the dead; well, it would be pretty hard to forget them if they were sat in your front room. And really it's not too different from having a bowl of plastic fruit in your kitchen instead of the real stuff. I guess this would be one up from that.

If you think about it, there are more dead people on the earth than living and yet we never see them. Maybe if we did we might talk about it more openly, which might also help us not to fear it so much. I told Angelina about my idea of private plastinates.

ANGELINA: I think it would not be a good idea. I mean, for the generations who are still alive and have a relationship to that person, maybe it would make sense to some extent. But once the mourning is over, it may become just an object. And have you thought about these specimens staying around more or less for ever? They are permanently preserved. They will not rot for the next decade, hundreds, maybe even thousands of years to come. Once our generation has passed away, who would care for your girlfriend?

I don't know why she turned on the idea. I'm not the one running a factory full of dead people playing football and doing star jumps! As for taking care of specimens, the same could be said about gravestones, as loads of them are not being looked after. You can't walk through a graveyard without seeing badly damaged headstones and overgrown weeds everywhere. If we were to get to a point where we were really relaxed around these plastinated bodies, they could possibly take the jobs of mannequins in shop windows. Since the birth of online shopping, it's always reported that town centres and high streets are dead. Why not make a thing of that and use the dead to get people back to the shops? You could pay your respect to Granddad as he's modelling his favourite chinos in Top Man. Some of these plastinates have more life in them than a lot of shop assistants I've come across.

Angelina took me to meet Vlad, who worked in the lab. I was to help him pose a body for the exhibition. The first thing he told me was that he didn't call them bodies – once the person was in the hands of the plastinaters it should always be referred to as a specimen. He then proceeded to give me a crash course in the various steps involved in plastination. The first stage involves pumping a formaldehyde solution into the body through the arteries to kill bacteria and stop tissue decay.

On reflection this was the toughest stage for me. The specimen was being held in a refrigerated storage drawer on a trolley. Even though he was covered by a thin white sheet I could see he was a rather large man. Vlad told me he had died only a couple of days earlier. As we pushed the trolley across the tiled floor, the bloated stomach wobbled. Even though I'd been surrounded by death all morning, this felt different. He looked somehow deader than the plastinates I'd been hanging around with in their superhero poses. As we turned the trolley into position a hand slipped from under the sheet. I could see the rough chipped fingernails on his hand. I think it was these little details that made him more human than the well-presented plastinates.

While Vlad cut open the skin on the leg to get to the artery, I focused on the tools he was using. There was a spray gun on the end of a hose that is used to wash the bodies down, and it was exactly the same as the one I have at home for watering the garden. It was odd to see it in this setting. When I get a minute I must go online and write a review for it on Amazon: 'Multi Spray Gun, Five Stars. Excellent sprayer with lots of different spray modes. Ideal for spraying lawn and plants, and washing blood and guts from dissected bodies! Would highly recommend this product :).'

We left the specimen, as it would take quite a while for the chemical to fill the body. Vlad wasn't much of a talker, but this could be due to him spending most of his waking hours with the dead, so I just followed him to another part of the huge laboratory where I was greeted with another specimen. This one was at the dissection stage. Again, the face was covered, but the skin on the chest area had been cut and acted as a lid to the organs. Vlad just lifted it up as if lifting the bonnet on a car, revealing all the workings inside. I helped to cut a few tubes here and there so we could remove the organs from the body in one piece, leaving a hollow carcass. I'd say that was probably the most insane thing I have done, and will ever do, in my life. It was like emptying a suitcase by picking everything up in one go and putting it in the washing basket – except surprisingly this didn't smell as bad.

Vlad let me have a go at carefully removing fatty tissues from the arm using a scalpel, which I found difficult as adrenaline was pumping

round my body and making my hands shake. It's quite a laborious job that he said can take months to complete.

The final specimen I saw was one that was ready to pose. All the water and fat had been removed and replaced with a kind of silicone rubber. The specimen was around five foot nine. Because the skin had been stripped away, there was no way of telling his age, though the bushy eyebrows, long ears and nostril hair would put him anywhere between my age and ninety. Vlad asked me if I had any ideas as to how we could pose the specimen. I came up with a couple of concepts.

The first thought I had was to place all of the organs from the body into a bag and have the specimen stand holding it. I would call the pose 'Bag for Life'. It would show just how much we carry around inside us to give us life. Vlad didn't seem blown away by the idea, but this could have been due to the slogan 'Bag for Life' not being known in Germany.

My second idea was to have the specimen holding a carving knife as if he was about to cut into the pile of heart, kidneys, lungs and liver that would all be placed on some kind of spike in front of the standing body. The title would be 'Donor Kebab' and it would promote organ donation. Donor cards could even be placed by the exhibit for the living public to take away.

I don't know what Vlad thought of it. I'd found it easier to read the faces of the dead people I'd seen that day but he was happy to help me try to create the pose. After using ribbons and clamps to stand the specimen up, I then tried to position the arm with the knife. I soon found that this wasn't going to be as easy as I first thought. Vlad explained that to do something like this the arms really needed to be placed into the required setting before they are filled with the silicone rubber. I tried to add a little bit of pressure to see if I could force the arm into position but it wouldn't move. Vlad watched on as I basically arm-wrestled a dead fella. This was when he explained that it can take 1,500 man hours to model a specimen into a pose. I only had an hour due to the fact that I had a plane to catch. I left after telling Vlad that maybe I'd meet with him again at some point in the future when I wasn't in a rush to go anywhere . . .

GROWING OLD WITH TIME

'GOOD JESUS?!' I said, as I saw my reflection in the mirror. What was staring back at me was my grim-faced, jowly eighty-year-old self. It had only taken three hours in make-up, but when my chair was turned to face the mirror it was as if I'd just been woken up from a coma after thirty-seven years. The prosthetic foam latex mask that had been fitted wasn't any old face. It had been made from a cast of my own head, so I could see me, but an old me. Every line and wrinkle had been made more prominent. Age spots had been added to give my skin the appearance of perfectly cooked lasagne. The hair that was left on my head had parted even further and was white, wild and wiry. I also had eyebrows to match. If this was how I was going to look when I was older I doubted many kids would have the nerve to come and knock on my door to ask for their ball back.

The point of all this was for me to get a taste of what time can do to your body.

Once my face had been aged, it was time for the rest of my cracking body to catch up. When I say cracking, I don't mean cracking as in 'sensational', I actually mean it's cracking! There's no way I could be a cat burglar nowadays as my joints make way too much noise. When I make my way upstairs Suzanne thinks I'm eating a Dime bar.

LOOKING LIKE A CROSS BETWEEN MY DAD AND MY TESTICLES.

To age my body I was kitted out with a suit created to mimic some of the troubles that the elderly face. It had actually been designed for nurses to wear to give them an insight as to what their patients feel when trying to perform basic tasks. It was made up of weights and straps that restricted my every movement to simulate joint stiffness. I also popped on a pair of heavy uneven shoes that caused me to shuffle and be unsteady on my feet.

What I ended up with was the head of my dad and the body movements of my auntie Nora. She's probably the oldest person I know. She's one of them people who has always been old to me and has been in and out of hospital for as long as I can remember. She's at the doctor's that often they ask for her opinion on soft furnishings for the waiting room. You think I'm joking. I don't know how much longer she has left but the amount she has to spend on pills, I'm hoping she leaves me her Boots loyalty card in her will.

My body now looked and felt physically old, I'd say about the age of eighty-two or eighty-three. I was to get a real taste of what may lie ahead when I was given a room in the Bay Vista Commons retirement home in Bremerton, Washington, USA.

I hobbled into my apartment and was greeted by a single bed. I suppose this is what my life may be like if Suzanne dies before me. I sat down feeling exhausted just from the short walk I had done from the car. I would normally be quite happy staying at home on my own while Suzanne goes out shopping or to see a mate. I just keep myself occupied with little DIY jobs that I show off to her on her return. But knowing Suzanne wouldn't be coming home and the effort it would take to move my old body, I really didn't feel like doing much. One of the things I thought I'd look forward to in old age was getting a B&Q diamond card, which gets you ten per cent off most gear on Wednesdays if you're an OAP. If there's one thing I've learned from wearing this suit it's that I'd have to leave the house on Tuesday if I wanted to take advantage of that offer. It was a real wake-up as to what my future could be like, with early death being my only get-out clause.

Simon the director said I should have a walk about the home rather than being miserable in my room, so I headed for one of the communal areas. The suit seemed to be getting heavier by the minute and was so weighty it was making me slouch. Every movement had to be carefully thought through. I found that I was always looking ahead for the next place where I could plonk myself down to rest. It was as if my life had turned into one big, very slow game of musical chairs.

KARL'S FACTS

The oldest person ever was a French woman who died in 1997 at 122 years old.

It shocked me how dejected I became in such a short space of time. The worse part about it was the way my brain knew what it wanted to do but my body took a while to actually perform the command. It was like using the TV remote when the batteries are starting to die. I found it hard to contemplate that my body could be in this state one day.

Before this experience, the idea of being in a home never bothered me. When I was at school me and a couple of mates were sent to an old people's home on the estate I grew up on. I'm not sure if it was a community thing or if it was some kind of punishment, but I do recall enjoying my time there. I was given the job of handing out biscuits, because I had the cleanest, least chewed fingernails of the three of us. We could help ourselves to tea and biscuits and watch the entertainment supplied by some local singers. I even sat and played seven-card rummy with a couple of the fellas. I loved it. It felt like we were on a cruise ship with all the free food and entertainment, but the residents were captains of this ship and would be going down with it. It never really entered my head that I would be as old as them one day.

I eventually found a communal room where a group of eight residents were sat playing bingo. They introduced themselves to me by giving me their name and then their age followed by when their next birthday would be. I wondered if this was because they were all living the same sort of life and it was only their age that made them different.

Maybe their next birthday was the only thing left to aim for. My dad mentions his age a lot more than he once did. He's always saying there can't be long left for him on the planet, joking that he no longer buys long-life milk as he may not be around to finish it. I put this down to the fact that most of his older mates died around the age he is at now. Friends Reunited is a walk round the graveyard for my dad.

A carer was calling out bingo numbers but nobody seemed to be playing by the rules. I think they just thought he was guessing their ages. It saddened me seeing how some of these people looked lost and confused. In some ways hanging around seemed a more frightening concept than dying if this was how my life was to go. Science is always shouting about how great the human race is and how people are living longer than ever due to medicine, but to me it seemed the only people benefiting from this were the ones selling the drugs, not the ones taking them.

Life can be pretty cruel in the way it leaves you behind, but everything moves so quickly these days it's difficult to keep up. I've got an iPhone 4 that no longer gets the software updates so it now runs slower and slower, and shuts down if I give it too many commands. In a way, that's how I feel at the age of forty-three. It's like I no longer get the updates. I can't imagine how confused I'm going to be in my later years. I wonder if this is why my arse came up with the idea of me and

Suzanne moving to Italy. I think it's a good place to be as you get older, as you don't have to deal with so many changes. In Rome there are buildings still standing 2,000 years after they were built, but when I go back to Manchester after being away from it for nine months, buildings have been replaced and roads have moved so my brain has to work out new routes. Honestly, I think the A to Z is now printed weekly, there's so many changes. That would never happen in Rome, and it would be one less thing to confuse me in later life.

Next I was headed to meet a man called Mike Walton at the Bremerton Memorial Stadium. He wanted to show me that though he was in his seventies he hadn't given up on life. He and many other retired people were taking part in a senior track and field event. When Mike introduced himself, he just told me his name without following on with his age like the folk back at the home. Mike was the same age as some of those people I'd left to play bingo, but you wouldn't have thought so. He had issues with his legs (both were strapped up to give them support) but he didn't let that stop him getting involved in the sports events. I suppose it's easy to sit back once you hit a certain age in your life, as in some ways it's expected of you. If you had an elderly relative who was going out for a jog in their seventies or eighties you'd probably be worried sick, but in some ways it's just as deadly to sit and do nothing.

I had a slow warm-up jog round the track with him.

MIKE: I started competing nine years ago. I was accumulating medals and doing pretty well, so I felt really good about myself – not only my competition standards, but maintaining my health and my longevity. Even the average person can still get out and exercise, or have a goal of competing in something and winning. You can't just give in. The people you saw in the home that are just sitting there are vegetables at sixty-five or seventy. They are people that have given up.

At the time I honestly thought I would have to be careful not to deflate everyone by winning all the races, but that wasn't going to be an issue. In my first race, which was a fifty-metre dash, I came in third after taking a tumble due to the weight of the ageing suit, which was over 30kg. Never mind the egg and spoon race, I was running with a week's worth of food strapped to me, and you can include a huge bunch of sour grapes in that, as things really didn't get much better.

THE DISCUS (80-84 age group)
RAY TIBEAU- **GOLD** :79.01
KARL PILKINGTON- **SILVER** :57.00
LAWRENCE POSEY- **BRONZE** :44.60

THE HIGH JUMP (70-74 age group)
GEORGE JOHNSON- **GOLD** :4.00
BOB SHEEDY- **SILVER** :3.10
KARL PILKINGTON- **BRONZE** :3.60

50 METRES (70-74 age group)
GEORGE JOHNSON- **GOLD** : 8.10
MIKE WALTON- **SILVER** :10.40
KARL PILKINGTON- **BRONZE** :12.25

A part of me wished I'd stuck to the bingo. I was shocked at how fast some of these people were. I was more concerned about catching my breath than catching up with them. I was knackered. It was no surprise really, as I've never been fit or good at sport and never won a race at school sports day. This was mainly caused by the fact that I was continually worrying about running into some dogshit as our school playing fields were used by dog walkers who never picked up the mess they left behind. I think it was my school that came up with the idea of the sack race as that was the only way to get across the field without getting shit on your trainers.

NAP OF HONOUR.

I decided to strip my old-age suit down just a bit, as my competitors were seventy to seventy-five and my suit was ageing me to around eighty-three years old. Plus I was still suffering with jet lag and had been up since 5 a.m. to have all the rubber put on my head. I took a few of the weights off my legs and wrists so I felt more like seventy-three years old and made my way back to the starting line. The OAPs were aware that I had removed some of the ageing suit, and so were the crowd watching. By doing this I had added more pressure on myself, as losing this race without the excuse of the suit would have been really embarrassing.

I was in lane two of five, and Mike was in lane one. After seeing some of the others run I knew that Mike was the one I had to beat. The starter pistol went off. I think the noise reminded the bloke in lane five of the war and he sprinted off to find a bunker. I noticed after a few metres that the fella in lane three had fallen and in turn slowed the bloke in lane four down. Now it was between me and Mike. This was like Man United v. Yeovil in an FA Cup game. The crowd was cheering but I could sense it was for Mike. There were only a few metres left to go and I gave it my all. Leaning as far forward as I could, I legged it.

And I did it. I came first in the hundred metres (age category seventy to seventy-four). My time was 19.56 seconds. Mike picked up silver at 20.09 seconds. I had won a gold. My first ever win. Okay, it was against a man who was old enough to be my dad, but a win is a win.

What I took from the experience was that no matter how old you are, you have to keep going and not use age as an excuse to not to do things. At the end of the day, life is one big race with some hurdles along the way and death as the finish line for all of us. You may as well have a bit of fun before going over it.

KILLING TIME

I've just had a thought. There is a strong possibility that no one will ever read this book. It could be like a message in a bottle that just floats around bookshops but never actually gets read. My AutoCorrect sometimes misses a few of my errors as I'm typing which means even my computer isn't raeding what I'm writing. It's feasible that even though you've bought this book it could still go unread, as we live in a world where there's always something else that you should or could be doing with your time. Even if you *are* reading this, no doubt you've got the TV on in the background and you're also uploading a photo of you and your cat to Twitter. Nobody is giving one thing one hundred per cent attention any more. It's odd that multi-tasking is talked about as if it's a good skill when I actually think single-tasking is a better gift to have, as it means you're really focused and can no doubt do things better and quicker and possibly even enjoy them more.

Iwonderifyouwouldbelessinclinedtodosomethingelsewhilereadingif bookswerewrittenlikethisasyouhavetoconcentratemoreatthetaskinhand asifyoulookawayfromthepagetomesswithyourphoneorlaptopyouwould losewhereyouwere. It's quite a good idea that, as it would also mean less paper would be needed, which is a bonus when you consider there's a possibility that no one could be reading it anyway.

How we choose to spend our 'free time' was what I was looking at next. It's interesting that we use the word 'spend' when talking about time as I think this shows just how valuable it is to us. We are constantly developing things that promise to give us more time – dishwashers, microwaves, Pot Noodles, Velcro – but what are we supposed to do with this extra time? Well, this is where hobbies come into play, which I've been thinking about quite a lot recently.

Cooking is a popular hobby, but as much as I love eating I'm pretty useless at making food. I can just about make ice cubes so I'd say that option is out for me. Suzanne bought me a bike for Christmas so I could go cycling, which seemed like a healthy way of spending some spare time, but I'm now finding it to be a royal pain in the arse. It's one of these bikes that is fitted with a quick-release seat, quick-release wheels and quick-release lights, which means they are also very quick and easy to rob! I'd only had it a week, and even though it was locked to a streetlamp someone still pinched my seat! So now every time I cycle to a café for a brew and a cake I have to take all the bits off so that someone doesn't steal them. I end up sitting in the café surrounded by so many bike parts it looks like a bloody Halfords roadshow. I've been contemplating painting it white so that it looks like a ghost bike, as criminals don't seem to steal those. Plus it would serve as a reminder for people driving past the café to slow down. It's a win-win situation.

KARL'S FACTS

Back in 1936 Patricia Salter had an unusual hobby for a twelve-year-old girl. She collected dirt.

I was off to meet a man named Kevin who had a peculiar hobby that I was going to try for myself. I rang his doorbell and had to wait quite some time for him to open it, due to him being on crutches as both of his legs were in plaster casts. I followed slowly behind him as he hobbled his way through to the kitchen before propping himself up against the sideboard. He was in a good mood. He wasn't suffering any pain now, and in fact he never had – he hadn't broken his legs, he is just fond of wearing orthopaedic casts. This was his hobby.

KEVIN: I actually really like the feeling of it. It feels cosy. It's kind of like being wrapped up in a warm blanket on a cold day, but it is rigid so it's kind of a different feeling.

KARL: It just seems like a lot of faff though, you know what I mean?

KEVIN: I am not certain what faff is . . .

KARL: A lot of messing about, a lot of extra work.

KEVIN: Yeah. I mean, it is all part of the ordeal. It's something I enjoy, I guess. I walk around Chicago and there are people in cars and some are like 'Hey, what happened to you?!'

KARL: Is that all part of it then, the attention?

KEVIN: Oh yeah, it is definitely a conversation starter. You know, it definitely engages other people to come up and talk to me. If it's a holiday like the Fourth of July I will have a red, white and blue cast. If it's St Patrick's Day, I'll go green. It's a conversation starter and people are like 'Oh, cool cast!' I am actually kind of socially shy and I cannot just go up and talk to random people.

KARL: But then what happens when you tell them that there is nothing wrong with you?

KEVIN: I've told them fibs – you know, stories. And it is kind of funny because sometimes when I tell people the truth, they think that it is a made-up story.

KARL: (*to Kevin's mum*) What do you think brought this on?

MOTHER: When he was a small child, maybe two or three, there was a little girl that he used to play with. And he went out one day to go play with her and she had broken her arm, and her arm had this cast on that looked like a marshmallow had swallowed her arm, and so he came running to me and was holding on to me and wouldn't let go and was hysterical, crying . . . He couldn't figure out what was going on.

KEVIN: I have no recollection of this . . .

MOTHER: After that he started playing with toilet paper and wrapping it up on his leg, kind of like she had it on her arm. So I think that is what started it.

KARL: At the end of the day it's not the worst thing your son could be up to, is it?

MOTHER: Not at all. Actually I am kind of proud of him. He is doing great.

The plan was for me to get my arms cast, so I could try and get an idea of what Kevin got from doing this. My immediate thought was that it was a total waste of time, and none of us like wasting time. For me the worst is having to wait in for a delivery. It drives me mad. You have to be up early in case you're the first drop-off and then just sit and wait from 7 a.m. to 8 p.m. It's an odd thing as I love being at home. I've got everything around me that makes me happy and yet I can't relax if I'm waiting for a delivery. I put it down to the fact that it's someone else controlling what I do with my time. I keep nipping out to check that the battery on the doorbell is still working, but still don't trust it so end up standing by the window until their arrival. I half wonder if this is a big government ploy to lower street crime. Rather than having police patrolling the streets they have us lot staying in all day gawping out the window waiting for deliveries. Like a new version of Neighbourhood Watch. Just a theory, but it's a good one, innit? I pace around muttering to myself how it shouldn't be this hard to get a delivery while glancing at the clock every thirty seconds and getting angrier as each minute passes. That's the other odd thing with time. It definitely goes slower when you clock watch. It must be a right pain in the arse to work in a watch shop as the day must really drag.

JASON'S OTHER PASTIME IS TURNING INVISIBLE WHEN SAT IN HIS WHEELCHAIR.

In just over an hour I had been cast in plaster, and it was now rock hard. I couldn't move my arms at all as the cast wrapped around the top half of my body, around my shoulders and down my arms. It was like wearing a very rusty suit of armour. My arms had been positioned so I could push Kevin in his wheelchair. Apart from that, they were pretty redundant. I was a human lobster. It was a very strange sensation and one that I've never had before, as fortunately I've never broken an arm or leg. I can't say I was enjoying it at this point. I suppose it's because I'm a bit of a control freak. I can't even handle being in a sleeping bag, so this was always going to be a bit of a challenge.

I quickly became agitated, and I didn't feel myself as I think my arms play quite a big part of me – not just in helping pick things up and carrying stuff, but also in how I express myself. My arms and hands move around quite a lot when I speak, to the point that you could easily think I was giving a running commentary for the deaf. I felt like a part of me had been muted.

I was now really dependent on Kevin. I had to ask him to apply some sun tan lotion to my head to protect it from the sun. He's a mechanic by trade so his hands were really rough. It felt like he was sanding down the top of my head with a brick. We hadn't even left the house yet and I was already feeling pissed off.

We headed to a local restaurant to grab a bite to eat. Kevin's not a small fella, so by the time we got there I was hot and knackered from pushing him in his wheelchair. I couldn't complain though, as I know I would have struggled if I'd gone for leg casts as I suffer with restless leg syndrome, which means I have the irresistible urge to move my legs. It's hard to describe the sensation but it's like my legs have energy trapped inside them that needs to be released. It's not too much of a problem in the day, when I'm free to move around, it's at bedtime when it becomes more of an issue. Suzanne says it's like being in bed with Michael Flatley of *Riverdance* fame on some nights. The only solution I have is to throw my legs out of the side of the bed and let them shuffle from side to side until they calm down a bit. It's an odd thing when your own legs have to stay up later than you do, and what's more annoying is that they tend to wake me up when they come back to bed.

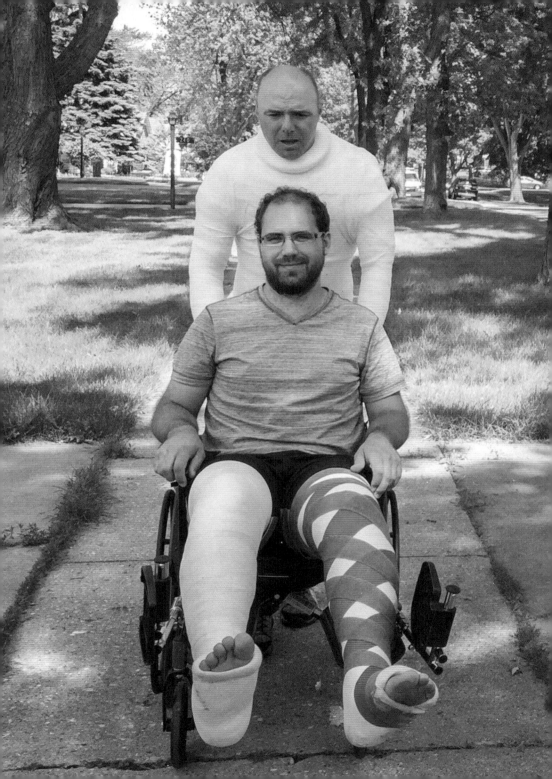

When I got to the counter to order our food, the lady who was serving asked me what had happened, which proves what Kevin had said was true: people do show more of an interest when you are wearing a cast. But I didn't want to lie to her so just said, 'Oh, you really don't want to know,' as I was too exhausted and miffed to want to get into a conversation. Kevin popped the tray of food on his knee, and I weaved in and out of the busy restaurant to a table that had a bit of space around it for Kevin's outstretched legs. He then had to feed me, which really took away the enjoyment of eating – so much so that I left most of it.

Things got worse when some people at another table started cheering. It turned out it was someone's birthday and the whole group started to sing 'Happy Birthday'. That's another thing that has taken up time in my life that I'll never get back. I really hate that song. It follows you through every year of your life and takes at least twenty-two seconds for people to sing. I'm forty-three now, so that adds up to fifteen minutes of my life listening to that shitty birthday song! There was a news story about the oldest living woman in the world, who was 116 at the time, and the clip they showed was of her sat there as her family sang that bloody song for the 116th time in her life. That works out at around forty-three minutes of her existence taken up with it.

Everyone in the restaurant started clapping. Except for me as my hands couldn't reach each other and they just hopelessly flapped about like the arms on a pinball machine.

The only positive that came out of this was that Kevin and I were forced to talk, which is a good thing. I've given up seeing some mates due to them being obsessed with all that social media stuff. I'd be out with them feeling like a spare part while they were all sat there typing away and talking to people they don't even know.

KARL: How much did you say you'd probably spent on this over the years?

KEVIN: Erm, probably quite a bit!

KARL: What sort of figure though, because every hobby costs money, doesn't it?

KEVIN: Probably around five thousand dollars or so.

KARL: And what about your job? Does this not get in the way?

KEVIN: No, no. I mean, I work forty hours a week, Monday to Friday, so it leaves the weekends open. You know, I put the cast on at the weekend so it doesn't get in the way.

So like a lot of people, Kevin spends his weekends getting plastered. He went on to explain that another thing he got out of casting was how it gave him new challenges. He took me to a local games park to show me what he meant. I tried my hand at baseball in a cage where a machine fires a ball at 70mph. I had to turn the whole top half of my body to swing the bat. I managed to hit the second ball, but then the third got its own back by hitting me. I didn't even see it coming, and typically it whacked me on an area of my body that wasn't protected by the cast, right on my inner thigh which produced a fairly nasty bruise.

Next we had a game of crazy golf. Though we made it even crazier. The toughest part wasn't getting the ball into the hole, but getting it out. I had to crawl on all fours to scoop the ball up as there was no way Kevin could bend over with the cast on his legs. I was getting a right sweat on from the extra work that was required to play. I know most golf players have a handicap but this was ridiculous. The interesting thing was, no other players complained about us.

I had a mate when I was a teenager who played golf. I liked the idea of it as I like walking and getting fresh air and don't mind a bit of healthy competition. But I wasn't any good with my swing, so rather than keep on getting beaten, I decided to change my style by not using clubs at all. While he was hitting his ball using a 7 iron, I would just throw my ball by hand. I enjoyed playing it this way as it took a bit of skill to work out how hard to throw the ball and whether to go over arm or under arm before trying to roll it carefully into the hole. I played that way a fair few times. But then the day came when my mate was given a memo saying he would be banned if he continued to bring his friend who insisted on playing with no clubs. So that was the end of that. The funny thing is, I reckon if I'd have had one of my arms in a cast I probably would have got away with it, as the club would have been too worried about coming across as disablist to stop me.

It was now 7.30 p.m. I'd been wearing the cast for over eight hours and desperately needed to pee. I decided to try and crack my way out of the cast. I found if I bent my arm as hard as I could, I could hear the cast

cracking and weakening. After a few strains I had managed to break the cast at the elbow which meant I was free to move my arms again. And I was free to pee. It was the best part of the whole day. There really is nothing like the relief you get when you can finally take a piss after holding it in for a long time. I think they call it a peegasm. Maybe this could be my new hobby. Not so much a pastime, more of a pisstime.

'I WONDER IF HAVING US ALL STAY AT HOME *waiting for* DELIVERIES IS A GOVERNMENT PLOY TO LOWER STREET CRIME. *Like a new version of* NEIGHBOURHOOD WATCH.'

OUR TIME ON EARTH

They say that when you travel you discover things about yourself you never knew. I believe this is true, as on the last day of my trip I found out that my eyebrows didn't work.

I was out on a mission wearing a space helmet and backpack that was providing me with air, when sweat started to run down my forehead, through my brows and into my eyes. It burned like hell. I used to leave my brows to grow. I liked being able to see a few hairs dangling in front of my eyes as it took me back to the time when I had a fringe. But Suzanne dug out an old photo of me from over a decade ago and they were ridiculous. It looked like I'd taken a selfie with two members of ZZ Top. It made me a bit self-conscious so now I let Suzanne trim them if she thinks they need it.

HOUSTON WE HAVE A PROBLEM.
MY HEAD IS ITCHING.

The whole point of the eyebrow is to function as a kind of gutter, to prevent sweat and water from running down into your eyes, but because Suzanne had trimmed mine too much they hadn't done their job. I suppose that now we live in a world where most jobs involve sitting behind desks and moving very little, we don't work up a proper sweat very often and so the eyebrows are a bit unnecessary. This is why most people trim them to a point where they are barely visible. It's this aversion to body hair that I blame for rising sea levels. If you think about the amount of hairy people who used to be knocking about on the planet, all going into the sea on holiday, they would soak up the water and then get out taking a pint or so with them in their hair. These days everyone is bald as a coot so the sea levels have gone up. It's obvious.

I wonder if the eyebrow could be the next big evolutionary change. I think they'll move from above the eyes to below them. Like I said, we no longer sweat as much as we used to, but people cry a lot more. You can't watch TV these days without seeing someone blubbing, so give the eyebrows a new purpose – let them catch the tears. Health reports are always saying people take in too much salt and blood pressure is increasing. Well, I don't think salt from food is to blame. It's from the tears rolling into the mouth from all that sobbing!

Anyway, I'm wittering on. There I was, with sweat stinging my eyes that I couldn't wipe away due to my space helmet. I had to shuffle slowly so as not to stumble across the uneven rocky terra firma beneath my feet while trying desperately to keep up with the rest of Crew 149. I asked the commander if we could stop for a moment to take a breather while I dealt with my problem. Using radio comms he spoke to engineer Sullivan, one of two members of the crew who were back at the Mars research station.

COMMANDER PAUL: Hab, this is EVA lead. We've ascended about a third of the way up the hill. We're taking a five- to ten-minute pause to catch breath and reassess. We expect we will continue on in about ten minutes. Over.

I sat on one of the huge orange rocks that surrounded us while squeezing my eyes tight to try and ease them. Once they had calmed down I took in what was around me. A dusty, barren landscape that went on for as far as my sore eyes could see. The only thing that stood out was the small, white cylindrical building that looked like a pressure cooker.

They call it 'Hab' (habitat). This was home to the seven members of Crew 149. A diverse, professional bunch of individuals from Canada, Belgium, Romania, Japan and the United States who were all dedicated to supporting the exploration and colonisation of Mars. The thing was, we were not on Mars. We were in a rocky corner of the Utah desert.

Even though we were millions of miles away from the real red planet, this place was a dead ringer for it, and while I was with Crew 149 I had to treat it as though it was the real deal, as the most important rule was to simulate everything as authentically as possible. This was the reason I couldn't remove my helmet to wipe my sweaty head.

The whole point of the Mars Desert Research Station is to help the human race survive the next mass extinction that is bound to come one day due to climate change and other factors. Stephen Hawking has even put a time on it and reckons we won't survive another 1,000 years if we don't escape our fragile planet. So this research station was set up to develop the skills and knowledge needed to prepare humans for Mars exploration. If you ask me, I'm really not arsed. Obviously it won't be nice to be around when the shit does hit the fan, but the idea that human life ends at some point doesn't bother me in the slightest. If anything, it annoys me that we think of ourselves as being so important that we must survive no matter the quality of life. Thousands of species become extinct every year and, as bad as that is, life carries on. Just a few days ago there was a report on the radio that some sea sponges are close to extinction. It really is no wonder sea levels are at an all-time high!

The way I look at it is this: the dinosaurs came and went, and one day it'll be our turn to move on. Who ever thought that Woolworths would close down? But it did, and life went on. We've been around for about 200,000 years, which isn't a bad innings, is it? I see young people wearing fashion from the '80s and I've heard they're making *Top Gun 2* – to me that just says we're out of ideas. Let's clear the way and let something new have a go.

KARL'S FACTS

We have a good idea of what other planets would smell like based on their atmospheric composition. Venus and Mars would smell like rotten eggs.

As I sat resting on a red rock the other crew members were using equipment to measure the amount of moisture and acidity in the ground, which was part of their research during their two-week stay at the base. I was nervous that the dust they were causing was going to sneak in through a gap in my ill-fitting helmet and make me sneeze. That would have been embarrassing, as if I have to sneeze, due to my bad back, I have to let it out or I end up pulling a muscle. Luckily it didn't happen, otherwise I'd have been stood there doing an impression of a used condom.

Even though I'd only been there a short time I couldn't imagine this being my life. I don't have a fancy existence but something I do like is a good walk and fresh air on my face. I can only stay in the Westfield shopping centre for about an hour before I need to get out of there, so living like this would do my head in. There would be no sounds of nature from birds, crashing of waves on the shore or wind blowing through trees. These are things that you might take for granted but once they weren't

there you would definitely miss them. It would feel like a punishment and make me really unhappy. And due to the days being thirty-seven minutes longer on Mars, I'd be unhappier for even longer.

After moving a rock that was blocking some mobile communication tower, Commander Paul asked me to help put up the Mars flag, which was red, green and blue. We're obsessed with flags. We haven't even got a human to the planet yet and there's a bloody flag for the place. Cats like to pee on things to mark their territory; we stick flags up. It was one of the first things Neil Armstrong and Buzz Aldrin did when they landed on the moon. God knows why. There's no wind on the moon so it seems like an odd thing to have taken with them. What else did he have in his rucksack, a bloody kite?!

I'd have thought one of the only good things about taking over a new planet would mean we'd start afresh and get rid of daft things like flags. I've never quite understood the point of them, as there's too many of the buggers to remember which flag is from where, and on top of that they're normally flapping around so you can't even make them out. I just think they're a waste of material. We should turn them into tea towels so that once washed you can show your love for your country on your washing line.

We made our way back to the Hab as our backpacks were getting low on air. When we got there we had to spend six minutes in the decompression chamber before we could enter and remove our helmets. I think this is where the extra thirty-seven minutes a day would get used up, hanging about in the chamber. You have to go in every time you leave and re-enter, so if you go out three times a day that's your extra time eaten up. This is the funny thing with time; we'll always find ways to fill it.

IS THERE RICE ON MARS?

It was an awkward six minutes too. The sort of uneasiness you get in a lift. I'm not sure what it is that causes this feeling. I don't think it's nerves about getting trapped that does it as they must be the safest mode of transport available. Maybe it's just the feeling of being trapped with strangers. But if I'm not happy getting in a lift to go up a few floors, what are the chances of me being happy getting in a rocket with a bunch of people for six to eight months to get to Mars?!

Once inside the two-storey, eight-metre-wide Hab, everyone got on with their duties. Some prepared meals using powdered food, others looked at rocks under microscopes, and Commander Paul wrote up his EVA (extra-vehicular activity) report while I was given the job of cleaning the toilet.

Commander's Report 2/17/2015
Greetings Mission Support!

1　We continue to support the two projects still in the Hab that were initiated by previous crews. When we receive instructions, we will harvest and measure Cyprien's experimental crops.

2　The majority of our day was spent accommodating a visit by a temporary crew member, Karl Pilkington. We trained Mr Pilkington on Hab systems, protocol, and maintenance. Mr Pilkington also participated in the day's key EVA to the summit of what our crew calls 'Sentinel Hill' to test comms signals. (More details in EVA 149-10 report.) In all, this was a very successful visit, and we enjoyed his company.

3　We conducted the third and likely final test of the ozone laundering system. Our temporary crew member was pleasantly surprised at how effective the device was, in comparison to the control method of just airing out, at mitigating the odor of a pair of particularly horrid socks. Out of respect for my crew, I will not identify the donor of the study socks.

4 At lunch, we tested the palatability of US military MREs. Generally speaking, the crew opined that they are 'not bad', which is pretty good for food that is designed to survive and remain stable in sub-zero temperatures, jungle heat, and air drops from 10,000+ feet.

5 We have a follow-up Geological resource survey EVA scheduled for tomorrow. We may elect to delay this EVA until the following day, depending on how rested the crew feels in the morning. Crew 149 has begun to shift gears already – we are packing up projects that have been completed, and are winding up the remainder of our studies.

It was a satisfying day here in the Tharsis Quadrangle. Our time here is growing short, so we have redoubled our efforts to squeeze the most out of each remaining day.

Respectfully submitted,

Commander, MDRS Crew 149

I met engineer Ken and public affairs officer Kellie, who said if the opportunity came up for them to move to Mars for real, they would take it.

KEN: Yes, I think most of us would, if it comes up as a real possibility.

KARL: Really though?! Really? Have you thought it through?

KEN: Yes, oh yes.

KARL: Do you have family at all?

KEN: Yes, I have four children. The youngest is about one year old. But it is going to take some time, they are going to be grown up. Once they are teenagers I will be begging to get off the planet! Seriously

though, my honest hope is that my children will be past high school and college and grown up with their own lives before I ever go up. It is a long-term goal.

KARL: And what about your wife then? Would she get to go or would you leave her behind?

KEN: I think she would be just fine. She'd find other people who weren't such an asshole as to abandon the family like me!

KELLIE: It depends how you look at it. If you look at it as an opportunity for the species, you know, it is because of how much we love our family and friends at home and how much we care about survival of our species that we want to make sure that this capability exists.

KARL: Yeah, you say that but I can't imagine it . . . I am just thinking 'forget it'. Other people can go if they want but it ain't for me.

KELLIE: I think that something our crew definitely has in common is that we all are dedicated to leading an example, and we are not going to say that someone else should solve the problems that we are not willing to commit to ourselves.

I don't know if it's because I'm evil or if it's just because I accept that all things eventually come to an end that makes me feel the way I do. I have the attitude of a panda – if their habitat isn't there due to us ripping all the trees down, why should it want to live? It's the way I feel about having to be on a planet that doesn't work for me. I think the only reason WWF doesn't want the panda to die out is that they use it for their logo and it's cheap to print as it's just one colour. God help them if the parrot is ever close to extinction.

After getting a taste of what Mars could be like, I know for sure that it isn't the place for me. A hostile planet, blanketed in toxic soil and zapped with radiation! This would be one giant leap too far for this man. I think I'd prefer to just sit with Suzanne and the cat and take whatever is coming.

THANKS TO:
Jodie Krstic (Series Producer);
Richard Yee (Director/Executive
Producer); Krishnendu Majumdar
(Executive Producer); Celia Taylor
(Executive Producer, SKY 1);
Will Yapp (Director); Jamie O'Leary
(Director); Simon Smith (Director);
Lynda Featherstone (Editor);
Mark Williams (Editor); Sam Hardy
(DOP); Mike Carling (DOP);
AJ Butterworth (Sound Recordist)
Mus Mustafa (DV Director); Gavin
Whitehead (DV Director); Carmelina
Palumbo (Production Executive);
Claire Jutla (Production Manager);
Jenny Hargreaves (Production
Manager); Kelly Lloyd (Production
Coordinator)